D0429325

Your Interfaith Wedding

Also by Laurie Sue Brockway

Wedding Goddess

The Goddess Pages

Pet Prayers and Blessings

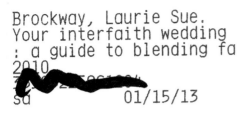

Your Interfaith Wedding

A Guide to Blending Faiths, Cultures, and Personal Values into One Beautiful Wedding Ceremony

Laurie Sue Brockway

AN IMPRINT OF ABC-CLIO, LLC
Santa Barbara, California • Denver, Colorado • Oxford, England

Library of Congress Cataloging-in-Publication Data

Brockway, Laurie Sue.
    Your interfaith wedding : a guide to blending faiths, cultures, and personal values into one beautiful wedding ceremony / Laurie Sue Brockway.
        p. cm.
    Includes bibliographical references and index.
    ISBN 978-0-313-37801-0 (alk. paper) — ISBN 978-0-313-37802-7 (ebook)
    1. Interfaith marriage services.   2. Interfaith marriage.
3. Weddings—Planning.   I. Title.
    HQ1031.B79   2010
    395.2'2—dc22   2010021208

ISBN: 978-0-313-37801-0
EISBN: 978-0-313-37802-7

14   13   12   11   10   1   2   3   4   5

This book is also available on the World Wide Web as an eBook.
Visit www.abc-clio.com for details.

Praeger
An Imprint of ABC-CLIO, LLC

ABC-CLIO, LLC
130 Cremona Drive, P.O. Box 1911
Santa Barbara, California 93116-1911

This book is printed on acid-free paper ∞

Manufactured in the United States of America

To the wonderful couples who have allowed me the special honor of being a part of their weddings. They have shown me time and again that even the most unique and diverse blended families can find a common bond when love is present.

And to Ray Summer, who left us too soon.

Contents

PART THREE   RESOURCES I: A MULTIFAITH VIEW
OF WEDDINGS

PART FOUR   RESOURCES II: CEREMONIES TO INSPIRE YOU

Acknowledgments

I have to thank all my wonderful brides and grooms who allowed me to share their stories. Almost all the weddings mentioned in these pages are weddings that I had the honor to officiate. I am so grateful that these lovely couples selected me as their wedding officiant and allowed me to play a role in their sacred experience and in coaching them through the wedding journey. Marrying couples in love has been a great joy in my life, and working with interfaith and blended-culture couples has been a special honor. It is through working with them on creative and personalized ceremonies that I have gained the wisdom to share in this book, to help other brides and grooms.

Blessings and a special thank-you to Rabbi Joseph Gelberman, founder of the New Seminary, where I studied and was ordained in 1999. I was trained in the rites and tenets of all faiths and prepared to work with people from diverse religious backgrounds. The motto of the seminary is "Never instead of, always in addition to." I call on that wisdom daily in my wedding ministry.

Thank you to the many teachers and guides who were there for me in my early days as a wedding officiant, and I am truly grateful for their willingness to share their wisdom and expertise, including: Rev. Deb Steen Ross, Rabbi Roger Ross, Rev. Judith Marcus, Rev. Diane Berke, Rev. Julie Omstead, Rev. Joyce Lichenstein, Ph.D., Ms. Audrey Sparks Fussa, Rev. Paul Michael, and Barbara Biziou. I would also like to thank my favorite role models, Daphne Rose Kingma and Charolette Richards, and make a special remembrance of Dr. Rose McAloon.

I thank my colleagues at Beliefnet.com for their inspiration and express my gratitude for the existence of a Web site so devoted to multifaith inspiration and filled with so much wisdom and truth from many traditions.

A special thank you to my amazing husband, Rev. Victor Fuhrman, for his contributions to this book and for being my partner in life, ministry, and in exploring the sacred; and to my son Alexander, who has seen me through 14 books since he was a baby and is now pursuing his career as a broadcaster.

Preface

THE SOUL KNOWS NO BOUNDARIES WHEN IT COMES TO LOVE

At the soul level we are always open to that person who is a different color, speaks a different language, or who comes from a radically different background. We are always brought to exactly the experience of love that our soul needs. And this is the power of the soul. It is here to challenge the ego and pull us off the paths that feel familiar. In this lies the surrender that allows us to be surprised by the true nature of love.

—Daphne Rose Kingma

I believe in the power of true love. I believe in soul mates and that the couples who are meant to be together have the ability to see one another through the eyes of the soul. These couples allow many feelings about so-called differences to melt away.

In my wedding ministry, time and again, I have met lovely people who clearly are meant for each other but who do not come from the same background or faith. They have found a way to embrace one another and, in most cases, one another's families, despite any inherent challenges.

It has become clear to me that love and commitment come in many packages, shapes, sizes, shades, languages, backgrounds, and faiths. Love simply does not limit itself to existing only between people who are of the same faith, nor does it merely join together people who have the same skin tone or accent. And it does not insist that a man born in one part of the world must only love someone from his country or culture or that a woman born into a religious household will find her beloved in the same faith of her family.

Love is a force with a mind of its own, and it transcends the limited thinking that we must "stick with our own kind." Many modern men and women are coming to see that true love is a gift, even when an adoring, committed partner does not quite fit the ideal of our fantasies or arrive in the outer package our parents imagined for us.

While some men and women fancy the idea of rebelling against an overly religious or restrictive upbringing, I've yet to meet a bride or groom of a certain faith, culture, or ethnic background who woke up one morning thinking, "Hey, I'm going to find someone who comes from a completely different background and marry that person. That way, I can abandon my own upbringing, make my parents crazy, and challenge my own hidden prejudices. Wow, that sounds like a great idea!"

More often, it just happens one day that this person meets someone who feels like home; a person with whom he or she feels comfortable, attracted to, happy about, and loved by. One thing leads to another, and the two fall deeply in love. Eventually, they decide to marry.

Our souls are drawn to inner radiance first. It takes some people a while to realize that they are falling for someone who is of a different faith or culture or even to realize that the people they love have parents who might want a ceremony in a Hindu temple or who could not bear it if their children were not to marry in a Catholic church.

Urged on by their love and desire to build their lives together, they begin the journey toward the altar. This experience is a microcosm of married life together, so it is a chance to grow more fully into their love and learn how to build and navigate family life together.

My philosophy is that love between two people is a sacred union, and it adds a dimension of holiness to our world that cannot be categorized by religion or culture.

Are there challenges? Yes, and for some couples, the situation is more complex than for others. But I have also witnessed many couples rise above the roadblocks to their relationships and successfully blend their beliefs into married life.

Warmly,
Rev. Laurie Sue Brockway
New York City

Introduction: The Prevalence of Mixed Marriages

Give all to love; obey thy heart.

—Ralph Waldo Emerson

This is not the first and won't be the last book about interfaith and blended weddings. We live in a world where these matches are becoming more commonplace every day, and people are searching for ideas on how to join two lives in a way that celebrates where both come from and honors what they have together.

Once considered taboo, couples from all faiths, cultures, and racial combinations are making their way to the altar. We hear all the time about celebrities of different faiths, cultures, and ethnic backgrounds falling in love and getting hitched. These couples are a microcosm of the bigger picture and the changing landscape of love, where average men and women fall for one another and are willing to rise up against the odds, or ignore them, to build a life together.

Filmmaker Mel Brooks and actress Anne Bancroft were pioneers decades ago; so were comedians Jerry Stiller and Anne Meara. In recent times, the list of long-lasting couples in interfaith and culturally blended unions continues to grow and includes luminaries such as Cokie and Steve Roberts, Kevin Kline and Phoebe Cates, Sarah Jessica Parker and Matthew Broderick, Courteney Cox and David Arquette, and Christina Aguilera and Jordan Bratman. Everyone was fascinated when Christian Chelsea Clinton announced she would marry Marc Mezvinsky in an interfaith ceremony, giving the famously churchgoing Bill and Hillary Clinton a Jewish son-in-law to look forward to.

In the United States, about 2.3 million couples join the ranks of the about-to-be-married each year, and interfaith marriages in the United States are on the rise. While it is difficult to assess the exact statistics, it is estimated that over one third of all couples now marry someone from a different faith background than their own and that this trend will increase over time, as the world becomes even more of a global community.

The Today Show reported recently that 28 million Americans are in interfaith relationships. Steve Waldman, cofounder and former editor in chief of leading multifaith site Beliefnet.com, estimated 33 million Americans live in interfaith households. Citing a 2008 study by the Pew Forum on Religion and Public Life, *Time* magazine reports 37 percent of married adults in the United States have a spouse from another religious tradition. Among Jewish Americans, that figure rises to almost half of all marriages.

The Pew study also tells us that more than a quarter of Americans have abandoned or switched from the faith of their birth (and infers this is in part due to intermarriage). And it also says 16.1 percent consider themselves unaffiliated, which sheds some light on the increase in nondenominational weddings, sometimes between people of different faiths who are not practicing a faith.

Here are some statistics on different religions (reported by Rev. Susanna Stefanachi Macomb, in her book *Joining Hands and Hearts*, and by other sources) that point toward the trend in intermarriage and couples marrying outside of their houses of worship:

- Nearly 50 percent of Jewish people are marrying outside the faith.
- Over 40 percent of marriage-age Catholics marry outside the Church, a figure doubling since the 1960s.
- Marriages between Catholics and Protestants are now accepted by the vast majority of those faiths.
- In the Greek Orthodox faith, the number of interfaith marriages has increased ninefold in the past half century, with approximately two out of every three marriages (66%) being with someone outside the faith. With the large number of adults marrying outside the church, some estimates put the number of interfaith marriages at 80 percent.
- Three in 10 Mormons are now in interfaith marriages, although Mormons are encouraged by their church to marry within their faith.
- The number of Jewish-Christian couples doubled to one million during the 1990s.
- Four in 10 Muslims, whose religion allows men, but not women, to intermarry, have chosen non-Muslim spouses.

- Buddhists and the unaffiliated are most likely to marry outside their faith.
- According to the most recent U.S. Census, the percentage of couples who are interracial has increased sevenfold from 1970 to 2000.[1]

The advent of couples from different faith backgrounds marrying one another, combined with the trend in couples from all faiths choosing to marry outside their houses of worship, has transformed the tone, content, and spirit of the American wedding ceremony. An entire industry and culture has grown to serve the needs of interfaith and blended-culture couples—from interfaith officiants to multiethnic DJs to wedding planners who specialize in creatively meeting the demand for culturally diverse weddings.

Interfaith, interethnic, and interracial marriage is so prevalent these days that many couples simply go about it with a sense of ease about blending their lives. Often this means they come together in the spirit of love—rising above dogma and outdated beliefs—and embrace the idea that they cannot be separated due to religion, culture, or skin color.

Then there are those who must deal with challenges before they get to the wedding altar. They need support, information, insights, blessings, and prayers that appease their parents, smooth out issues between relatives, ease cultural clashes, and fully bless their marriage. They need to learn more about each other's faiths and understand the mind-set of each other's families. Some need spiritual counseling to help them sort things through.

Then again, there are some brides and grooms of different backgrounds who do not consider themselves religious or who are disconnected from faith altogether. Many are atheist, unaffiliated, or just do not care much about including religion or God in their weddings.

Of the group of unaffiliated individuals cited in the Pew study, about 4 percent say they are agnostic or atheistic. Just over 12 percent say they are connected to "nothing in particular." So they may still believe in God, but not religion per se.

It appears that a fair number of people are making choices to follow a path that is personally fulfilling or not to follow one at all. The fluidity of people's religious beliefs is obviously opening the door to increasing numbers of interfaith unions. The evidence that such a large number of Americans have stepped away from organized religion also points to the increased demand for nondenominational or nonreligious wedding ceremonies.

The spiritual diversity of all these couples is reflected in interfaith ministry today and comes alive in thousands of wedding ceremonies each year.

WHO IS THIS BOOK FOR?

This book is designed for interfaith couples from all backgrounds (Jewish/Hindu, Buddhist/Christian, Muslim/agnostic, etc.) as well as intercultural and interracial couples. I use *interfaith* as an umbrella term to cover the variety of heritages couples may be blending. This book is also a helpful guide for nondenominational couples who may want to dip into the rituals and traditions of other cultures because they are not beholden to one faith. In addition, this book is suited for the "alternative" couple who might seek to weave elements into their wedding ceremonies to be different and make things personal. This book is also a helpful guide for other interfaith and nondenominational ministers. It is the book I wish I'd had when I began my wedding ministry and it represents many years of experience in this wonderful field.

At the heart of this book is the articulation of a heartfelt belief that love is not ruled by religion, race, or culture and that true love can find its way to bring two hearts together and, in many cases—but not all—two families.

Many interfaith couples need an alternative to the wedding traditions of their birth or a ceremony in addition to a traditional religious ceremony. *Your Interfaith Wedding* shows them how to select the wedding vows and rituals that are truly meaningful.

Quiz: Are You Ready for an Interfaith Marriage?

While we have seen an amazing increase in cross-cultural pairings, interfaith marriages, and a huge movement toward fellowship of people of all faiths, we all have very deep-rooted beliefs about religion and about merging families from different faiths and cultures. It is important to shine a light on what we truly believe and how ready we are to step out of the box of upbringing to marry the person we love. Please answer the following questions honestly, and at the end we will share your "readiness scoring."

1. **Prior to falling in love with the one I will marry, this is the kind of love life I had:**

    A. I turned away suitors of different faith, culture, or race.
    B. I was intrigued by people who were different but thought I should not go out of my way to mix it up.
    C. I've always been attracted to people who are different from me.
    D. I spent time with people I truly liked and did not choose based on faith, culture, or skin color.

2. **This is how I would describe my relationship to religion:**

    A. I actively practice my faith and attend worship services.
    B. I celebrate only on holidays but feel I should do more.
    C. I am more culturally religious than devoutly religious.
    D. I am not religious or have my own personal practice.

3. **I was brought up a certain way, and many of those beliefs remain with me today. Deep down, I believe that**

   A. God will punish me if I go against the teachings of my faith.
   B. I should marry someone of my own background.
   C. Dogma is not as meaningful as the spirit of religion.
   D. People of all faiths and backgrounds can and should get along.

4. **My family is devout and believes I should marry someone of my own background. I feel**

   A. Heartbroken that they won't support my marriage.
   B. Angry at them for being closed-minded when they should be more understanding.
   C. Hope that we will have their blessing and that they will come around.
   D. I must follow my heart despite their beliefs.

5. **I don't consider myself prejudiced, but when I am totally honest, I admit that somewhere inside, I am worried about raising children who**

   A. May not look like me or like they are from the same family.
   B. Have a different religion and belief system.
   C. Celebrate a culture that is foreign to me.
   D. Become confused about their heritage because of their mixed parentage.

6. **I am concerned my beloved's family may have problems with my faith, race, culture, or family differences. My biggest worry is that they will**

   A. Emotionally manipulate my mate into following their ways.
   B. Be rude or disrespectful to me and my family.
   C. Not come to our wedding.
   D. Never give me a chance to bond with them.

7. **His mother is heartbroken you are not to be married in her house of worship. Your reaction is:**

   A. Maybe we better not get married.
   B. That's her problem.
   C. Maybe I should convert.
   D. Let's find a way to honor her beliefs in our ceremony.

8. **When I think of making a public declaration of our love, some of these thoughts come to mind:**

   A. People will stare because we look different.
   B. Our families will never get along due to different faiths or cultures.
   C. Loving someone from a different background will be a challenge sometimes.
   D. I am so blessed to be loved and have someone to love me.

9. **Even though you are a tolerant person, how would you react to having in-laws who speak a different language, look different from your family, or have cultural customs that seem very odd?**

   A. I would find it embarrassing and weird.
   B. I would worry that my family and friends would think it is odd and that I should not be involved with this family.
   C. I would spend time finding out more about how they live and what they believe and celebrate.
   D. I would love them, no matter how different, because they are part of my mate's life.

10. **If your interfaith or mixed-culture child came to you someday and said he or she wanted to follow your spouse's religious beliefs and not yours, you would**

    A. Cry your eyes out or get angry and feel you have lost a battle.
    B. Try to talk your child out of this decision.
    C. Be glad that he or she at least has *some faith* in something.
    D. Find out more about what he or she loves about the religion and look for ways to celebrate it together.

11. **If I have any concerns about our relationship, they are that**

    A. Our children will be confused or rejected.
    B. We will have a hard time figuring out how to blend our backgrounds on a day-to-day basis.
    C. We will have to communicate with extra care to make sure we stay on the same page, and it feels a little scary.
    D. We may overthink our relationship instead of just being present with each other.

12. **If you heard there was a way to celebrate both faiths and cultures and have the best of both worlds, you would**

    A. Ignore it.
    B. Doubt it.

    C. Investigate it.
    D. Celebrate it.

READINESS SCORING

If you got four or more in any of the following categories, please see the message for you in the category.

If You're an A

If you got four or more As, you need to review your mind-set about religion and religious beliefs as well as some of the beliefs of your upbringing and check in to see if you can truly open your heart to someone of a different faith or background and love that person without worrying that you are betraying your faith or your parents.

If You're a B

If you got four or more Bs, you still have a lot of shoulds and should-nots attached to your idea about mixed pairings, and there is still a great deal of hesitancy. We all are products of our cultures and belief systems, so give yourself some time to sort out the issues and consider counseling with someone who specializes in interfaith issues. It can help you both work on hesitancies to embracing your love.

If You're a C

Full speed ahead with wedding planning. You are almost there and are just working out some last-ditch hesitations about your love. Open the lines of communication with your beloved, and make sure you lean on each other and talk things through at every turn.

If You're a D

You are definitely ready to marry your mixed-match mate! Open your heart and have a great wedding!

Part One

Clearing the Path to the Altar

Marriage is a huge commitment. Loving and marrying someone of a different faith or culture can bring an additional set of challenges. But it can also be an amazing, awesome adventure in building a life with the one you love. Look for ways to meet challenges head-on. Seek ways to heal anything that is out of balance. And learn to accept that you cannot please all people all the time. This section is designed to inform you more about the joys and challenges of interfaith unions.

1

You Can Express Your Love in a Sacred Ceremony That Includes Everyone

Most beloved of the sacraments is the one of marriage. It symbolizes the fulfillment of earth's sweetest dream. Almost any sensitive person can testify to the emergence of power that is broadcast during a marriage ceremony. This force is created by the beauty and intent of the rite itself. The spiritual fusion of two individualities into a duad of love generates an energy and luminosity that reaches even the most impersonal onlooker.

—Rev. Flower Newhouse, *The Meaning and Value of Sacraments*

Every time I officiate at a wedding ceremony, I am awed by the extraordinary energy that becomes available when two people in love literally *step up* to commit themselves to sacred union. As an interfaith minister, I am frequently called on to solemnize marriage vows outside traditional religious settings, and I have seen time and again that a holy temple can be created *anywhere* love is present.

I serve many diverse couples, from many different backgrounds and points of view, and often create ceremonies that weave together different cultures, traditions, faiths, personal values, and families. The common denominator with all my couples boils down to this: whether they opt for traditional religious elements or a sprinkling of familiar rituals, or forego God altogether, they want their ceremonies to be sacred, and they don't want to offend anyone.

It is my aim with *Your Interfaith Wedding* to show you how to create a sacred ceremony that is personally meaningful to you and to guide you in ways to include your family and friends while focusing on your love and commitment. The first thing I want to share is a very special secret that not every bride and groom or parent or grandparent can understand while planning a wedding: having married hundreds of brides and grooms from all faiths, cultures, and backgrounds, I have come to understand that the wedding altar is the neutral territory where everyone learns to speak the sample language. The language is love.

When I am up there with the bride and groom, it feels as if we are standing in a love bubble—sacred, pure, and protected. This energy is so powerful that it radiates to everyone in attendance; guests in turn send love to the couple. A holy presence surrounds the couple and up-lifts them, along with those they love. Love rains down on all.

While some couples are stressed before the wedding and worried about family issues related to differences in beliefs and background, time and again I see those issues melt away in the presence of such profound love. Couples can seize the opportunity to allow their ceremony to be a healing experience—for them and their loved ones.

Although many of us grew up attending traditional weddings, in churches, synagogues, and temples, in recent years we have seen the emergence of a new type of wedding, where couples marry outside a formal house of worship. Because of the increase in interfaith pairings and also an increase in couples seeking nondenominational wedding services, they often opt for ceremonies that are nontraditional, personal, and unique.

While many couples strive to have interfaith unions that follow the traditions of both faiths evenly, and maybe even have officiants from both religions presiding, there are many who prefer less religion and more spirit. This is the trend I see in my wedding ministry and is the kind of wedding in which I specialize. Some people call it "cherry-picking," meaning that they select the most meaningful parts of their culture and faith, leaving behind the dogma and any outdated traditions that do not feel right for them.

Many couples relish the idea of a memorable and special sacred ceremony—but they want to tread lightly on some of the traditions and trimmings that relatives with strong religious beliefs would find upsetting or offensive. They also want ceremonies that are welcoming to loved ones and can easily include the participation of friends and family.

The modern interfaith or blended-culture wedding ceremony is one that has to be crafted by and for each individual couple. It's personalized and has to include elements that will help that couple truly seize on the energy of the moment. That is why this book presents so many ideas and options for brides and grooms putting their ceremonies together.

It doesn't have to *look like* a classic Jewish or Christian ceremony, or a Hindu ceremony, or a Buddhist ceremony, or seem like a reenactment of the sacred ceremonies of ancient times. It can be a groom in a tux and a bride in white who walks down the aisle or a shoeless couple on a beach. It can contain elements or rituals of existing traditional or nontraditional ceremonies; it can include any religious, spiritual, cultural, or family traditions the couple chooses. The main ingredient is their love and their conscious intent to express that love to one another—and share it with their community—in a way that is holy and sacred to them personally.

I have seen and been part of some extraordinary healing moments, and in this book I share some of the amazing experiences and ceremonies of brides and grooms of differing faiths and backgrounds who have made their weddings a great celebration for all. And I have seen some devastating moments when bride and groom are rejected by family or criticized for wanting to marry a mate who happens to be from another culture, religion, race, or caste. It is important to share those, too, to illustrate how some family members simply cannot get past the differences. Fortunately, even some of the most stressful wedding experiences have had happy endings.

THOUGHTS TO PONDER

I would like to share some of the questions people most frequently ask about interfaith weddings and my role as an officiant of mixed marriages.

What Is an Interfaith Marriage?

People tend to think of *interfaith* as Jewish and Christian, but it is actually an umbrella term for many diverse pairings. The combinations are unlimited. When any two people of differing faiths and/or cultural backgrounds decide to marry, it is considered interfaith. On one end of the spectrum is a Catholic marrying a Lutheran—both are Christians but technically of different faiths. Or it could be a union between a Hindu from Trinidad and an African American Jehovah's Witness. In that scenario, there is a blending of both religions and cultures.

What Kind of Couples Have You Married?

As an interfaith minister, I have had the honor of marrying many diverse couples, from many different backgrounds and points of view. Just recently, the faith and cultural pairing of some of my couples included: Christian and Hindu; Hindu and Buddhist-Christian-Jewish groom; American lapsed Catholic and Sri Lankan Buddhist; French Canadian Lebanese and Dominican Republic Catholic; Wiccan and atheist; Muslim and Hindu; Hindu and Jewish (both from conservative families); Scottish traditional to Church of England British; Catholic of Mexican heritage and religious Jewish; Russian Jewish and Russian Christian; and African Christian and American Jewish.

Estimates Say 25 Percent of Marriages Are Interfaith Unions. Why Do You Think the Number of Interfaith Marriages Is on the Rise?

There are a number of factors:

1. First of all, one of the things that most people want in life is to find true love with a devoted partner. In our global community and our daily lives—where we live, work, and travel in blended communities—it is so easy to meet and become attracted to someone who may come from a different faith, culture, country, or skin color.
2. A lot of people today are open minded enough to opt for love over the package that love comes in, and in the process, they find the package is quite lovely as well.
3. Many people feel disconnected from the religion of their birth, so they don't actively seek a mate by religious standards. A recent study showed us that 16 percent of all Americans do not consider themselves to be of any faith, and 25 percent of Americans "switched" faiths at some point in their lives, and some believe this is in part due to interfaith marriage.

Do People in Interfaith Marriages Have to Convert?

There are some faith traditions, families, and individuals who feel this is a requirement in order for a marriage to be recognized by a religious body or by the family. I recommend that couples clarify the protocol of their differing faiths as well make peace with their families on this issue whenever possible. But I do not see conversions much in my ministry because I am the officiant people seek out when they are choosing a ceremony created for their unique union and family.

Is There Such a Thing as a Typical Challenge That Interfaith Couples Face? Or Is There a Common Issue That You See?

The most common challenge I come across is that a bride is worried about appeasing a religious or very traditional mother, father, or grandparent. For example, the family might be having a hard time with the idea that a couple is choosing to get married at a wedding venue rather than in a church. Or the parents might be pressuring the bride and groom to have two weddings—one with me and one that is a traditional wedding with which they are familiar and they feel is the correct way to marry.

Or on some sad occasions, I've dealt with an intolerant parent or two or the pain a couple was going through because of it. I've had at least two weddings where the father of a bride refused to come to his daughter's wedding because she was marrying an African American man. I've had a Jewish mom refuse to partake in a nondenominational candle lighting that was part of her son's marriage to a beautiful African doctor (what she was really saying was she was not supportive of the marriage). But overall, when a couple is OK inside themselves about their marriage choices, we see more acceptance from all involved.

With Couples So Diverse and Their Wedding Needs So Wide Ranging, How Are You Able to Serve Each Couple's Individual Needs? Do You Have Any Religious Restrictions or Religious Protocols to Which You Must Adhere?

I do not have to follow any religious protocol per se, although I do have a legal responsibility to uphold the marriage laws of the state and city. I consult with couples to find out exactly what kind of ceremony they want, and I include only the rituals, prayers, blessings, and words that they feel will help them honor their families and their relationship while maintaining their personal values. The ceremonies mainly focus on their love for each other. That's the central theme.

**Many Clergypeople Refuse to Conduct an Interfaith Marriage
Ceremony or at the Very Least Are Uncomfortable with the Idea.
What Is Your Personal Philosophy on Love and Marriage?**

My philosophy is that love between two people is their business and
their choice. Love adds a dimension of holiness to our world that
cannot be categorized by religion or culture. A temple can be created
wherever there is love. I believe in soul mates, and I feel that the couples who are meant to be together have the ability to see one another
through the eyes of the soul. That allows many feelings about so-called
differences to melt away. I don't feel it is up to me to decide who can
or can't marry based on religion, race, or culture. But I certainly understand the restrictions to which other clergypeople must adhere and the
beliefs they hold dear.

**Of Course, Many People Worry about the Children. When Your
Couples Seek Counsel from You on How to Raise Their Families,
What Do You Suggest?**

I personally believe in *blending.* This is not for everyone; some couples
will need to select one faith to follow and stick with it to give their kids
a religious identity. If they are choosing to raise their kids in one faith,
then they need to really look at what that will mean for both families
and family celebrations such as religious holidays. For example, will
it be OK with a Catholic dad if his kids celebrate Passover with their
Jewish mom's family, and not celebrate Easter with his family?

But when couples are unsure, I tell them to look into their own
childhood for the rituals and celebrations they most loved from their
religions and to make a list of what they would like to give their children from column A and column B, and to factor in ways their children
can partake in family celebrations, time with grandparents, visits to
houses of worship—all in a way that fits with their personal beliefs.

**What Is the One Common Denominator That You See
in All Interfaith Couples?**

The common denominator with all my couples boils down to on thing:
love. They love one another, and therefore they are willing to rise up
against the odds, or ignore them, and build a life together.

And Your Role in It All?

I am just a facilitator for love and perhaps a bit of a cheerleader for love, as well. I make no judgments and I have no rules about who can marry whom. If a couple is in love and they have committed to building a life together, then I consider it a blessing and privilege to officiate for them. It is an honor to create unique ceremonies to match their unique unions and to make their wedding experience all it can be.

Do You Believe Interfaith Unions Will Affect the Bigger Picture?
Can They Add to Peace on Earth?

I do. By virtue of loving one another, each couple brings more love to their circle of friends, their families, and their world. Devoted love of any kind is sacred, and when it brings two faiths and cultures together, it expands fellowship between families and communities of different faiths. It doesn't have to be Romeo and Juliet, the Capulets versus the Montagues. Although interfaith couples have dragons to slay—all relationships do. I think overall, interfaith marriage is a very positive thing.

2

Facing Your Fears

Talking It Through Together

My partner and I focused on the wedding as a gateway to the rest of our lives together. We spent time discussing where we had been in our relationship, as well as discussing our future vision. This included talks on how we would blend our lives and raise our kids, and chats on anything that worried us.

—Monica

The most important part of your journey is to communicate with your mate and create a sacred boundary around your relationship that no one can penetrate or disturb. The first step is to tell the truth—about your fears, worries, and concerns for the future—to yourself.

In a perfect world, love and commitment would be the most important part of any marriage. The fact that two people found one another would be celebrated and their decision to wed would be honored by friends and family. Most important, their feelings for and about one another would be clear, and they would harbor no secret fears or worries about whether they have chosen the right partner.

I have seen many couples like that in my ministry. They just know they are meant to be together and they plan a wedding, deal with any bumps in the process, and then stand up at the altar to pledge heart and soul. Making plans to spend the rest of their lives together seems completely natural to them, despite any differences between them and their families.

But I think it is fair to say that it is more natural for most couples to have a few fears or concerns about taking this huge step in their lives, and that this is seen as a natural part of the process as you get ready for marriage. A wise minister once said to me, "Every relationship has a dragon to slay."

Interfaith couples, and couples who blend cultures and ethnicities, sometimes have a dragon or two more to deal with in the form of prejudice, ignorance, fear of straying from tradition, limiting religious or cultural dogma, and just a sheer lack of insight about other people's faiths and beliefs. But these things are not always generated by the people around us—they can live within us, as well.

The first step to clearing the pathway to the altar is to acknowledge your own inner truth—without judgment and shame. Ask yourself the questions that will help you define your own identity and those that will help you understand your feelings about merging your identity and life with someone who may not have the same viewpoints on religion or who has grown up in a completely different culture.

Some mixed marriages bring together pairs from dramatically different backgrounds, and some bring together families where there are seemingly tiny differences. How each partner truly feels about things and what issues will be important to explore in your marriage are as unique as the two of you.

I have seen some of the most complex situations resolved between couples, so I am completely convinced that love will find a way when challenged, if there is a strong commitment, but it requires looking inward first. And it also requires time. The journey of exploring feelings should begin before the wedding, but couples need to know it is an ongoing process of discovery and growth.

Jill and Jean Paul were in love and planned to marry in the fall. She was Jewish from Boston, and he was Catholic from Haiti. He'd lived in New York for most of his life, and while he seemed devoted to his faith or to honoring God in their ceremony, he was also very devoted to making her happy and comfortable and was willing to compromise. He struck me as being very spiritual, wise, and open hearted. She was culturally Jewish and not truly practicing the religion; in fact she seemed to resent her faith.

When we first met, Jill told me that she had already accepted the fact that her conservative Jewish parents would not come to the ceremony because they could not accept that she was marrying a non-Jewish man, let alone a nonwhite man.

She was so angry at them for their prejudice that she never took the time to sort out her own feelings. Quite unexpectedly, several months before their planned wedding, Jill got pregnant, and the couple decided to move up the marriage. It was when they asked me to do a brief ceremony to make their union legal that Jill confided in me she was beset with worry about how she would feel about her own child. She realized that part of her parents' prejudice was also a part of her, and she was worrying that her baby could end up a different religion from her, and also would perhaps look more like her husband.

Although Jean Paul was loving and accepting of Jill, and understanding about the feelings she was having, he admitted that he, too, was feeling a little upset at her parents' behavior and about the deep anger Jill had about her religion. He wanted his children to know God—regardless of religion—yet Jill also seemed mad at God. Underneath it all, he worried that the woman he loved could be as closed minded as the in-laws who had rejected him without ever meeting him.

They felt the rush to the altar was the right thing to do for their baby on the way, but they had worries about what would lie ahead. So they took on the task of using the time of the pregnancy for counseling and clarifying what was truly in their hearts and addressing their own hidden feelings about each other's faiths and families. When they began to dialogue about these things, it strengthened their bond. Jill was able to see that initially, she was attracted to her husband because he *was* so different, and deep down she knew this would anger her parents. She realized there was a part of her that wanted to hurt them and turn her back on them. It wasn't just their anger she was dealing with, it was her own. In fact, her parents were a reflection of her own inner rage toward them.

By the time they arrived at their original, planned wedding date, they went ahead with a small gathering to celebrate their union. They had worked through the dragons within and were happily married and awaiting their first baby. Fortunately, this couple worked out their challenges. (And eventually, her parents could not resist their first grandchild.)

Love hits some couples like a bolt of lightning, and once a couple decides to marry, wedding planning can take on a life of its own. Since wedding planning can have its own stresses and demands, some couples tend to shuffle emotional and spiritual issues under the rug, figuring they will deal with it after they get married. Couples who give some thought to the issues beforehand often feel like they have things more under control—or at least they feel they have a game plan to guide them.

Donald and Jami were looking forward to a summer wedding ceremony. This couple seemed to be made for each other—they were the same age, had similar careers and interests, had the same friends, loved the same kinds of movies, music, and activities. They were both from the East Coast and had lived in New York for years. In terms of their day-to-day life, culturally, they were completely in tune. They were also devoted communicators and chose to be completely honest with each other, and sought spiritual counseling when they felt they could not figure things out on their own.

Although Jami's mom was a church music director, Jami did not feel personally called to practice her Protestant religion. She did, however, love the traditions of her faith—Christmas, Easter, listening to church choirs. Donald was born into an Orthodox Jewish family and raised with all the religious trimmings, but he did not follow his faith with any sense of spirit—it was more out of obligation. Regardless, he felt strongly that he wanted his children to be raised Jewish and to have all the same religious experiences he had as a child—Bar Mitzvah, Passover Seders, Hanukah candles.

Since Donald was so clearly wedded to the idea of raising Jewish children, Jami was willing to make that compromise, but she needed something, too. So we talked about including the things she loved about Christianity in their home and lives—a small Christmas tree, holiday music, Easter eggs. She was happy with those touches. The problem they both faced was feeling OK about participating in each other's traditions—he did not want to go into a church, she did not feel she could physically sit through a bris (the Hebrew tradition of welcoming a boy into the world on his sixth day).

When they peeled away the layers of their religious feelings, it turned out that they both actually were in a similar place—they'd had it forced on them as kids and did not care for it as adults. On top of that, neither of them truly believed in God, so they were trying to set up a game plan for raising their children with some sense of religious identify, while neither of them had one.

We realized that we would not have all the answers before their wedding day. So I gave them the assignment of spending their first year of marriage learning more about each other's faiths and cultural traditions, of testing their tolerance for each other's religions (she would go to High Holy Days at the synagogue and he would go to midnight mass at Christmas), of exploring interfaith worship where both their faiths are honored, and most of all, of exploring whether they wanted to create a relationship with the divine in some way. Their task was to define what religion is to them personally and to see if the faiths of their birth held anything genuinely meaningful that they would want to pass along to their children someday. What looked slightly irresolvable before the wedding began to take clearer form as they worked at it.

Ultimately, Donald sealed his commitment to raising the children Jewish by deciding to make peace with his own religion and practice it with more spirit. Jami, on the other hand, found herself on the other end of the spectrum, still not finding spiritual substance from faith but feeling open minded about finding her own true spirituality. There was a part of her that worried about how to raise Jewish children, but she and Donald agreed the responsibility for that rested with him. "I am not going to be able to answer their questions about God and I will not be a hypocrite in trying," she said. Donald found enough meaning to his religious life to comfortably share it with kids someday.

Making the effort to sort through fears and worries, challenges and concerns, before the marriage can put your mind at peace in some cases and help highlight the issues you will face as a married couple in others. There may not be a perfect solution for interfaith dilemmas and cultural challenges in immediate sight, but couples can take on the commitment to continue to fine-tune their relationship and will often find, over time, that they develop their own personal approach to living as a blended family.

THOUGHTS TO PONDER: DISCOVERY EXERCISE—
36 QUESTIONS TO ASK YOURSELF

Any relationship requires a bit of bending and meeting in the middle of certain issues, but there are some things that none of us would change or could change for another. Couples who come to love from different backgrounds sometimes have to work extra hard to be on the same page with their beloveds—even if it is to agree to disagree. It is important for each partner to understand his or her own wiring—his or her religious beliefs, cultural standards, beliefs about relationships, and level of tolerance for other people's points of views and cultural references.

Religious intolerance has created disharmony in our world since the beginning of time, so of course, some of us come into the world with that DNA, but if you two can work it out, you bring healing to our world. When you hail from different cultures, ethnic backgrounds, countries, and worldviews, the dance of intimacy has additional challenges. You have to ask yourself, are you up for these challenges? Do you know what they are? Do they even matter to you?

It is so important that you be completely honest here. Take a separate sheet of paper and pen, and give some thought to these questions.

Where Do You Stand Personally on Religion?
- What is the religion of your birth?
- Do you consider yourself religious?
- Do you attend regular worship services?
- Are you more of a spiritual person than a religious person?
- What is your personal spiritual practice?
- Do you belong to a spiritual community?
- Is spiritual community important to you?
- Is your spirituality your foundation for living?
- Do you get more spiritual as you age?

Where Do You Stand Personally on Cultural Difference?
- What is the culture of your birth?
- Are you proud of your heritage?
- Do you feel particularly connected to a certain race or culture of people?
- Do you ever spend time with people outside that race or culture?
- Do you hail from a tolerant family?
- Is it important to be with someone of similar ethnic background, nationality, and culture?
- Do you seek a mate from a culture or background different from yours? Any culture in particular? Why?
- Would it be OK if your mate came from a different culture or race and yet shared similar personal values and beliefs?
- If culture is not that important to you, would you want a mate who shares that sentiment?

What Are Your Family Influences?
- Is your family very religious?
- Do they attend regular worship services?
- Do they have a family clergyperson?
- Were they raised with strong cultural influences or traditions?
- Do they have strong beliefs about their faith or culture?
- Do they adhere to certain marriage customs?
- Do they assume they will have a say in who you should marry?

- Will they pressure you to marry according to their beliefs?
- Do you fear they will be mad or reject you if you do not follow their wishes?

What Is Your Ability to Tolerate Differences?
- If religion is important to you, could you be happy with a mate who does not share your religious views?
- If religion is not that important to you, would you want your mate to share that sentiment or even want your mate not to believe in God?
- Could you be tolerant of your mate's religion if it were important to him or her?
- Would you feel comfortable going to worship services at a church or in conjunction with a religion that is not your own?
- Is there any particular religion that you do not tolerate well or feel comfortable with?
- Are you drawn to any other religions or spiritual philosophies that you would like to share with your mate?
- If your new in-laws come from different religious points of view, can you embrace those views or accept them and feel good about being connected to your mate's family?
- If your new in-laws come from starkly different cultures, can you embrace the differences, as odd as they might seem?
- Could you enjoy celebrating with in-laws from a completely different world, or would you feel out of place?

PARTING THOUGHT: WHAT ARE YOU READY FOR?

As you explore the pathway to love, intimacy, and partnership, it's important to know what you are really ready for and how much you are willing to grow into your relationship and new family life. Marriage changes us. Mixed marriages can change our life cultures and points of view significantly. Seek spiritual and emotional counseling for any issues with which you need help along the way.

3

Winning Over Mom and Dad

Family Issues

Stay true to yourself and what you want. You shouldn't be pressured by "tradition" or what "everyone" does. Do what you want, even if the whole family screams to the heavens. It's your day. Have grace. Patience. Listen to annoying information with open ears. Respond honestly, clearly, and be grounded in your decision.

—AnaMaria

Weddings are notorious for stirring up the emotions of the clan. Add the element of intermarriage and even the most loving people might exhibit some of the stereotypical behaviors that have long plagued mixed-culture brides and grooms—the mother who is wounded because the wedding is not in a church, the grandmother who thinks your children will be cursed if you don't marry "your own kind," and the stubbornly conservative father who just can't see beyond his own tradition. It's not easy to deal with these kinds of issues with your parents, but understanding them will help you keep your footing.

Planning a wedding is often the first place couples begin to truly get some experience in the art of compromise. Interfaith couples especially are given many opportunities to work on the balance between "including everyone" and doing certain things to "keep the peace." Couples must also form good boundaries to protect themselves and their relationship when parents do not agree with their choice of mate—or the break in family tradition the marriage might bring.

The best approach to dealing with worried parents is with empathy and trying to understand their points of view and feelings—and then giving them time to adjust. Ultimately, you have to decide what is right for you. But attempting to hear their point of view is an important part of the process for all. It is an exercise in understanding the culture from which your family or in-laws hail and allows you to prepare for married life. The issues that surface during planning a wedding are a microcosm of the issues that may underline your ongoing family relationships. These are the things that will get exacerbated during family functions, holidays, and when the children come.

A Hindu bride with a very religious mom called me recently about her wedding and told me her mother had yet to meet her mate. "She has totally rejected the idea of this marriage and my husband-to-be," said the bride. "It's gotten to the point where I am not talking to her." She wanted to know if I had any ideas for helping her parents fall in love with the man she was about to marry. I suggested she start by opening the lines of communication and moving them toward a family dinner. While it will not solve everything, when they see how much this man loves and adores their daughter, firsthand, they may relax. My advice, always, is to keep the lines of communication open whenever possible and talk with your parents. Rather than fighting about faith traditions, focus on letting them know how happy you are and how in love. Ultimately, for many parents, your happiness will be the most important thing.

WHAT ARE SOME OF THE ISSUES WITH INTERFAITH PAIRINGS?

In my ministry it has been a blessing to see that most families who have religious or cultural issues come around eventually, and there can be healing of rifts and cultural disagreements. Yet there are some situations where, despite best efforts, parents will not change their minds about intermarriage or the mate you have chosen. The challenge then becomes knowing when to move forward, without their blessing, while leaving the door open to acceptance someday.

Interfaith and intercultural issues usually come with many layers; they may be more complex or serious depending on the culture from which your family hails, their personal religious values, and their attachment to their traditions. Over time I have identified certain issues that repeat themselves. You might encounter one or more of the following:

Your Parents May Be Upset Because
1. You are marrying outside your religion.
2. You won't be marrying inside their traditional house of worship.
3. You are not having a ceremony according to tradition or following the family traditions.
4. You are downplaying or leaving out God.
5. You are not wearing the expected wedding apparel or going through the expected rituals.
6. You are wearing wedding apparel from your beloved's culture and/or going through rituals of his or her culture.
7. They fear you may honor your mate's tradition more than your own.
8. Deep down they are prejudiced or suspicious of people from different backgrounds, countries, faiths, and cultures.
9. They are afraid of what relatives, friends, and community will think and worried that they will be judged for your choice of mate and style of wedding.
10. They are so set in their ways, combined with any number of the preceding issues, that they can't deal with or accept your choice in mate or style of marriage.

They Worry Because
1. They think you and your children will suffer or be shunned.
2. They are concerned your marriage (and hence children) won't be properly blessed by God or the family clergyperson.
3. They realize that if you are not married formally in your religion of birth, it many not be considered an official sacrament by their faith, religious institution, or clergy.
4. It may be an embarrassment to them in front of family and friends.
5. They may feel they have not done their job properly as parents or they have failed.
6. They feel they are betraying their traditions by participating in the marriage and/or they are concerned they will have to participate in spiritual rituals that are against their own faith.
7. They fear that they—or you, or both—will be punished, ostracized, or blamed by relatives and the community.
8. They feel they have lost control of their family and their dreams for you, and they feel threatened.

9. You may not carry on the heritage of which they are proud.
10. Your heritage or faith may be watered down if you blend your life with someone from a different background.

TRY TO UNDERSTAND THEIR FEARS

Many parents will articulate their concerns very clearly, but often there is another issue running beneath the surface. At Edward and Lola's wedding the bride's family was in traditional African wedding attire and the groom's family were in yarmulkes. This couple was completely in love. The bride was a doctor—brilliant with a great future. She was highly educated, and her parents were both physicians. They looked slightly out of their element in this New York gathering, but they were kind and accepting and willing to participate in anything their daughter asked of them. The groom's mother, on the other hand, had a meltdown a half hour prior to the ceremony, refusing to partake in the family unity candle lighting. She said it was against her religion. It seemed, though, that she was acting out her upset over her son's selection of mate. She was wounded, and she felt participating in the ceremony was betraying her heritage. It could be said she was unable to rise above her prejudice and was acting out her feelings in a childish way, but it turned out also that the groom had never really discussed his marriage and ceremony with his mother. He was so afraid of her reaction that he never shared the depth of his love for his bride and never took the time to listen to any of his mother's concerns. He was so worried about her anger and rejection, he was afraid even to tell her that she was scheduled to participate in the ceremony. On top of all the other issues, the groom's mother was feeling disconnected from her son. It was so hard for her to participate lovingly in the ceremony with all this going on, but eventually the groom's family helped her see how important it was that she was included. During the candle lighting in the ceremony, I talked about how the couple's love was bigger than their differences and their fears, and the groom's mother seemed to surrender to love in that moment. She looked over at her son and daughter-in-law and got a glimpse of the love in their eyes. She smiled. She was a little more at ease. Did it change her deepest feelings? Probably not. But it opened the door to possibility and, it is hoped, better communication between the newlyweds and the groom's mother.

Know When to Compromise and When Compromise Is Too Painful

I have noticed time and again that when it comes to weddings, some couples and families become *suddenly* more interested in religion and culture. While many are genuinely practicing their faith, some just feel they do not want their family faith underrepresented. This ends up putting a lot of parental pressure on brides and grooms. It helps to be able to honestly clarify your own beliefs and your level of true de- votion to your faith and also to make the distinction between what is important to you personally and what you are willing to compro- mise on to relieve parental pressure. Karen, a nonpracticing Christian who was marrying Amram, her nonpracticing Muslim boyfriend of six years, said in all the times they were together, he never showed inter- est in his religion. "He drank, smoked and ate all day during Ramadan [Muslim fasting holiday] and has not been in a mosque for years," she said. "And he never prays." She believed she was more spiritual than he was, but when they decided to wed, the groom suddenly got very focused on religious values and insisted that they be followed some- how in their Western ceremony and in raising their children. The bride challenged him to truly follow his religion and make it important in his life, in preparation for marriage and children. He could not. But as the wedding grew nearer, his mother was pressuring him more. Although his mother was not actively practicing her faith either, she feared their marriage would not be proper because they were having a nondenomi- national ceremony in the United States. The mother refused to fly in for the wedding unless there was a *nikah*, a traditional Islamic ceremony. This tension put the couple in counseling for months. Finally, they came to a compromise: they decided to go ahead with their Western ceremony but make it religion-free, and they opted to have a *nikah* in a mosque that same day, led by an imam, a traditional Islamic cleric. This satisfied the groom's mother, but it did not help the couple clarify the future of religion in their lives. When one side is more religious or more demanding, it often means the person who is least religious has to bend the most. The bride did most of the religious compromising here, but in many ways, the groom did, too, because he was not authentically devoted to his faith, so they *both* bent to do something that felt forced, and it was not healthy for their relationship. It is absolutely fine to have a second ceremony to honor family heritage—couples do it all the time—but it is equally important to find ways to make it meaningful for you as a couple. In this case, the couple did not even enjoy making the groom's mother happy because the spirit of the occasion had been lost to a religious demand that was not really suited to the couple.

Have the Courage to Follow Your Heart

I once attended a wedding of a friend that broke my heart. It was a wedding officiated by a Hindu priest, but I had come to offer my blessings to the bride and groom because I knew they needed a little extra spiritual support. The family behavior I saw that day was unlike anything ever witnessed; it was in fact surreal. When Ladita married Arjuna, her father and his entire family stood in the back of the temple marriage hall—crying. When it was time to participate in the wedding rituals and blessing, they came up to the front of the room and did so without even looking at the groom. They seemed totally disconnected and did nothing to hide their upset. Why? Ladita, a Brahman, choose a beloved from a different caste. Not only did she not allow her father to choose her mate, she married for love, and the man was not the doctor husband her father hoped for. Her dad seemed totally willing to throw away his wonderful relationship with this amazing daughter because of this marriage. To her credit, the bride and groom had their wedding anyway and enjoyed all the traditions. The bride's mother and sister did all the work on the ceremony, as the other relatives sulked. They had planned a second ceremony with the groom's family a couple of months down the road, and they felt that they would then have all the family blessings they needed; they did not let the small-minded behavior of the bride's clan disrupt things. I went up to the bride's dad at one point, and he looked me in the eyes, with tears, and said, "This is not my tradition." I wanted to tell him to snap out of it, but instead I offered a hug. When I went to the bride and groom, they shrugged and said it was his loss. I sensed he would come around someday, even though he was far from accepting their union on their wedding day. Sure enough, a year or so later, he threw a huge baby shower bash when his daughter became pregnant with his first grandchild. Is he in love with his son-in-law? No. But he is in love with his grandchild and they have all, finally, made peace.

Keep the Door Open for Healing

True and utter family disharmony can wreck a wedding ceremony. If the opposing parties are going to disrupt the wedding or act out, it may be better if they do not come. If your parent does not like the groom you have chosen or your grandmother thinks marrying the woman of your dreams is a complete betrayal of faith or family, then sometimes we simply cannot win them over—not when you are planning the wedding, anyway. The family issues that challenged soul mates Jennifer and Omar throughout their relationship flared up on the way to the altar. Jennifer comes from a traditional Roman Catholic Italian background, and Omar's family is practicing Baptists. They are also African American. Jennifer and Omar met in college in their second year in 1995 and fell in love, but when school ended and Jennifer moved back to her family home, her father pressured her about their interracial romance. Family disapproval led to their breakup, but neither had truly gotten over one another. They were both living in New York when Omar, then a social worker, was working at a homeless shelter and missing Jennifer. A Catholic priest colleague urged him to call her. He did. Their relationship rekindled, and they decided to marry. Jennifer's father had issues about the marriage, and he verbalized them and said he would not come to the wedding. As painful as this was, both bride and groom began to resent having to deal with such small mindedness. The situation became so uncomfortable that even when her mother said her father might change his mind if she called him, she decided not to because at "that point it was too weird." Both bride and groom felt a huge gap that her father did not come to the wedding, but they accepted it and decided to go on with their big day and their future together. "As soon as I realized that Omar was the most important thing, we felt it doesn't matter what our families thought," said Jennifer.

The Thanksgiving after the wedding, Jennifer's aunt went to Florida to see her dad. She had taken some photos of the wedding with her, and he asked to see them. "After that he called my mom and told her he did not want this to be an issue anymore. So that Thanksgiving, my father came up and met Omar for the first time. They had a bit of an exchange of words; Omar promised he would take care of his daughter." Omar and Jenn were able to determine that her very traditional father was worried about his side of the family and what they would think. Omar also admitted that prior to the wedding, his mother had had her concerns. "My mom wanted me to marry someone who looked like her," says Omar. "But she said, if this is what makes you happy then do what you feel you need to do. I accept it."

Although this couple has a few years of married life under their belt and they look forward to their future, there will always be a tinge of sadness that Jenn's father is not in the wedding photos and perhaps that he never really apologized for his actions at the time. And Omar says, "I still get a little nervous about her dad, but I don't let it get in the way of my love for Jenn or my love for her family." All parties have made an attempt to move forward and reestablish family ties. It was not easy, but healing can come even after bitter family breakups during wedding planning. Omar and Jenn are happy that they followed their hearts and for the magic between them. "Our relationship was something meant to be," says Omar. "Ever since we got married so many positive things have happened."

When They Run Screaming from the Room

In the 1971 movie *Made for Each Other,* Renée Taylor and Joseph Bologna play Pandora and Giggy, an interfaith couple who meet in group therapy, fall for each other, and then break up. Ultimately, Pandora pushes for a reconciliation and insists Giggy take her with him to a Sunday dinner visit to his old-fashioned and wacky Italian Catholic family, despite his protests.

They take their seats with parents, grandparents, and siblings. Giggy's father, portrayed by Paul Sorvino, tries to cut through the uncomfortable silence and make conversation. But the mother, portrayed by Olympia Dukakis, is visibly upset. A dysfunctional family ruckus ensues when, in the middle of dinner, she has an outburst because she senses Pandora is Jewish. "If you marry her," screams Giggy's mother, "I'm not coming to the wedding."

The father calms the mother and grandparents, yet eventually the whole family gets into an uproar, projecting that this Jewish woman and Catholic man are going to end up betrothed. In desperation, Giggy and Pandora run out to the car. By then, the father is leading the whole family in running after them, screaming, "I'm not coming, I'm not coming, I'm not coming!"

I mention this movie because I always tell my couples, when planning a wedding, you don't want to put anything in the ceremony that will make one side of the family "run screaming from the room." However, sometimes we have to accept that the marriage itself may make them run screaming—initially.

This humorous and dramatized protest of an interfaith marriage happened on film in the 1970s, but the attitudes were not completely off for that era. The script for *Made for Each Other* was written by Taylor and Bologna, a real-life Jewish-Christian couple who wed in 1965. Their interfaith union also inspired *Lovers and Other Strangers*, a play, and then a 1970 movie that took a comedic look at the coming together of a Jewish-Christian couple at time when it was not the norm.

Four decades later, a marriage between a person of Jewish heritage and a Christian is one of the most common interfaith pairings. Family reactions are far more civil these days—or at least they are not completely disruptive, if they do occur. And some couples have absolutely no specific interfaith issues as they head to the altar. But not every mixed couple's decision to marry is at first greeted warmly by parents and family. Over the years, I have heard from hundreds of couples grappling with issues related to faith, culture, and race and looking for ways to appease parents while having the wedding of their dreams. I have been called on to coach many couples through difficult family situations.

Dealing with family dynamics can be a very complex situation, and it will be different for each couple. In real life, Taylor and Bologna's families were not wild about their interfaith union. In later years, they went on to renew their vows every few years, celebrating by having a ceremony from different faiths and cultures. They've made their interfaith marriage work for 45 years.

THOUGHTS TO PONDER

1. The first thing you need to think about is how much involvement you want your family to have in your weddings and how important their "blessings" are on your union.
   If having them involved and happy about it is important, clarify and identify what the issues are with your parents or family.
2. Short of canceling the wedding, are there ways you can compromise that can also be meaningful to you as a couple?

   - Would either of you consider or want to convert or change religions?
   - Would you consider having two officiants or two distinct ceremonies?
   - Would you travel for a ceremony or celebration in your partner's hometown?

3. Can you give your family the time and space they need to adjust to the new change in their lives without having them miss the wedding?
4. How would you feel if they did not come to the wedding?
5. Would your family be helped by spiritual counseling?

Part Two

How to Put Together Your Ceremony

What would be the best wedding ceremony for you? How much religion and tradition do you want to include? Would you like friends or family to offer readings or unique tributes? Perhaps as you start the journey to your wedding day you are not yet sure. The following chapters will give you the suggestions as well as spiritual and creative ideas to help you design a wedding ceremony that enables you to truly express your love and commitment in a personalized and memorable way, with the words and rituals that are meaningful to you both.

4

Deciding on the Kind of Ceremony You Want

What was most important to me was to focus on our life together. I enjoyed every moment of my ceremony. The rain that fell around us couldn't do anything to ruin the wonderful feelings I had inside.

—Deborah

Every culture has its customs. When you have been raised with a certain way of thinking about weddings, it sometimes takes a little effort to adjust your mind-set to the idea of creating your own personalized wedding ceremony.

For example, one of the most ancient and yet still prevalent traditions is the arranged marriage. Devout Hindus, Sikhs, Muslims, and Hasidic Jews are among those who still expect to follow that path to the altar. In that scenario, your parents select your mate and you marry according to the traditions of your family, faith, and culture. The path to the altar and married life is set forth by a set of values and rituals that have been passed down through generations. In certain countries and cultures, even if a marriage is not arranged, when couples of the same background and culture fall in love, they often follow long-standing protocols of their tradition. So if you come from a family where arranged marriage or same-faith marriage is considered the "right way" to marry, you (or your parents) might struggle a bit with the idea of a ceremonial experience that strays far from the traditions of your birth.

By the same token, some brides and grooms have to adapt to the idea that they can actually approve of and in fact control the content and spirit of their wedding ceremony. In the West, it used to be that a man would propose, the couple would pick a date, and the parents of the bride would pay for and arrange a wedding in their hometown house of worship. The bride and groom would be married by the family priest or rabbi. No one ever asked about the form or content of the ceremony. Who even thought to—or would dare—question a religious leader about his or her area of expertise? More likely, bride and groom would simply go along with whatever they were told to do, often standing there dazed at the wedding altar. Many brides and grooms can't even remember what happened between the processional and the recessional. As one woman told me of her wedding more than two decades ago, a time before couples sought the kind of personal touches brides and grooms can hope for today, "We got married by a rabbi who did the entire service in Hebrew. We had no idea what was being said, or what it all meant. To this day, we still have no idea what really happened during our ceremony."

An interfaith couple is not a likely candidate for a cookie-cutter wedding ceremony. There simply is no one-size-fits-all kind of service. Sometimes there are only two faiths to blend—such as a Christian-Jewish interfaith wedding—and in that case a couple might prefer to have clergy from both sides officiate, bringing in elements from both faiths. But sometimes there are far more layers of faith, culture, ancestry, and family life to blend or consider.

In my wedding ministry, I have seen just about every combination of faith, culture, race, and age, along with blending in children from one or more prior marriages or unions. For example, the bride may be Buddhist with a Buddhist mother and a Catholic dad. Perhaps her groom is Christian but has a father who is part Chinese, Irish, Native American, or Jewish. Maybe one of them has been married before—or both—and have one or two kids, so there is another dimension of spiritual and family union to bring into the ceremony.

This is why it is so important to open your minds and hearts to the possibility of a truly unique and personally tailored ceremony. You can get married in a way that honors your ancestors, acknowledges your faiths, and most important, celebrates your love.

You can meet all your needs as well as your yearning for elements of tradition. It will take a little more clarification and finesse than the average same-faith ceremony, but the results will be memorable and extraordinary.

There are many options for personally tailoring a ceremony, so it's important that you two figure out the general tone you would feel most comfortable with—religious, nondenominational, civil, offbeat, humorous, solemn, a little of each—as well as decide on the kind of wedding officiant with whom you would most like to work.

Unless you choose to be married in a religious ceremony that will follow a time-honored religious protocol, you can be as creative as you like. We live in a new age of weddings.

THE MENU OF WEDDING OPTIONS

Many brides and grooms are surprised to know that there are *so many* ways to approach a wedding ceremony; it is almost overwhelming when they discover they can blend aspects of many different kinds of ceremonies into one uniquely loving, expressive, and personal wedding. The range of options is vast. Here are *some* of the flavors of weddings today.

1. **Traditional religious.** If you are both of the same faith and have decided to marry in a traditional house of worship and/or select a traditional clergyperson to officiate at an outside venue, you are signing on for a traditional religious ceremony. Your clergyperson will speak, offer prayers, and include rituals from the holy books of your faith. This kind of ceremony generally follows a specific form and has very specific content. You can request the inclusion of personal vows; depending on the clergyperson, you may be able try for those and other touches. Like it or not, you can't expect to edit religious protocol—you wouldn't tell a Catholic priest to leave Jesus out, suggest a Buddhist monk chant in English, or tell a rabbi to skip the seven blessings over the wine. You can certainly ask to see the ceremony beforehand or be advised of what it contains so you are aware of what you are in for. Keep in mind that many traditional clergypersons have done so many weddings that the content of the ceremony may be in their memories and not on paper somewhere.

2. **Nontraditional religious.** If you are both of the same faith but do not relate to the traditional ceremonies you've witnessed or gone through, or you have been precluded from marrying through traditional channels, you might want to have a ceremony that honors the faith you were both raised with but goes easy on religion. You can have a lovely ceremony that celebrates your love and your belief in God and can include only the parts of the ceremony that are personally meaningful to you. For example, a Catholic couple had a double challenge. She'd

been divorced (and not annulled), and he never completed all the sacraments required before marriage. So they opted for a restaurant wedding that included Catholic vows and readings and prayers in the name of the Father, Son, and Holy Spirit, but they decided to modify the language and make the ceremony more about their commitment to one another than their commitment to God and the Church.

3. **Interfaith.** If you and your beloved are of different faiths, you might choose a ceremony that honors both. This can be done in a number of ways: co-officiated by a clergyperson from each of your faiths or by a single interfaith or nondenominational minister. If both or one of you is religious, or if your parents are, you might want to have a religious ceremony that includes a balance of prayers and rituals that both you and your families will recognize and feel comfortable with. If you are not terribly religious but would like to *honor* aspects of your faiths or heritage, you can *blend in* symbolic traditions from each faith. For example, a Jewish groom and Catholic bride might have a reading of *I Corinthians* as well as unity candles from the Christian side and the breaking of the glass along with a Hebrew prayer from the Jewish side. If your wedding is officiated by two clergy from different faiths, they might want to structure a more traditional format or each do their own ceremony, one at a time. With an interfaith or nondenominational officiant, you can choose the level of religion included. For example, a Buddhist bride who did not consider herself very religious had a prayer written by her dad read at the ceremony, while her Hindu groom decided to include vows from his own faith, without the ritual aspects. On the other hand, an atheist Korean groom and a somewhat spiritual American bride elected to go with two officiants doing two distinct ceremonies. One was a nondenominational minister who did a *slightly* spiritual ceremony in English, and one was a Korean minister who did a service in Korean.

4. **Nondenominational or secular.** If you consider yourselves spiritual but not religious, and you are not marrying in a house of worship, you might want a beautiful ceremony that honors marriage and honors God or Spirit but does not include *any* aspects of any religion. You might not even want to use the word God and might prefer to personalize the prayers to "Divine Spirit," or "Creator," or even "Mother, Father, Great Spirit." The idea is to honor your spirituality and celebrate your relationship in a sacred yet secular way. Many brides and grooms—interfaith, same religion, and nonreligious—love the nondenominational option because it seeks to honor the most common denominator and takes a middle ground, which makes *everyone* feel comfortable.

5. **Multicultural and culturally inclusive.** In addition to interfaith, some couples are from very different cultures or perhaps from the same

faith but from—literally—different worlds. Other couples have simply adopted many traditions along the way in life and would like to include them. A multicultural approach to a ceremony can be interfaith, religious, or nondenominational. It means including customs from more than one culture; sometimes from several. For example, one couple got married in Brooklyn with the New York City skyline as the backdrop and included the Native American custom of calling in the directions, an adaptation of the seven steps from Hinduism, a Hawaiian sand ceremony, and the Jewish custom of the breaking of the glass. An American bride and her beloved, born in Spain, had a nondenominational ceremony that included readings in both English and Spanish.

6. **Civil.** Typically this is a no-frills ceremony that includes just the legal aspects of solemnizing vows—a question of intent and free will and the pronouncement of you two as husband and wife. Although some states do include a mention of God, most people tend to think of a civil ceremony as one that is brief and contains no religion or religious references. A traditional civil ceremony is performed by a justice of the peace, a judge, a notary public, or a mayor, for example; it might be in a judge's chambers, a town clerk's office or City Hall, or a restaurant. *Civil* is sometimes interchanged with the word *nonreligious* and used to describe a ceremony that has no mention of God or religion yet has a creative or romantic spirit. An interfaith couple who married in Central Park in New York insisted on a traditional civil ceremony but asked for a slight cultural twist. He was Australian and she from Sri Lanka. They included an adaptation of the Sri Lankan custom of tying strings around their fingers instead of exchanging rings, and they ended by eating Sri Lankan wedding cake.

7. **Spiritual marriage or sacred love ceremony.** The emphasis is on an even greater spiritual connection between the couple. Rather than relying on "God above" to create and strengthen their union, the couple is empowered to see their own divinity and the divine light within each other. This theme is common in ceremonies in some of the pagan traditions, such as Celtic handfasting, and also in some Hindu or Tantric traditions, where the bride and groom come to the altar as God and Goddess to declare their love. The sacred love ceremony gives marriage an extraordinary start. It doesn't have to look like a Hindu or pagan ceremony. It can be a groom in a tux and a bride in white who walks down the aisle or a shoeless couple on a beach in Maui.

8. **Contemporary, creative, personalized.** Every wedding is a sacred event that holds profound meaning and potential for the two people who step up to the altar in the name of love. This kind of ceremony can pull together elements from *any* kind of ceremony and be personalized and unique from start to finish. You can literally create your own wedding.

THOUGHTS TO PONDER: HOW TO FIGURE OUT THE KIND OF CEREMONY YOU WANT

It is perfectly permissible to blend tradition with creativity and romance. And don't be surprised if you also find yourselves *yearning* for or leaning more toward tradition. Even nonreligious people tend to "get religious" when it comes to a wedding; you might look forward to a ceremony that is based on or includes elements of your faith tradition. These traditions are pleasantly familiar because you've seen them so many times at the weddings of friends and family. Tradition is a wonderful thing, and it is important to assess, together, how much of it you want in your ceremony:

- **Ask yourselves, where does religion fit in?** For example, if you've not stepped into a synagogue since a childhood Hanukah party, would you want a Jewish ceremony in a temple with a rabbi or a cantor? Or would you perhaps just like a symbol of the religion such as the breaking of the glass or a Hebrew prayer? If you missed out on most of the sacraments of the Catholic Church, are you going to cram to catch up so you can experience the seventh sacrament (marriage) in a church, or would you be more comfortable lighting a unity candle or offering a prayer to Jesus outside the traditional church setting?
- **What type of ceremony is most suited to you?** Would a traditional ceremony be most suited to the two of you—or not? Or would you rather blend in *aspects* of your traditions in a nondenominational ceremony? Or would something romantic and offbeat be more your style? On the spectrum between a formal and traditional ceremony and the wackiest exchange of vows you can think of, where are you? Somewhere in the middle, or somewhere on the edge, wanting to be different?
- **What are your special needs?** Think about the requirements you each may have. Is one of you more religious than the other? Is one of you more traditional than the other? Is one of you more influenced by parents than the other? Is one of you atheist or agnostic? If you are an interfaith pair, are you interested also in your mate's background? Do you hail from different cultures? How much do you want to honor your heritage and the traditions of your parents and family? Is there anything you abhor about those traditions and would never want in your own ceremony?
- **What do you two truly want?** Most important, be completely honest with one another (and then with your officiant). Honor your heritage and your parents, but make sure you are creating this ceremony for the two of you—not just to please others.

5

Finding the Right Officiant

Choosing an officiant who was spiritual, down to earth, and open to alternative ideas was paramount. We were lucky to find someone who imbued these qualities and was able to help us create a ceremony that was unique and wholly ours. We chose readings that spoke to us as well as rituals and blessings from our cultures and other cultures that were meaningful to us.

—Jackie

To select the right kind of wedding for you, you have to select the right officiant—or officiants. You want the person who facilitates and guides this important milestone in your lives to be someone you *both* feel comfortable with and confident about, someone who makes no judgments about your union and whose only concern is providing you a ceremonial experience that is all you want it to be. It would be wonderful—and in many ways essential—to work with a clergyperson who is caring and who knows you or is willing to get to know you.

Perhaps you have in mind a family minister or a clergyperson from your own faith. There are many kinds of clergy and officiants available to serve modern couples, including Unitarian and Humanist ministers, open-minded rabbis and former Catholic priests. Or perhaps you were hoping to have your best friend ordained, like Joey, who presided over Monica and Chandler's weddings on *Friends*? (Just make sure that kind of ordination privilege is available and legal in your state.) For a civil ceremony, you might prefer a retired judge.

There is also a new genre of officiants and interfaith ministers who are trained by interfaith seminaries to create *any kind* of personalized ceremony for couples of all backgrounds. Many of them are hip, open minded, and willing to create the wedding service you truly want. They are often very glad to co-officiate with other clergy and even friends or relatives.

Seek someone who makes you feel so at ease on so many levels that *you can relax on your wedding day,* knowing you will be taken care of— and that there will be no surprises or unwanted preaching. One bride had a clergyperson who unexpectedly launched into a tirade of religious political commentary about Palestinians and Israelis in between her vows. "I found him offensive," she says, "and could barely focus on the ceremony. It was so distracting."

The right officiant is a must. This is the person who will lay down the foundation for your married life with a ceremony that celebrates your hopes and dreams and—it is hoped—blesses your union in a personal way. Sometimes this means talking your childhood clergyperson into flying in for your wedding or seeking a less traditional officiant.

You do not have to settle for a ceremony that is completely controlled by someone else. Even if you two decide to go the traditional route, ask to make adjustments to any language you cannot live with. (One bride couldn't bear the idea of being pronounced "man and wife" and asked her clergyperson to make sure he said "husband and wife"; another asked her minister to replace the phrase "till death do you part" because "it was too negative sounding.") Even in traditional settings, look for the most open-minded clergypeople and, at the very least, request information on what will be said in the ceremony and what you will be asked to do.

THOUGHTS TO PONDER: CONSIDERING WHO WILL OFFICIATE

Give some thought to who should have the honor of presiding over your wedding. Ask yourselves these questions:

- Do you want one officiant or would you rather have two—one from each faith or representing each family?
- Do either of you have family clergypeople you'd like to include? Will that person co-officiate an interfaith union?

- Do you prefer a male or a female officiant?
- Do you want someone who has a prepared script, or are you interested in co-creating or at least having input into your ceremony?

Always insist on meeting with potential officiants beforehand and ask some key questions, or at least have an in-depth phone conversation with your clergyperson. The initial consultation should be free. Find out what this person is truly able to offer you—a canned ceremony or a personalized approach.

6

What Are the Elements of the Wedding Ceremony?

The fact that we wrote the ceremony ourselves, including our vows, reinforced our investment in the actual event. We included two poems that reflected exactly how we were feeling. We loved creating our own special day!

—Courtney

Beyond selecting the level of spirituality and the general tone, you can put your imprint on every segment of your ceremony. *The ceremony is the wedding* and the wedding is the start of the most intimate relationship of your lifetime. When you work on the details of the ceremony together with your officiant, and you each take the time to add input and ideas, it will enhance your wedding experience in so many ways.

This is the part of the wedding day that allows you both to step up to the plate and formally declare your love, commitment, and intentions for marriage—before family, friends, and the world. The language of the ceremony literally sets forth the foundation for your life together.

HOW TO PERSONALIZE YOUR CEREMONY

Everyone's relationship is unique, so you want to make sure, whenever possible, that the words, readings, and vows expressed in the ceremony uniquely represent the two of you. The language of the sacred is very subjective. Every couple should have the opportunity to choose (or at the very least review) all that will be spoken and relayed at their wedding as well as the opportunity to write and speak their own vows.

How Much Can You Personalize Your Traditional Ceremony?

When planning a traditional ceremony based on religious protocol (especially if in a house of worship), you may not have as much freedom to "tweak" or personalize your wedding. For example, a Catholic priest is not likely to alter the traditional wedding ceremony; while there are some priests who will allow personalized vows, many will not. Flexibility depends on the faith tradition, the protocol of the house of worship, the clergyperson who has been asked to officiate, and how much leeway that individual has or is willing to take given his or her religious responsibilities. If you are working with an officiant outside of a house of worship (with the wedding taking place at the reception venue), it sometimes grants more flexibility in the content of the wedding. Make sure you ask questions about where he or she is willing and able to tailor the ceremony to your needs—whether it is through personal vows, readings you select yourself, music, or participation of family members.

How Specially Tailored Can a Contemporary Interfaith or Nondenominational Ceremony Be?

If you have opted for a creative contemporary ceremony, the sky is the limit. Whether you write it yourself or work with a loving officiant who will help craft your dream wedding, you can handpick the elements of both your faiths, selecting only those that are personally meaningful. The term people sometimes use for this approach to weddings is *cherry-picking*, which in essence means you can assess what fruit is available and pull the best from the tree. This means you can review the wedding traditions of both your faiths and cultures—those you grew up with and those you have adapted along the way—and select the aspects that you both love or that you agree are important. You can add in any special rituals and readings you like. You can look for ways to include family and friends. For example, in a Christian-Jewish ceremony, your main focus might be on love and commitment, but you can honor both traditions and include things that are familiar to both families—candle lighting and a reading of I Corinthians from the Catholic side, a Hebrew prayer and breaking of the glass from the Jewish side.

What the Law Requires

The requirements for a ceremony outside a house of worship are minimal—similar to the requirements of a civil ceremony. Other than following state laws of whatever locale is home to your wedding, you are free to create the wedding of your dreams. Check requirements state by state. In New York, for example, you require a valid marriage license, a witness over 18, and an ordained or otherwise legally empowered officiant who can sign the license, ask a question of intent, and pronounce you husband and wife.

CEREMONY OUTLINE

Your most important tool is an outline of what *can* be included in a wedding ceremony. The following will help expand your awareness of the possibilities as you to begin to formulate ideas, including where to place rituals, readings, and vows. Sit down together and go through these elements in an organized, step-by-step manner. Find out the ideas you both have for the ceremony. You will learn a lot about one another in the process! A well-versed officiant will be able to help fill in the blanks by getting to know your style, showing you sample ceremonies, and offering many creative ideas for making the ceremony special.

This basic structure and outline can be used for a nondenominational, interfaith, and any contemporary creative wedding ceremony. It was adapted from the standard ceremony format used in *Sacred Threshold*, by Gertrud Mueller Nelson and Christopher Witt, and from Daphne Rose Kingma's book *Weddings from the Heart;* course materials from the New Seminary; and other sources.

- **Processional.** Figure out the order and plan on music that will bring the relatives and bridal party down the aisle, and then select something special for the bride. In the Jewish tradition, the groom's parents walk the groom first and the bride's parents walk her last. Many modern couples like this touch, regardless of their religion.

- **The Greeting.** This is where we hear the minister/officiant on TV say, "Dearly beloved..." In real life, he or she simply welcomes everyone and thanks those gathered for being there on this special day.
- **The Opening Prayer/Invocation/Convocation.** A sacred space is created by a prayer to God (the Creator, Spirit, the Divine), and a petition is made for a strong, loving marriage filled with good fortune. This can also be offered as a general blessing, without evoking the Divine. For Buddhists and nonreligious couples, you can open instead with a moment of silence.
- **Wedding Reading.** A favorite poem or scriptural passage (or even a song you love) is read by the minister or a friend or family member. (There can be more than one reading. Additional readings may be placed here or elsewhere in the ceremony, perhaps after the officiant's message or at the end of the ceremony.)
- **Officiant's Message.** The minister offers loving advice for a long, strong marriage. This is a great place to include insights into your relationship, your love for each other, and your intentions for marriage. This is also a good place for the officiant or one of your friends to share a story about your relationship.
- **A Special Wedding Ritual or Tradition.** You may light a unity candle, do a wine ceremony or a sand ceremony, or include some religious tradition. The ritual might also be placed elsewhere in the ceremony such as a handwrapping and blessing after the exchange of rings.
- **The Declaration of Intent.** These are the "I dos." This can be done in the form of a question (Do you, Jane, take...), or you can declare your intent to one another (I, Jane, take you, Jim, to be my lawfully wedded husband. I promise to...). They can be classic, traditional, or hip and modern. As long as you say I do, it's a done deal. *This is a legal question that signifies you have come of your own free will and it must be included.*
- **The Vows.** These are optional but highly recommended. Writing your own vows is a special way to declare your loving intentions for marriage. You can borrow from existing vows or even read a poem that fits. You can read them to your beloved or do this in repeat-after-the-minister style. (See the chapter on vows for more details.)
- **Blessing and Exchanging of the Rings.** There are many ways to do this. It can include audience participation—such as asking people to silently bless the rings by filling their hearts and minds with good thoughts for you two—and can include a ring vow such as "with this ring, I pledge my love" or the classic "with this ring, I thee wed."
- **Pronouncement.** This is where the minister says something like, "I now pronounce you husband and wife" and formally declares you husband and wife. *This is a legal requirement.*

- **The Kiss.** You know what that's about! But you may not realize that it doesn't always have to be encouraged with the statement "you may kiss the bride!" You can also ask your officiant to say, "Please share your first kiss as a married couple" or "You may kiss" or, even, "Seal it with a kiss!"
- **Closing Cultural Tradition.** If you are including the Jewish tradition of breaking the glass, this is the time. Also, the jumping of the broom, an African custom, comes now.
- **First Act as a Married Couple (Optional).** Many guests are used to the wedding being over with the kiss, but you can choose to include another meaningful moment or two. You can exchange a rose or a gift, or you can invite the community to shower you with personal blessings, called out from the crowd. Hindus throw flowers, and Orthodox Jews sometimes throw candy. Some couples hand out cones or bags filled with rose petals to be thrown as they go up the aisle.
- **Benediction or Closing Prayer.** If you want to end the wedding on the kiss, this can come before the pronouncement. A beautiful prayer or poem will bring the sacred ceremony to a close and send you on your way with love and blessings. Many couples like the Apache Wedding Blessing or the scriptural "May God bless you and keep you." It can be very short, even just one line.
- **Recessional.** Congratulations! You're married. You head up the aisle as a married couple. It's a nice touch if the clergyperson allows your moms and dads and even grandmothers to step out from their seats and head up the aisle as part of the recessional.
- **Receiving Line.** After this, you will likely want to consider a receiving line or figure out a different way to greet your guests and let them congratulate you.

THOUGHTS TO PONDER: IS THERE ANYTHING SPECIAL YOU'D LIKE TO INCLUDE?

- Are there elements you have always dreamed of having in your wedding ceremony?
- Is there something you have seen at someone else's wedding you'd like to include?
- Is there a significant wedding ritual or tradition from your faith or culture that would make you feel truly married?
- Remember also to consult your parents and grandparents to find out about any traditions from their weddings that might make a special touch in yours.

Choosing Meaningful Wedding Vows

The most sacred thing that we did as a couple when organizing our wedding was when we wrote our vows.

—Jodie

Wedding vows are the hallmark of the wedding ceremony in many faiths and cultures. Some interfaith couples elect to use vows from each of their faiths. For example, one Hindu groom included the vows that are part of Saptapadi, the seven steps around the sacred fire in his tradition, and his Jewish bride called on the ancient statements from Song of Solomon in Hebrew—*Ani L'Dodi, v'Dodi Li.* They also shared the English translation—"I am my beloved's and my beloved is mine"—so there was something for everyone.

Blending your family's faith or native language into your vows can be a lovely way to honor both traditions, but you can also decide to create or select beautiful vows that have no particular religious significance. The most important thing is that you create, select, speak, and/or agree to words that have meaning to you and that come from the heart.

You can select from classic vows or create vows that represent a unique and heartfelt way to express your love. Although your whole ceremony can be an expression of that love and commitment, the promises you make to one another are among the most sacred moments of a ceremony.

Public speaking may not be your thing, so it is important you do not stress yourself over vows, but it is so helpful, together, to give the vows some careful consideration and thought. Contained within those vows are intentions for marriage and deep declarations of love. These are the seeds of dreams to come true.

GET FAMILIAR WITH DIFFERENT KINDS OF VOWS

Question of Intent Vows

In every ceremony, there is a question put forth by your officiant that gives you a chance to declare that you freely choose to marry the person standing beside you. It's called the "question of intent." In many states it represents a legal aspect of the ceremony in that it tells your officiant you come to the wedding altar of your own free will. If you two feel you do not want to speak much during the ceremony because you are shy or because the thought of it makes you too nervous, you can have an extended question of intent that satisfies the legal requirement for a question (such as "Do you, Jonathan, take Annie to be your wife?") and gives you a chance to agree to certain declarations. This would be asked by your officiant. For example, a classic vow many people are familiar with is as follows:

> Do you, Annie, take Jonathan to be your husband,
> To have and to hold from this day forward?
> In sickness and in health?
> In good times and bad times?
> Will you love, honor, and cherish him
> All the days of your life?

Here's a more modern approach to the same kind of vow format:

> Do you, Jane, take Adam to be your husband?
> Do you promise to grow with him in mind and spirit,
> To always be open and honest with him,
> And cherish him for all the days of your life?

To either, you will, of course, answer "I do."

Repeat-after-the-Officiant Individual Vows

Alternatively, you can also have a set of vows spoken individually *in addition to* the question of intent (right after or before) or spoken as part of your ring vows (during the blessing and exchange of rings). These vows should be of a manageable length and fed to you in bite-sized pieces by your officiant so that you don't have to memorize anything and so that they will be easy for you each to repeat. Here's an example from Sophia and Zvonko's ceremony:

1. **Here is the basic vow outline,** with each partner speaking the same vow:

   I, Sophia, promise
   To trust and respect you...
   Be patient and understanding...
   Openly share my thoughts,
   And share my fears and dreams...
   Watch after your well-being...
   Nurture your growth...
   And bring lightness and joy to our lives.
   I will be a loving and supportive partner.

2. **Sharing a longer vow.** If you have a vow that is on the long side, instead of having you both repeat the same lines, you can each speak part, and then you can together repeat the final lines. This can also be done in repeat-after-the-officiant fashion. Chris and Lori adapted this vow, in part, from Roy Croft's poem "Love":

   Chris First:

   Lori, I love you
   Not only for what you are,
   but for who I am
   when I am with you.
   Not only for what you have made of yourself...
   But for what you are making of me.

   Now Lori:

   Chris, I love you
   For helping me to see
   the dreams I have for life
   more clearly than ever before.
   One of those dreams is becoming realized
   right now,
   As we come together as a family.

Now Lori and Chris Together:

I promise to you today
That I will forever fulfill my role
as your partner
in the life we are building together.

3. **Vows exchanged with rings.** If you prefer to speak your vows along
   with your rings, which is common in the Christian tradition, you might
   have a vow like this one that Elizabeth and Ross found in *The Everything Vows Book:*

Take this ring
As a sign of my love for you
And my commitment to this union.
This is the beginning.
I will be with you until the end.

4. **Simultaneous vows.** A unique, memorable, and modern approach is
   for you each to speak the same vow simultaneously. This is like stereo
   vows—you hear it consciously and subconsciously—and it is really a
   nice touch to share your sentiments and promises to each other at the
   same time. It represents partnership and working in the spirit of harmony and cooperation. For example, you might have a vow like this
   one. I wrote it for a couple who were stressed about writing vows but
   not about speaking them:

On this day,
a new adventure begins.
I want you to know
That I will stand by your side
As your partner in life.
I look forward to laughing with you,
Crying with you,
Comforting you,
And being comforted by you,
Inspiring you,
And being inspired by you.
I will always cheer you on
As you follow your dreams,
And I will let you help me achieve mine.
Let us grow together,
In mind and spirit,

And stand together to face the world.
I will cherish you always.
You are my one and only true love.

Reading Vows to One Another

If you have a lot to share with each other, it may be a little too un-
wieldy to approach vows from a repeat-after-the-officiant style. And
perhaps it is redundant to read the same long vow to one another. Mix
it up! You can always call on the classic approach of writing or adapt-
ing vows you read to each other. Or try a unique approach to reading
to one another, using a favorite poem or song. Once in a blue moon, a
brave soul will memorize or speak from the heart, but unless you are
a professional actor, I don't recommend trying to memorize on your
wedding day!

Many couples fear that reading their own vows will bring on a down-
pour of wedding tears—it might—and some shy away from reading
their own vows, fearing they will be too nervous. Yet raw nerves and
real tears are often what make the exchange of vows so authentic. Here
are some ideas for highly personalized vows.

1. **Writing and reading your own vows.** Of course, the time-honored
   way to share vows is to each write your own separate vows and read
   them to one another at the wedding altar. Many couples like to coordi-
   nate their vows, preferring to write them together, share them before
   the wedding, or each read the same vow to each other. Some couples
   choose to surprise each other and share the vows for the first time on
   the wedding day. Either way, it is always a beautiful touch.

Some couples opt for completely unique vows and others choose
also to add in some traditional sentiments such as these vows from Katerina, of the former Yugoslavia, and Xingmin (pronounced *Shin-min*),
who was of Chinese descent. We printed their vows on beautiful scroll
paper, for an elegant touch.

Katerina:

Xingmin, I love you for being gentle, kind, and tender.
I love you for hearing my thoughts, sharing my dreams.
I love you for filling my life with joy and loving me without end.

I love you for accepting me as I am.
With you, I can be completely happy and completely myself.
From this day, I promise to love, honor, and cherish you,
in sickness and health, in good times and bad.
I pledge myself to be ever faithful to you, with my body, my mind, and
my heart.
I freely take you as my husband.

Xingmin:

Kaca [her nickname], I consider my decision to learn ballroom dancing
the best decision I ever made in my life. That's how I met you, got to
know you, and fell in love with you.
I love you because you are beautiful, intelligent, and kind.
I love you because you make me happy and you make me whole.
From this day, I promise to love, honor, and cherish you,
in sickness and health, in good times and bad.
I pledge myself to be ever faithful to you, with my body, my mind, and
my heart.
I freely take you as my wife.

Then there are couples like Brad and Karin who each take a completely different approach to their vows. Karin blended in traditional
thoughts with her own heartfelt sentiments, and Brad wrote something unique to their relationship in the form of a humorous rhyme.
This American businessman and Scandinavian businesswoman had
spent much of their relationship trying to stay connected long distance
or meeting up with each other in different countries. These vows acknowledged where they had been and the new promises they were
making on their wedding day.

Karin:

Brad, I take you to be my lifetime partner,
secure in the knowledge that you will be
my constant friend, and my one true love.
I promise to encourage and inspire you, to laugh with you,
and to comfort you in times of sorrow and struggle.
I promise to love you in good times and in bad,
when life seems easy and when it seems hard,

when our love is simple, and when it is an effort.
I promise to cherish you, and to always hold you in my highest
regard
These things I give to you today, and all the days of our life.

Brad:

Karin, we have traveled together
from Barcelona to Budapest
and Thailand to Tuscany
Tahoe to Mexico and places in between.
And the journey we start today
Is the beginning of more sights unseen.
And all along the way
I promise you this…
I promise you my life
To help navigate a course
That delivers love
From an everlasting source.
I promise you my dreams
To be shared as they come
Not hidden but joined
Together as one.
I promise you truth
When we're rich or poor
Whether it be sweet
Or bitter to the core.
I promise you trust
Because on this we are built
It is the cover of love
An everlasting quilt.
So thank you, my love
For taking my hand
To become my wife
In every land.

2. **Alternation line vows.** You can also decide to divvy up the lines and
   alternate reading to one another. This is a very creative and somewhat
   theatrical way to share your vows. Here are the vows Tony and Summer (he's a director and she's an actress) read to each other. We made
   it easier to follow by printing the bride's and groom's lines in different
   colors (using their favorite wedding colors).

Summer:	My darling Tony, you are the magic of my days.
Tony:	My darling Summer, you help me to laugh and teach me to love.
Summer:	This I promise to you:
	I will always be honest, kind, patient, and forgiving.
Tony:	This I promise to you: I will encourage your individuality because that is what makes you unique and wonderful.
Summer:	I will nurture your dreams because through them your soul shines.
Tony:	I will help shoulder our challenges because through them we'll emerge stronger.
Summer:	I will share with you the joys of life, because with you they will be that much sweeter.
Tony:	I will be your partner in all things, working with you as a part of the whole.
Summer:	I will be a true and loyal friend to you.
Tony:	I will cherish you, hold you, and honor you.
Summer:	I will respect you, encourage you, and cherish you, in health and sickness.
Both:	Through sorrow and success, for all the days of my life, I will love you with all of my heart. These are my sacred vows to you, my equal in all things.

Similarly, Andrea and Pat alternated lines in their vows and opted to speak the last segment simultaneously.

Pat:	I promise to love you always, without reservation or restraint.
Andrea:	I will honor, trust, and respect you, my one and only love, for all of my life.
Pat:	I will faithfully support you in all of your hopes and dreams and stand with you through all your challenges.

Andrea: I will be your companion, your lover, your best friend, and your equal as we take this greatest journey of our lives together.

Both: I will without fail
In summer's light
In dark of night
In love
With respect
In joy
With honor
Devote myself
To you, my love.

3. **Other ideas for vows.** Be as creative as you would like! If you would rather select or adapt vows from poetry or a song, go for it.

   a. Tim and Patty adapted favorite songs. Tim read the lines from Chicago's *Inspiration* and Patty shared sentiments found in *From this Moment* by Shania Twain and had a guitarist and singer play it live immediately after she and Tim exchanged vows.
   b. Maria and Michael used poetry. The bride was shy about speaking, so Michael read Oriah Mountaindreamer's stirring poem "The Invitation."
   c. Steven and Deborah chose not to speak vows themselves and instead had their officiant *read* their favorite song, "My First, My Last, My Everything" by Barry White.

4. **Speaking from the heart—and from the hip.** Some brides and/or grooms prefer to speak without prompting from the officiant or reading from a piece of paper. As mentioned, I never recommend that you try to memorize your vows—too stressful on your wedding day—yet by all means, if you or your beloved prefer simply to "share" what is in your hearts, do so.

When Kelly and Ron married in Central Park, it was only the bride and groom and two witnesses, yet more than 100 bystanders quietly gathered around us during the ceremony. In a move that surprised all of us, the groom suddenly shared with his beloved—and hence those observers in Central Park—how much he adored, honored, and cherished her. The bride recalled, "The part of the ceremony that most strengthened our union was when Ron started to speak from his heart. It wasn't planned, rehearsed, or read from a card. It was just from the heart."

The words truly poured from him in a waterfall of loving tributes that day, and when he was done, the crowd applauded. There was not a dry eye in the house.

Neither of you should feel forced to speak or pressed to write vows if writing will stress you. By the same token, if one of you would love to speak and the other is super shy, you can find a way to make it work for you both! After Ron shared what was in his heart, Kelly *read* Ron what was in her heart.

If freeform sharing feels natural, by all means do so. But don't needlessly stress yourself. If in doubt, keep a piece of paper at the altar or a card with your vows on it—it is absolutely fine to keep a little cheat sheet handy in case you blank out. One groom showed up to his wedding at the United Nations Chapel with an eight-line vow scribbled on a napkin. He thought he'd be able to speak the vows without referring to the napkin, but I kept it close by in case—and he was happy I did!

VOW WRITING EXERCISE

The first thing I give brides and grooms is a writing exercise to help them bring out their feelings of love, friendship, and appreciation. They know they love and adore one another but don't always have the language to express it. It would be so helpful for you and your beloved, together or individually, to take some time to ponder and answer these questions. Your answers will give you insight on ways to personalize your ceremony as well as inspiration for things to express in your vows.

Questions to consider:

1. How did you meet and what first attracted you to one another?
2. What do you love about each other?
3. What does getting married mean to you?
4. What are some of your dreams and intentions for married life?
5. What story do you want to share about your love?

Personalized vows can be a way to celebrate your relationship and have some fun sharing some of the things you love—and also laugh about—together. Here is a process that will help you create the perfect vows.

1. **Find inspiration for your vows.** Look for the kinds of sentiments you want to express in wedding readings, poetry, popular songs that you love, or even greeting cards. Pour through vow books that share the words of love used by other couples. Find ideas from the faiths or cultures you were born into or the spiritual traditions you love.
2. **Connect to the feelings.** When you are ready to write, take a moment of pause or meditation to reconnect to the energy and magic that made you want to marry this person, and let the feelings flow.
3. **Ask yourself these key questions. Jot down some notes:**

   - What do you love about this man or woman?
   - What feeling pours over you when you think of his or her love for you?
   - What are your hopes and dreams for your married life?
   - What promises would you like to make?

4. **Write a first draft.** Begin by sharing what you love about your sweetie (you can include cute and funny reasons) and let him or her know how he or she makes you feel. Next, share things you look forward to experiencing together. Sprinkle in promises you would like to make. Summarize by sharing how grateful you are for his or her love and the opportunity to share your lives.
5. **Revise and perfect.** Then go through the first draft; edit or add in new thoughts. Don't be afraid to use humor—if that's your style (e.g., "I promise never to change the channel when the Yankees are on").
6. **Make sure you speak from the heart.** Let your sentiments come from the heart. They do not have to be long. Approach them with a K.I.S.S. (Keep It Simple, Sweetheart) and make them real. Those are the *best* wedding vows.

As Rev. Diane Berke, director of One Spirit Seminary, points out, "In general, I encourage couples to keep their vows short and pithy, going right to the heart of what they want to promise each other. That way, the vows can be something you can tuck into your heart, and pull out in those moments when you need to remember them most."

THOUGHTS TO PONDER: WHAT IS THE RIGHT APPROACH TO VOWS FOR YOU?

While you may have a certain reference or preconceived notion of what a wedding vow is meant to be, as you can see, there are many different options for the vows and promises you make on your wedding day. In selecting the approach most suited to the two of you, consider the following:

- Would it give you joy to write your own vows, or would you prefer to adapt vows from a book or someone else's writing?
- How comfortable are you both about speaking in front of friends and family, or would you rather agree to certain promises than speak them out loud?
- Would you prefer to read vows to one another or have your officiant support you in a repeat-after-me fashion?
- Would you rather skip vows because you are uncomfortable sharing such personal things and instead just have a question of intent?

8

Wedding Blessings, Prayers, and Readings

We had a special concern in creating our ceremony. I was raised Christian and my husband was raised in a Jewish family. We wanted to have a ceremony that would make everyone feel comfortable and wouldn't exclude anyone. So we decided to mainly have a nondenominational ceremony with a central theme of love. We selected wonderful readings that expressed our feelings. It was a sweet, spiritual, loving ceremony, and it helped set the tone for the evening and our marriage.

—Laura

In a religious ceremony, readings typically come from holy books, but in an interfaith or blended cultural wedding, you can draw from scriptures of one or more faiths or from the classic literature of the culture. Contemporary couples can choose *whatever* makes their hearts sing—a little of this and a little of that—and can find readings in favorite poetry, literature, or music. It can be any words that speak to your feelings for one another, express sentiments about love and marriage you can relate to, or that relay religious or spiritual sentiments you cherish.

This chapter offers a sampler of readings from different faiths and cultures as well as some from pop culture. These can be read by your officiant, yet readings are also a wonderful way to involve friends and family members.

CATHOLIC SCRIPTURE

I Corinthians 4–7

Love is patient, love is kind.
It does not envy, it does not boast, it is not proud.
It is not rude, it is not self-seeking,
it is not easily angered, it keeps no record of wrongs.
Love does not delight in evil but rejoices with the truth.
It always protects, always trusts, always hopes, always perseveres.

—New International Version

The Lord's Prayer

Our Father who art in Heaven,
Hallowed be thy name;
Thy kingdom come
Thy will be done
On earth as it is in heaven.
Give us this day our daily bread;
And forgive us our trespasses
As we forgive those who trespass against us;
And lead us not into temptation,
But deliver us from evil.

—Roman Catholic, traditional Matthean version

CHRISTIAN WEDDING PRAYER

Wedding Day Prayer

Most gracious God, we give you thanks for your tender love in sending Jesus Christ to come among us, to be born of a human mother, and to make the way of the cross to be the way of life.
We thank you, also, for consecrating the union of man and woman in his Name.
By the power of your Holy Spirit, pour out the abundance of your blessing upon this man and this woman.
Defend them from every enemy.
Lead them into all peace.
Let their love for each other be a seal upon their hearts, a mantle about their shoulders, and a crown upon their foreheads.
Bless them in their work and in their companionship; in their sleeping and in their waking; in their joys and in their sorrows; in their life and in their death.

Finally, in your mercy, bring them to that table where your saints feast
forever in your heavenly home; through Jesus Christ our Lord,
who with you and the Holy Spirit lives and reigns, one God, for
ever and ever.
Amen.

—*Book of Common Prayer* (1979)

Ecclesiastes 3:1–15

There is an appointed time for everything.
And there is a time for every event under heaven
A time to give birth, and a time to die;
A time to plant, and a time to uproot what is planted.
A time to kill, and a time to heal;
A time to tear down, and a time to build up.
A time to weep, and a time to laugh;
A time to mourn, and a time to dance.
A time to throw stones, and a time to gather stones;
A time to embrace, and a time to shun embracing.
A time to search, and a time to give up as lost;
A time to keep, and a time to throw away.
A time to tear apart, and a time to sew together;
A time to be silent, and a time to speak.
A time to love, and a time to hate;
A time for war, and a time for peace. Amen.

The Lord's Prayer

Our father, who art in Heaven,
Hallowed be thy name;
Thy kingdom come,
Thy will be done
On earth, as it is in heaven.
Give us this day our daily bread;
And forgive us our debts
As we have forgiven our debtors;
And lead us not into temptation,
But deliver us from evil.
For thine is the kingdom,
And the power,
And the glory,
Forever.

—Protestant orientation

JEWISH SCRIPTURE

Song of Solomon 2:10–13

My lover spoke and said to me, "Arise, my darling,
    my beautiful one, and come with me.
See! The winter is past; the rains are over and gone.
Flowers appear on the earth; the season of singing has come,
    the cooing of doves is heard in our land.
The fig tree forms its early fruit; the blossoming vines spread their
    fragrance.
Arise, come, my darling; my beautiful one, come with me."

—Old Testament

Hebrew Blessing

Ba-ruch A-tah Ado-noi E-lo-hei-nu Me-lech Ha-olom
She-heh-che-yah-nu Ve-ki-yi-ma-nu Ve-he-gi-a-nu Laz-man Ha-zeh.
Translation: Blessed are You, Lord our God, King of the universe, who
    has kept us alive, and sustained us, and enabled us to reach this
    moment.

—Traditional Hebrew blessing

KABBALAH: JEWISH MYSTICISM

The True Nature of Soul Mates

Each soul and spirit, prior to its entering into this word,
consist of male and female united into one being.
When it descends on this earth the two parts separate
and animate two different bodies.
At the time of Marriage, the Holy One,
blessed He be, who knows all souls and spirits,
unites them again as they were before,
and they again constitute one body and one soul,
forming as it were the right and left of one individual.

—The Zohar, book of Jewish mysticism

MIDDLE EASTERN

On Marriage by Kahlil Gibran

You were born together, and together you shall be forever more.
You shall be together when the white wings of death scatter your days.

Yes, you shall be together even in the silent memory of God.
But let there be spaces in your togetherness.
And let the winds of heaven dance between you.
Love one another, but make not a bond of love.
Let it rather be a moving sea between the shores of your souls.
Fill each other's cup but drink not from one cup.
Give one another of your bread but eat not from the same loaf.
Sing and dance together and be joyous, but each one of you be
alone—even as the strings of a lute are alone though they quiver
with the same music.
Give your hearts, but not in each other's keeping.
For only the hand of Life can contain your hearts.
And stand together yet not too near together:
For the pillars of the temple stand apart,
And the oak tree and the cypress grow not in each other's shadows.

—Kahlil Gibran, from *The Prophet*

PERSIAN/SUFI/MYSTICAL ISLAM

Marriage Blessing from Rumi

May these vows and this marriage be blessed.
May it be sweet milk,
this marriage, like wine and halvah.
May this marriage offer fruit and shade, like the date palm.
May this marriage be full of laughter,
our every day a paradise.
May this marriage be a sign of compassion,
a seal of happiness here and hereafter.
May this marriage have a fair face and a good name,
an omen as welcome
as the moon in a clear blue sky.
I am out of words to describe
how spirit mingles in this marriage.

—Jelaluddin Rumi, from *The Rumi Collection*

BUDDHIST

The Buddha's Sermon at Rajagaha

Do not deceive, do not despise each other anywhere. Do not be angry
nor bear secret resentments; for as a mother will risk her life and

watches over her child, so boundless be your love to all, so tender,
  kind and mild.
Cherish good will right and left, early and late, and without hindrance, without stint, be free of hate and envy, while standing and
  walking and sitting down, what ever you have in mind, the rule of
  life that is always best is to be loving-kind.

  The Buddha's Sermon at Rajagaha, Buddhist scriptures, verses 19–22

Buddhist Wedding Prayer

Today we promise to dedicate ourselves completely to each other,
  with body, speech, and mind.
In this life, in every situation, in wealth or poverty, in health or sickness, in happiness or difficulty, we will work to help each other
  perfectly.
The purpose of our relationship will be to attain enlightenment
  by perfecting our kindness and compassion toward all sentient
  beings.

—Lama Thubten Yeshe (1979)

HINDU

Blessing over the Seven Steps (Adapted)

1. May this couple be blessed with an abundance of resources and
   comforts, and be helpful to one another in all ways.
2. May this couple be strong and complement one another.
3. May this couple be blessed with prosperity and riches on all levels.
4. May this couple be eternally happy.
5. May this couple be blessed with a happy family life.
6. May this couple live in perfect harmony...true to their personal
   values and their joint promises.
7. May this couple always be the best of friends.

—Rev. Laurie Sue Brockway

NATIVE CULTURES

Apache Wedding Blessing

Now you will feel no rain,
  for each of you will be a shelter to the other.

Now you will feel no cold,
   for each of you will be warmth to the other.
Now there is no loneliness for you;
   now there is no more loneliness.
Now you are two bodies,
   but there is only one life before you.
Go now to your dwelling place
   to enter into your days together.
And may your days be good and long on the earth.

—From the 1950 movie *Broken Arrow*

IRISH BLESSINGS

Classic Irish Blessing

May the road rise to meet you,
May the wind be always at your back.
May the sun shine warm upon your face,
The rains fall soft upon your fields.
And until we meet again,
May God hold you in the palm of his hand.
   May God be with you and bless you;
May you see your children's children.
May you be poor in misfortune,
Rich in blessings,
May you know nothing but happiness
From this day forward.
   May the road rise to meet you
May the wind be always at your back
May the warm rays of sun fall upon your home
And may the hand of a friend always be near.
May green be the grass you walk on,
May blue be the skies above you,
May pure be the joys that surround you,
May true be the hearts that love you.

FRENCH LOVE LETTER

When two souls, which have sought each other for however long in
the throng, have finally found each other, when they discover that
they suit one another, that they understand one another, that they

hear one another, in essence that they are one and the same, then a union is created between them, fiery and pure as they themselves are, a union that begins on earth and continues forever in heaven. This union is love, true love…a religion, which deifies the loved one, whose life comes from devotion and passion and for which the greatest sacrifices are the sweetest delights. This is the love which you inspire in me.…Your soul is made to love with the purity and passion of angels.

—Victor Hugo, written to his beloved Adele Foucher (1821)

CLASSIC WEDDING READING

The Art of Marriage

Happiness in marriage is not something that just happens.
A good marriage must be created.
In the art of marriage the *little things* are the *big things* …
It is never being too old to hold hands.
It is remembering to say "I love you" at least once a day.
It is never going to sleep angry.
It is at no time taking the other for granted;
the courtship should not end with the honeymoon,
it should continue through all the years.
It is having a mutual sense of values and common objectives.
It is standing together facing the world.
It is forming a circle of love that gathers in the whole family.
It is doing things for each other, not in the attitude
of duty or sacrifice, but in the spirit of joy.
It is speaking words of appreciation
and demonstrating gratitude in thoughtful ways.
It is not looking for perfection in each other.
It is cultivating flexibility, patience,
understanding and a sense of humour.
It is having the capacity to forgive and forget.
It is giving each other an atmosphere in which each can grow.
It is finding room for the things of the spirit.
It is a common search for the good and the beautiful.
It is establishing a relationship in which the independence is equal,
dependence is mutual and the obligation is reciprocal.
It is not only marrying the right partner, it is *being* the right partner.
It is discovering what marriage can be, at its best.

—Wilferd Arlan Peterson (used with the permission from his estate)

ROMANTIC MODERN READINGS ABOUT LOVE

My Beloved Soul Mate

My Beloved Soul Mate,
I always knew you existed.
But I worried that I would never find you.
When you came into my life,
Everything changed, and became clearer.
I gained a deeper understanding of who I am,
By seeing myself through your loving eyes.
On this special day, we pledge our love
And we embark on the journey of life, together.
Together we will see the world,
And we will be the world,
For one another.
And so the journey begins.

—Rev. Laurie Sue Brockway

Merging Hopes and Dreams

You met, and fell in love.
You were drawn deeply to one another
And wanted to get to know each other.
Soon, you began to merge your lives.
And you began to dream,
and look toward a future together.
On this day, you merge your hopes and dreams,
Your challenges and disappointments.
You began this ceremony as two individuals,
Walking down the aisle toward each other.
You leave this ceremony as one,
Walking toward your new life together.
May this marriage be blessed in all ways.

—Rev. Laurie Sue Brockway

Just You and Me

The moment we met I knew you were the one.
Our relationship began with laughs and fun.
Over time we began to know each other very well
And we realized we were headed toward wedding bells.
Now we stand before those we love
And we stand before God above.

We pledge our love and fidelity.
And we look toward our life together,
Just you and me.

—Rev. Laurie Sue Brockway

Recipe for Love

Falling in love is the easy part.
 Creating a good marriage is a bigger task.
Here is a special recipe for building your lives together:
 Give life to your love.
Through small acts of kindness and caring
 Communicate clearly.
Always tell one another what is on your minds.
 Listen to each other.
Truly hear what your partner has to say.
 Have a shared mission.
Know what you want your marriage to be.
 Follow dreams together.
Decide on worthy goals that you can pursue together.
 Support each other's dreams.
Be the wind beneath one another's wings.
 Be there in tough times.
Conjure strength for each other in sorrow and disappointment.
 Cherish what you have.
Always treasure your relationship and the one you love.
 Hold on to each other.
Remember how valuable it is to love and be loved.
 Make this marriage the foundation of your lives.
Let it always be the home you return to,
and the safe heaven that the outside world cannot disturb.

—Rev. Laurie Sue Brockway

This Marriage Is Our Home

Let this marriage be our new home.
May it be warm, loving and inviting.
 Let us embrace those we care about most.
May they join us in a circle of happiness.
 Let us build a life and a family here.
May we welcome children and grandchildren.
 Let us bless the world with our love,
For surely we have enough to go around.

—Rev. Laurie Sue Brockway

Why We Love Weddings

The reason we love weddings so much is that we come together in
great happiness to celebrate the love between a couple who have
asked us to bear witness to their love.
That means we get to share in the joy, the reawakening, the inspiration of love.
Weddings help everyone present remember love.
As we journey through the ceremony, the love in the room rises and
everyone there becomes enfolded in it and elevated by it.
In that moment, through being present for this common rite of passage,
we all understand and have an experience of the power of love.
That's why weddings are such happy occasions. And why we love
them so.

—Rev. Laurie Sue Brockway

The One I Have Longed For

You are the one I have longed for,
The true love I prayed for,
The partner I envisioned,
The playmate I hoped for.
The best friend I needed.
The wise counsel I sought.
The dear one I wanted to hold near.
You came into my life,
And through the mirror of your love,
Showed me I could be all those things to myself.
Yet with you in it, my life is richer, and better.
Thank you for loving me.

—Rev. Laurie Sue Brockway

What Marriage Means

Take my hand,
And walk with me into our new life,
You and me,
Together,
Blending our lives.
Building our dreams,
Enhancing our passion,
Exploring the world,
Improving Ourselves,
Preparing for a Family,
Embracing the ones we care for,

Sharing our love,
Leaving our mark,
Creating our legacy of love.
Marriage means we will grow,
and grow older, together.
We will support each other,
And be there for each other,
Through the good,
and not so great times.
We are a pair now,
Partners in the game of life,
And we are meant to stick together,
No matter what,
You and me,
Together,
Holding on to each other,
And living the journey of our new life.

—Rev. Laurie Sue Brockway

What Is Commitment?

Commitment in marriage means:
You will be there for each other
Through all seasons
And through all life brings you.
In good times and bad,
In sickness and in health,
In happiness and sadness,
In success and disappointment,
In passion and despair,
In celebration and reevalution,
And even in those times
when you don't feel like being there.
Marriage has its ups and downs.
But you will learn to ride the waves,
And deal with the tides of change,
Together.
That is what commitment is about!

—Rev. Laurie Sue Brockway

Join Me at the Altar

Join me at the altar of our love
Here we stand before God,

And those we love,
Pledging ourselves to one another,
For all time.
    We come here of our own free will,
Having chosen one another,
And knowing that marriage is a big step.
    We come here in the spirit of love,
Filled with hope for our future,
And confident that our love can see us through challenges.
    We come here not knowing exactly what life will bring,
But knowing we want to experience it together,
And trusting our commitment is strong enough to last forever.
    On this day, as we pledge our love and devotion,
May God strengthen our bond,
Joining our hearts and souls for all our days.
    May we grow in love and respect for one another.
May we grow in our devotion to one another.
May this marriage be blessed in all ways.

—Rev. Laurie Sue Brockway

THOUGHTS TO PONDER: WHAT KIND OF READINGS WOULD YOU PREFER?

Think about the tone you would like to create with readings and blessings. Do you want to honor your faith, or honor your romance, or both? A ceremony typically has one or two readings, but you can opt for more.

Here are some additional ways to find appropriate wedding readings for the minister, family members, bride, and groom:

- The Internet (TheKnot.com, Beliefnet.com)
- The library
- Greeting cards
- Favorite books on love
- Favorite movies
- Love songs and popular music
- Poetry books

Also, feel free to write your own poetry or have friends and family write poems, blessings, tributes, and readings to share at your wedding.

9

Selecting Rituals and Customs

Our wedding was made special by candle lighting and handwrapping. The candle lighting allowed us to include family and friends, and the handwrapping really sealed our commitment to each other.

—Monica

There are many beautiful rituals and customs from world cultures and faiths. Woven into the wedding ceremony, they offer you the chance to affirm and celebrate your love as they seal the union between you two and acknowledge the family ties that are established on your wedding day.

Many brides and grooms have gone along with the rites of the wedding ceremony, sometimes not knowing much about what they mean. The modern interfaith couple can actively select the rituals in their weddings, learn more about what they mean, and even make sure that the rituals are explained by the officiant as part of the ceremony—or included on the wedding program.

"It's very important that we embrace rituals because they make our wedding experience so much richer," says event planner Collin Cowie. "Ritual brings us together; it helps us to understand where we come from and where we are going. The whole idea of a wedding ritual is to have a little reflection."

The rituals in your ceremony will serve to move you from your everyday state of being into a higher state of love and partnership, and toward deeper family bonds. These rituals are also meant to symbolically take you from singlehood and engagement into the realm of marriage. Just think about it: you start your journey down the aisle single...*and you leave married*!

Search for the rituals that truly sing to you and that you are comfortable partaking in. In this chapter you'll find a sampling of ideas of rituals from different cultures as well as nondenominational rituals. Feel free to select any that you like, even if they are not from your tradition.

HOW TO SELECT RITUALS THAT ARE RIGHT FOR YOUR WEDDING AND YOUR MARRIAGE

Wedding rituals and customs are typically symbolic markers of the occasion and of the intention of marriage. They may be religious or spiritual in nature, or they can be nondenominational and creative rites. Essentially, they celebrate union and commitment as well as acknowledge the transformations that marriage brings—going from single to married life, from one family to the merging of two.

The rituals and customs you choose to include in your wedding ceremony will depend on how you choose to honor the tradition into which you were born—if at all—and what rituals "feel right" for you and your beloved. Here are some of the most popular religious and cultural rituals and customs that modern brides and grooms might choose to honor their heritage, along with their traditional meanings.

1. **Jewish.** The breaking of the glass reminds us that while we are joyous, there is still suffering in the world, but that the love of the couple adds to the healing of the world.
2. **Christian.** Lighting of the family unity candle brings the light of two separate candles together to light the one candle that represents the new union. In a church, it typically includes the union between woman, man, and God and/or the Church.
3. **African American.** Jumping the broom takes a couple from single life into the land of matrimony. It is said to be a custom that originated when slaves would secretly marry as a way to acknowledge their union.
4. **Hindu.** Satipati, or the "seven steps," is one of the most important rituals, where bride and groom take seven sacred steps around a sacred fire. In the Hindu ceremony, this is considered the ritual that seals the marriage.

5. **Japanese.** The sake ceremony symbolizes the fusion of two lives and offers blessings for long life and good fortune as bride and groom alternately sip from three different-sized cups.
6. **Chinese.** The red string of fate celebrates the legend that soulmates are tied together at the ankle at birth to ensure they will find each other some day. The red goblet ceremony gives the couple a chance to take a sip from two goblets tied together by red string. It symbolizes unity and blessings for shared good fortunes.
7. **Native American.** Calling in the directions is a way to honor the ancestors and call in the support of the spirits from all corners of the universe. It is an invocation that is sometimes enhanced by setting up a wedding altar composed of natural items representing all the elements and directions—air/east, water/west, fire/south, and earth/north.
8. **Hawaiian.** The Hawaiian sand ceremony is a way to symbolically blend the lives of two as one. Bride and groom pour two individual containers of sand into one shared container, showing that while they will always be their individual selves, they will never be separate.
9. **Pagan ritual.** Handfasting is an ancient Celtic tradition of literally tying the couple's hands together to signify their bond. This originally was an engagement ritual for ancient Celts, and modern pagans refer to their entire wedding ceremony as a handfasting.

Below are the actual rituals, ceremonies and customs you can use in your wedding, based on these preceding nine. You will find additional customs and strictly nondenominational rituals as well as a wine ceremony and hand blessing.

NONDENOMINATIONAL RITUALS ADAPTED FROM DIFFERENT CULTURES

Over the years I have worked with my couples to craft ceremonies with nondenominational interpretations or what we sometimes call "religion lite." They are meant to bring in traditions of your families, faiths, and cultures yet to take a more universal approach to honor that you are blending traditions as you blend your lives.

1. The Breaking of the Glass (Jewish)

In the Jewish tradition we conclude the ceremony with the breaking of the glass. A wine glass or lightbulb is wrapped in a linen napkin or cloth and placed in front of the groom's right foot.

Officiant says: There are many interpretations for the symbolism of breaking a glass. Today this tradition reminds us that love can help heal our world.

Bringing together the hearts and lives of two people in marriage creates a dimension of holiness; it brings more love into families, circles of friends, communities. Thus this marriage shines the light of healing and wholeness and helps perfect our world even more.

In the Jewish tradition, we end the ceremony with the man stomping the glass with his right foot. So [groom's name], please break the glass!

Everyone cheers and shouts, Mazel tov!

2. The Lighting of the Unity Candle

Bride and groom light two separate tapers and join their flames to light one central unity candle. These are usually secured into a unity candle holder or on separate candle holders.

Officiant says: It has been said that "from every human being there rises a light that reaches straight to heaven. When two souls that are destined for each other find one another, their streams of light flow together...and a single brighter light goes forth from their united being" (this is a quotation from the great Hasidic master Bal Shem Tov).

The lighting of the unity candle symbolizes the light of two individuals coming together as one brighter light....It symbolizes the promise to merge two lives as one....And it honors the family ties that are created by marriage. As a gesture of unity between the two families that are united on this day, we ask the mother of the bride and the mother of the groom [anyone can represent the two families, or bride and groom can do this on their own] to step up here and light the solo candles from the one light that already burns on the altar. This light represents the light [of God] within us all.

Parents/family come to either side of the bride and groom. They light candles. Then the clergyperson asks them to "pass the light" to the bride and groom.

Officiant to the bride and groom: Please hold the candles for a moment....These two lighted candles represent the two of you, as well as your families, ancestors, the source of who you are. These two distinct flames represent your lives, up until this moment. [Pause] We now ask you to bring these two separate candles together to light the unity candle. *They bring candles together with unity candle.*

Closing blessing: May the loving light of Divine Spirit, family, community, and good friends always bless this marriage!

3. Jumping the Broom

Couples who use this ritual typically create or have a family member create an ornate broom or besom, designed with flowers and lovely trinkets. It should be ready at the altar. After the officiant explains the ritual, one of the attendants hands the broom to the groom, who makes sweeping gestures to eliminate any negative energy. The groom then hands the broom to the bride, who places it on the ground in their path.

Officiant says: We end this ceremony with the African American tradition of the jumping of the broom. As our bride and groom jump the broom, they physically and spiritually cross the threshold into the land of matrimony. Traditionally, jumping the broom was also a means of sweeping away all negative energy, making way for all things that are good to come into your lives.

It is also a call of support for the marriage from the entire community of family and friends. In honoring the ritual, [bride] and [groom] issue a hope and a prayer of sweeping away any hatred or prejudice between people of different colors, beliefs, or traditions. The bride and groom will now begin their new life together with a clean sweep!

—Larry James, CelebrateIntimateWeddings.com (used with permission)

4. Saptapadi (the Seven Steps)

*Traditionally, a brass plate (*puja *plate) is on the floor, set up with a fire crafted with a candle wick and ghee. This modified version suggests the* puja *plate with the fire can be on a small table that the bride and groom can easily walk around. They each have a handful of puffed rice and throw a little into the fire with each step. The couple walks clockwise.*

Officiant says: Now, the bride and groom will take seven sacred steps, to seal their marriage covenant. In the Hindu tradition, this is the moment in which bride and groom become husband and wife.

With each step, they also symbolically agree to the following seven marital vows.

Officiant reads these vows and the couple takes a step with each.

Officiant says: With God as your guide, please take

1. The first step to ensure that together you will share the duties and responsibilities of your home by protecting and providing for your family.
2. The second step to develop physical, mental, and spiritual health.
3. The third step to increase wealth by righteous means for proper use.
4. The fourth step to acquire knowledge, happiness, and harmony by mutual love and trust.
5. The fifth step to be blessed with a healthy family.
6. The sixth step to develop mutual respect.
7. The seventh step so that you become true companions and remain lifelong partners through this wedlock, the perfect halves to make a perfect whole.

Bride and groom come back in front of the altar. The rest of the ceremony continues.

5. Sake Ceremony (Japanese)

In this modified version of the sake ceremony, we use only two traditional sake cups and one small pot of sake. Pour before the ritual.

Officiant says: To celebrate your union we call on a Western version of a Japanese custom. This cup of sake represents your new relationship as husband and wife. Today, you blend all you are, and all you will become, into this one union. This represents all the celebrations to come—may there be many. And all the challenges you will handle together—may they be minimal. It is symbolic of all the hopes and dreams, as well as disappointments, you will share during a long life together as a married couple.

Officiant hands them the cups.

Share a drink now, together, to symbolize your willingness to share all of life. And may the cup of life be full to overflowing.

6. The Red String of Fate and Red Goblet Ceremony (Chinese)

Officiant says: This couple's unique love story brings to mind the Chinese myth of "The String of Fate." It tells us that at birth the Gods tie an invisible red string around the ankles of men and women who are destined to be soul mates and one day marry each other. As they grow, the string gets shorter and brings them closer. It is believed that they will find each other, "regardless of time, place, or circumstance. The thread may stretch or tangle, but it will never break."

It is believed it might take time for the man and woman to mature and recognize true love in one another's eyes. That's the thing about soul mates. It may take time and effort to bring them together, but once they recognize one another, they fall deeply in love and become inseparable—like [bride] and [groom]!

We celebrate that these soul mates have been united with the red goblet ceremony. They will sip from two red goblets tied together by red string. It symbolizes unity and blessings for shared good fortunes.

To couple: Please share a sip to a rich and soulful marriage. The color red represents courage, joy, passion, and good luck—elements needed for a strong and happy marriage.

As you drink from this cup, you acknowledge that now that you have found one another, marriage is the thread that will hold your lives together.

They sip, simultaneously.

7. Calling in of the Directions

This is often read as an invocation or opening of the ceremony. If you choose to build an altar representing the elements, set it up before the ceremony. This is a good custom to involve friends in, giving people a direction to call.

Officiant says: Our ancestors reveled in their connection to nature and to the elements of earth, air, fire, water, and spirit. They believed that great blessings can be bestowed from all corners of the universe. So we offer a very special blessing to the bride and groom, culled from an ancient Native American tradition.

We call to the spirits of the East. We honor wind and ask that this couple sail through life safely and calmly.

We call to the spirits of the South. We honor fire and ask that this union be warm and glowing and that their hearts are always filled.

We call to the spirits of the West. We honor water and ask that it cleanse this couple for marriage and sooth them so that they may never thirst for love.

We call to spirits of the North. We honor mother earth and ask that this marriage be abundant and grow stronger with each season.

We call to the spirits of above, of below, and within. With all the forces of the universe, we pray for harmony and joy as this couple grows with one another.

As they pledge their hearts and lives together, please bestow great blessings and grace on this couple that stands before us in the name of love. Please surround us all in a circle of light.

In this tradition, you thank the ancestors and the directions, as they are treated as living spirits.

At the end of the ceremony, officiant says: We thank the spirits of the east, south, west, north, of above and below and within. We thank the ancestors and the elements of our common being for blessing their marriage.

8. Sand Ceremony (Hawaiian)

Bride and groom select two different colors of sand and pour from two separate containers into one central container. This can be modified to include family members.

Officiant says: We are all made up of millions of molecules, facets, possibilities, points of views, experiences, desires, hopes, and dreams. Our very beings are as vast as a beach that stretches on forever and our makeup as complex and complete as the many tiny particles of sand that, when joined together, make the beach such a stunning sight.

In the modern tradition of the sand ceremony, a couple acknowledges their individuality, and their desire to merge their lives in marriage, by pouring two separate containers of different-colored sand into one empty vessel. This symbolically unites the many aspects of their individual selves and also brings together the families that are united by marriage.

To couple: You come to this day as individuals, whole and complete unto yourselves, bringing the many tiny aspects that represent the two of you together into one vessel that represents a joint venture that is a stronger, fuller, more powerful expression of your love.

Couple pours sand simultaneously, and when they are finished, clergyperson says: Your newly formed union is represented by the intertwined pattern of sand you have created together. It represents all that you both are, all that you both bring into your marriage, and all that you will become together. May this union be blessed in all ways.

9. Handfasting (Pagan)

Traditionally, a couple chooses colorful silk ribbons that represent different qualities they want to bring into their lives. For example, green represents fertility and prosperity; red is courage and passion; yellow is inspiration; white represents purity and the divine within yourself and your partner; purple is the deep spiritual and emotional connection you share; and gold and silver represent the connection to God and Goddess, divine providence, and the sun and moon. Couples figure out a way to braid the ribbons or secure them together so all can be tied on the couple's hands at once. In a traditional handfasting, the ribbons are often tied one at a time.

Officiant says: In the ancient Celtic tradition of handfasting, a couple's hands were literally tied together to symbolize spiritual and physical unity. Please face each other and hold hands so you may feel the gift that you are to one another.

I will tie your hands together with multicolored ribbons, symbolizing your desire to blend your lives.

Officiant ties hands together and then places one hand on the couple's hands.

> **Officiant:** I offer this blessing over the hands:
> What a great gift it is to be loved, and to have someone to love.
> Hold on to the hands that love you,
> Tightly when need be and lightly when need be.
> As you embark on this life adventure together,
> In one another, seek strength, but never seek the other as savior.
> Let the tides of time not alter your love, unless to grow it.
> Let the tides of misfortune never sway you, unless to move you closer.
> Look for what is right between you
> And gently accept flaws, your partner's and your own.
> Explore things of the Spirit together and express Gratitude for the life you share.
> Storms in life will come and go, but a true partner is hard to find.
> Cherish and protect each other's souls,
> And know God and Goddess are with you always.
> May these hands, these lives, and this union be blessed.

MORE RITUALS FOR YOUR WEDDING

1. Handwrapping and Blessing of the Hands

This nondenominational blessing of the hands can be done after the ring exchange or even as part of the pronouncement. Bride and groom can use their own sacred cloth or buy a special scarf for the occasion.

Officiant says: When you give your hands, you give your heart. Many cultures have different ways of blessing the hands of the bride and groom. In Thai ceremonies, the couple kneels as elder and married relatives pour blessed water from a conch shell onto their hands and offer words of blessing. In the ancient Celtic tradition of handfasting, the couple's hands are literally tied together to symbolize spiritual and physical unity as prayers and blessings are recited. In any tradition, a hand blessing is a ritual that is meant to draw you closer to one another. The left hand is connected to the heart, and a hand blessing symbolically brings two hearts together. Today we will use the slightly modern tradition of hand-*wrapping*.

To bride and groom: If you choose to become one with each other, please place your right palms together, and then place your left palms over them. This creates a figure eight, or infinity symbol, with your hands. It signifies hearts that will love forever. I will wrap them with a sacred cloth, also in an infinity symbol. This will signify a relationship that lasts forever.

Clergyperson lays a cloth or scarf across the clasped hands and brings its ends up over each other, also creating a figure eight or infinity symbol, and places a hand on the couple's hands and offers one of a number of written/ spoken blessings that can be used.

Officiant offers blessing over the hands:

Please look at each other's eyes but hold hands so you can feel the
  love between you.
Shakespeare said, "Now join your hands, and with your hands, your
  hearts."
As your hands are bound together,
imagine also that your lives and spirits are joined.
Choose a union of love, trust, and mutual support.
Heart to heart, soul to soul, body to body. And so it is.

2. Wine Ceremony

The bride and groom share a sip from one chalice. Grape juice can replace wine.
Officiant says: This cup represents your new life together. It contains your hopes and dreams, your fears and concerns, and all the possibilities that lie before you. Sharing a sip from this cup symbolizes that your two lives—once separate—are now joined. Now, take a sip to celebrate your sacred union. May you never thirst for love!
  They share a sip.

3. Tasting of Four Elements

Place all four elements in small cups and have them handy at the altar. It works well to have attendants on either side of the bride and groom holding two elements each. They pass one to the bride, then one to the groom, and then the couple exchanges the items.

Officiant says: There is a Yoruba/African tradition in which the bride and groom taste four flavors representing different emotions within a relationship (sour, bitter, hot, and sweet), symbolizing that they will get through the hard times and in the end enjoy the sweetness of their marriage. We will ask our attendant to help.

- Attendant hands the groom the lemon and he then shares it with the bride.
- Attendant hands the bride the vinegar and she shares it with the groom.
- Attendant hands the groom the cayenne and he shares it with the bride.
- Attendant hands the bride the honey and she shares it with the groom.

Officiant says: No matter whether life brings you the hot or the cold, the bitter or the sweet, may you always have each other to share all life has to bring.

4. Step into the Rose Petal Wreath/Circle

This requires a bag of fresh rose petals. Bride and groom create the circle together at the start of the ceremony, creating a half circle each and joining each other's rose petals in the middle. They step into it at the start of the ceremony, or they can step in at the end.

Officiant says: Let us begin by asking the bride and groom to step into the beautiful wreath of rose petals that they have designed for their wedding altar.

This wreath represents a circle of love. It is the circle of love in which they choose to live the rest of their lives. It is the circle of love in which they will include their children, and it is symbolic of the closeness, the unity, and the oneness of the relationship they share.

As they step inside, let us pray: God, Goddess, Divine Spirit of all that is, please bestow great blessings and grace on this couple who stand before us in the name of love. And so it is.

5. The Bonds of Marriage

Many cultures include customs that bind a couple in marriage by, literally, creating a bond. You might want to adapt some aspect of these customs to symbolize a bond that will go on. In a pagan handfasting, the hands of bride and groom are tied together with individual ribbons of different colors that each represents a certain quality or blessing the couple hopes for. In some Buddhist traditions, the hands are wrapped with a prayer shawl. In the Hindu seven steps (Satipati), the bride's sari or sari shawl is often tied to the groom's coat in what is known as the "wedding knot" as they take seven steps around a sacred fire. In the Greek Orthodox Church, bride and groom each wear a crown of flowers that are tied together, as they take their first steps as husband and wife around the altar. In Thailand, an elder ties a "sacred thread" like angel halos around their heads, joining them both by a long thread that connects them in a symbol of unity. In the Native American tradition, the couple cozies up under a blanket that is wrapped around them during the ceremony.

THOUGHTS TO PONDER: WHAT KIND OF RITUALS ARE RIGHT FOR YOU?

There are many different ways you can strengthen your union and seal your commitment. First, you both have to get a sense of how much ritual you would like and from which or how many different traditions. Some couples prefer a very low key and ritual-free wedding—this includes skipping the rituals of their faiths and cultures—and some vote for "wedding theater," which has more fanfare and more participants coming up to read and offer blessings. Before you decide on which rituals you want, ask yourself these questions:

- Do you both love the idea of the ritual aspects of weddings—such as candles, wine, small ceremonies within the ceremony—or do both or one of you find yourself turned off by it?
- Would you prefer something simpler or prefer to express your love mostly in words spoken by the officiant?
- Do you want to honor your religious backgrounds and heritages by choosing rites that your parents had at their weddings?
- Do you want to combine rites and rituals from your different backgrounds, or would you rather not call attention to differences?
- Would you be most comfortable addressing the most common denominator in your wedding ceremony and choosing rituals that are completely neutral?
- Would you consider including rites from traditions that are not your own, simply because you like them?
- Would you feel comfortable asking mothers and grandmothers to share any family traditions that might be fun to include?

10

How to Include Family, Friends, and Children in Your Ceremony

I got my mother and my mother-in-law to search through the family photo albums so that I could create a family photo tree of both our immediate families. We set up a memory table outside the chapel and then moved it into the reception. I had photos of us together, us as kids with our siblings, and our parents, grandparents, and my great grandparents on their wedding days.

—Mimi

Many couples grapple with ways to include family and friends in the ceremony—it is not a phenomenon specific to blended couples. You might be seeking a way to honor your heritage and family traditions, to acknowledge specific loved ones, or merge the new family that is formed by your marriage. The trick is to do this in a way that doesn't make anyone feel pressured or excluded and that is true to the spirit and tone of your ceremony. The ideal is to make *everyone* feel included and welcomed.

The ceremony can be a hot potato when you and your beloved hail from different backgrounds or if you are a nontraditional pair and your families try to impose their own beliefs and needs. Some inclusions take a little more *finesse* than others because you want to avoid any tricky religious issues, cultural clashes, or family politics.

For example, it might be easy to honor both your mothers, or pay tribute to the best friend who introduced you two, yet if you or your beloved has a child or children, or if one or both of your families is super religious and you're not, it requires a little creative thinking to appropriately include the kids or honor the parents.

The wedding can truly be a healing experience. It is there that families tend to be not just civil but celebratory and happy. So to the best of your ability, look for ways to acknowledge that marriage is not just the coming together of you and your mate but the merging of two families, two life stories, and two or more different traditions. Here are some ways to cast a circle of love that includes the whole family.

HOW TO INCLUDE THE PEOPLE YOU LOVE IN YOUR WEDDING

Here's a tip: it is good to get a sense of how open your family is to participating, but it is wise also to give some thought to whom and how you want to involve loved ones—before you bring it to the family for open discussion. This will save you the chaotic feeling—à la *My Big Fat Greek Wedding*—of people trying to randomly pitch in however they feel like it.

That said, there are many ways to include the people you love. Mothers and fathers can come up and light unity candles or read prayers. Siblings and friends can offer blessings and readings. If a relative has a great voice or plays an instrument, that person can sing or perform. Your children can light candles, participate in a modern-day sand ceremony, sip grape juice while you sip wine, and be included in the rituals and prayers. You can also lovingly remember those relatives who have passed on as well as those who could not physically be present.

If you want to give *everyone* close to you something to do in your ceremony, consider some of these ideas: you can have group candle lighting; an organized time for calling out blessings; or a cultural ritual such as the tossing of flower petals at a designated moment (as Hindus do). You can also choose to assign certain blessings to a group of people such as having seven friends offer the seven blessings (Jewish) or speak the intentions of the seven steps (Hindu), or you can have four friends call in the directions (Native American and Goddess traditions).

Consider some of these suggestions and see which are most appropriate for you. These ideas come from dozens of brides and grooms who have walked the path before you.

1. **Organize the clan and let them contribute.** One of the loveliest ways to include family (or ease tensions in parents and family) is to let loved ones help with the spiritual aspects and in some cases add their own

special touches. For Sanjai and Shari's Hindu-Jewish wedding, the bride had her mom bring the family kiddush cup for the wine ceremony, and the groom asked his mother to prepare the Hindu elements of ghee candle, *puja* plate, and rice; she added in a sari for the officiant. Karen and Paul worried their parents would be offended by their nonreligious ceremony, so they let their pious parents offer blessings of their own. Lilly's mom was asked to provide the unity candles and bring holy water from her church the day she married John. Moments before Henry and Jona's wedding, the groom's sister organized a Chinese tea ceremony to honor their grandmother. When Cindy married Alexi, her mother baked the traditional Slovenian wedding loaf. At Christopher and Negron's wedding, the bride's Iranian mom set up an elaborate traditional Sofreh-ye Aghd wedding altar to use in the Persian ritual in their ceremony and showed the groom's Jehovah's Witness mom how to partake in the traditional ritual by offering coins to the bride. It is so much fun when the family comes along for the ride on your unique interfaith and blended-culture journey.

2. **Use symbolism.** Have something that represents the family or a particular member or person at your wedding altar. In the famous phrase "something old, something new," the *something old* is meant to be something the bride carries or wears that is passed on to her by a relative. For example, Sue carried her grandmother's handkerchief when she married Joshua. At Jackie and Tom's wedding, the bride carried a bouquet of eight calla lilies that represented eight important people in her life, including her mom and dad, her groom's mom and dad, her grandparents, her uncle, and her best friend. She made note of this on her wedding program and added that "the bouquet was tied by the groom . . . as a symbol of the love and unity that brought us here today."

3. **Give them a shout out in the ceremony.** A simple yet powerful way to include the family is to mention them by name and thank them. Alice and Paul created a list acknowledging the qualities in each of their parents and grandparents, and stepparents, and spoke about how much they admired each of them. Leo and Betty acknowledged the strength and spiritual lessons they had learned from their Buddhist and Christian families. Paulo and Jane adapted the bride's Chinese tradition of honoring the relatives and ancestors (usually done at the dinner banquet) as part of the ceremony. Amy and Shawn's wedding honored the parent by saying, "The light of love that illuminates this marriage would not be possible without the love passed on to Amy and Shawn by their families. We would especially like to thank the parents of the bride and groom. You have all, in your own special way, brought forth love, and this bride and groom are certainly a reflection of this."

4. **Unique walks down the aisle.** When Jane married Adam, she made sure everyone in her groom's family were represented as well as her posse of *five assorted parents:* her mom, dad, ex-stepmom, ex-stepdad, and current stepdad all walked down the aisle. At Tim and Patty's ceremony the bride wanted to have her former in-laws *and* her two uncles *give her away.* Her parents and her first husband were deceased, and she was very close to her first husband's parents as well as her uncles. So the in-laws walked her to one point down the aisle, and the uncles brought her the rest of the way. When Raquel and Matthew married in a nondenominational Filipino ceremony, they honored the custom of "sponsors" who participate in ceremony rituals by inviting 20 loved ones to walk down the aisle and also take seats of honor on the aisle. Martha made her entrance to marry Gavin led by a bagpiper (to honor the groom's Scottish heritage) and nine bridesmaids.

5. **Having loved ones at the wedding altar.** It is traditional to have the bridal party at the wedding altar with you, or, when it's a tight space, just the best man and maid of honor stand. Yet you don't have to stand on tradition; in fact, you can adapt tradition to suit your needs. At Xiomara and Brian's Hindu-African ceremony, the bride and groom skipped having attendants and instead had the groom's Hindu parents from Guyana and the bride's Jehovah's Witness parents at the altar throughout. This fit in with their theme of honoring the ancestors. When bride or groom hails from the Jewish tradition, you can honor family and roots with a huppah, a canopy on poles that represents your new home. It usually involves at least four people to hold the poles, or a canopy that is set up at the very start of the procession. At Dan and Amy's wedding, the groom built a special huppah to honor his bride's heritage. He asked everyone at the wedding to sign it in lieu of a guest book. It was then attached to the poles. With the loving blessings of friends and family just over their heads, this symbolically brought the love of all the people they care for into their marriage and their new home.

6. **Opening or closing with a musical loved one.** If you have a talented relative who is willing, by all means include a personalized musical offering. At Safia and Kenneth's interfaith and multicultural ceremony, the bride's younger sister opened with a stirring rendition of the Andrew Lloyd Webber's piece *I'll Go with You.* At Michael and Amanda's ceremony the groom's sister rocked the house when she ended the ceremony with the soulful sounds of *I'll Always Love You.* At Mary Anne and Barry's Christian-Jewish nuptials, the bride's family heritage was honored by having a dear friend sing *Ave Maria* for the processional. Musician Peter and choreographer Jodi had professional Broadway singer friends perform both classic and made-up songs at

their wedding, and the groom played the processional music with his father and brother before joining the bride at the altar. At Rachelle and Sanith's Christian-Buddhist wedding, the bride's musical family sang throughout the ceremony, and the groom's Sri Lankan parents sang right afterward, followed by the bride serenading her groom.

7. **Rituals that merge the families.** There are many lovely rituals that can gather in the family.

- **Sand ceremony.** A sand ceremony that includes parents and/or children of the bride and groom is a creative and fun way to symbolically blend families together. This would require different-colored sands and separate containers for each participant and one central container into which to pour the sand. Grandparents would pour first; then parents, representing the ancestors; then bride and groom; and then children, representing the future. (See more in chapter 9.)
- **Unity candles as the common ground.** Unity candles hail from the Christian tradition, yet they also serve to bring light and connection to families of any faith, any culture, and who speak any language. Moms usually help light the candles and then return to their seats. But if your moms hail from different faiths, or one or more of them is very religious, it is a nice touch to invite them to offer prayers from their faith traditions or special blessings just before they light the candles. At Martin and Jana's wedding, the bride's mom offered a Hebrew prayer of celebration, and the groom's mom, who was Catholic and hailed from Quebec, offered a Christian blessing in French as part of the candle-lighting ceremony.
- **Family welcoming/rose ceremony.** There is a nondenominational tradition of offering flowers to the moms or to significant family members. Usually, the bride and groom give a red and a white rose—colors that represent unity—to each of their moms. It is particularly nice if bride and groom each give one flower to each mom, followed with a hug. This would also be a good time to publicly acknowledge your moms and thank them. Here is the rose ceremony from AnaMaria and Jose's wedding.

Officiant: As this bride and groom come before us to be married, they wish to acknowledge and thank their families for their love and support. As a gesture of unity between the families that are united on this day, and as an acknowledgment of the special people who have loved and nurtured this bride and groom, they will present a very special gift of flowers to their mothers. (AnaMaria presented roses to her groom's mother, and Jose presented roses to his bride's mom).

With these flowers, they welcome one another's families into the new family that is created by their marriage today. These flowers symbolize the love Jose and AnaMaria feel for each other, extended to their loved ones. They are also symbolic of the merging of two families in love and unity.

- **Ritual blessing from elders.** You can adapt blessings from any tradition and ask your family to participate. At Jackie and Brian's wedding, the four parents of the bride and groom called in the four directions, a Native American custom. Dawn and Dominick wanted to bring a blessing of elements to their marriage, so they asked their parents to each bring a small item up to the wedding altar that represented the elements—water, air, fire, earth—as the officiant read a blessing on behalf of each parent.

Officiant: Marriage is more than the coming together of two individuals. It is the joining of two families. To honor the family ties that are created by this marriage, and bless the union of their children, the parents of the bride and groom will perform a blessing for new beginnings.

We ask the mother, father, and stepmother of the bride, and the mother and father of the groom, to step forward as they are called. They each have a special offering to place on the wedding altar. Let us all join them in blessing this marriage with the elements of our common being—earth, air, fire, and water. *Parents come up one at a time, except for bride's father and stepmother, who come up together. After placing their item on the altar, they stand off to the side.*

Air: *Mother of the bride brings a feather that represents air.* We bless this marriage with the element of air, which represents intelligence and spirit. We ask that this union be granted gifts of communication, wisdom, and understanding.

Fire: *Father and stepmother of the bride bring a candle that represents fire.* We bless this marriage with the element of fire, which represents illumination and passion. We ask that this union be granted gifts of vitality, passion, and creativity.

Earth: *Father of the groom brings a crystal that represents earth.* We bless this marriage with the element of earth, which represents a strong and solid foundation. We ask that this union be granted gifts of stability, strength, and abundance.

Water: *Mother of the groom brings a vessel of water.* We bless this marriage with the element of water, which represents the clear and holy spirit of purity. We ask that this union be granted gifts of love, intuition, and trust.

Thank you, moms and dads. You may all be seated.

8. **Inviting loved ones to offer readings and blessings.** Your officiant can read poems, readings, and blessings you select, but it is always nice to ask a loved one or two to participate. There are many creative ways to do this. Typically, a wedding will have one or two readings. You can select scriptures or readings you love and then consider who you might like to read them, or you can ask people you love and trust to select or write a reading. Consider including parents, siblings, or best friends, or the person who introduced you. Here are some of the creative ways couples have asked people to partake.

- **Shared readings.** If you want to keep the number of readings down, you can have two or more people each read a stanza or two. When Jane and Adam married, they invited their three siblings to read one poem. They came to the front of the room and then took their seats again. Elle and Eddie asked Elle's three daughters to share the stanzas of a Celtic blessing.
- **Very personal tributes from friends.** For her wedding to Jose, AnaMaria asked two close girlfriends to come up with readings. The results were both hysterical and poignant. The bride gave them carte blanche and did not ask to know the content beforehand. One friend, Reshma, told the story of this couple's love like only a friend could. She highlighted how this couple had been best friends for years, when they finally professed their love for one another. Here's an excerpt.

  You realized that the One, the guy you've been waiting for, the one who has been waiting for you, is right in front of you. He's your best friend. Why didn't you see him before? He tells you that he's been waiting for you all along and you're speechless. You are struck mute in your kitchen. He holds out a hand full of flowers, and you check your pulse. You cannot move. Your fuzzy slippers might as well be made of concrete. And suddenly, the heavens seem to open up and the opera of "no more dating" rises to a rushing crescendo. You fall back onto your refrigerator door, slide to the floor, and cup your hands to your face. And that's it. You came for friendship, but somehow you take away love. It's not a science, and it's not predictable. The rest is history, as they say.
- **The whole gang.** When Jackie and Brian married, they were intent on having their ceremony be a multicultural community event. They had 17 readers! The way this was accomplished in a ceremony of 35 minutes was to give each person just one or two lines. A number of the prayers and blessings were divvied up between participants, who sat in the

audience and stood only when it was time to speak, passing the microphone from person to person. For example, drawing from the Hindu tradition (although neither were Hindu), the final blessing was shared among seven friends.

Officiant: Culling from the Hindu tradition, where man and woman are married as God and Goddess, we conclude this ceremony with seven blessings. These are adapted from the ancient rite of Satapadi, whereby the bride and groom take seven steps around a ceremonial fire and agree to seven vows that will make their marriage strong. This ritual is said to seal the marriage forever.

We capture the essence of that soulful commitment in these blessings on this union. Jackie and Brian, concentrate on these seven blessings as they are spoken and allow them to formulate the foundation of your new life together. The blessings will be offered by seven loved ones.

> **Vicki:**   May this couple be blessed with an abundance of food and comforts and be helpful to one another in all ways.
> **Kim:**   May this couple be strong and complement one another.
> **Phoebe:**   May this couple be blessed with prosperity.
> **Debbie:**   May this couple be eternally happy.
> **Erica:**   May this couple be blessed with a happy family life.
> **Pam:**   May this couple live in perfect harmony.
> **Denise:**   May this couple always be the best of friends.
> **Officiant:** Your two lives are now joined in one unbroken circle.

- **Having a special friend or family member co-officiate.** When Andrea and Patrick married, they wanted the groom's dear friend, a Buddhist psychologist, to play an important role, so they hired a local ordained clergyperson who could write a ceremony, co-officiate, and sign the license locally. When John and Dana wed, they had their heart set on the bride's father, a deacon, officiating. Since the bride's dad was not authorized to sign the license, they also were able to find a flexible clergyperson who could co-officiate and make the ceremony legal. Some states allow couples to have a friend who is ordained for a day, or on the Internet, officiate, but it is best to check state laws.

9. **Honoring family traditions and language.** Sometimes it is extremely important to acknowledge your parents and family by honoring your heritage and your family's native language. Some wedding gatherings are filled with relatives who do not speak English; any way you can include them is helpful. Some couples hire an officiant who is bilingual or a

second officiant who speaks the language of those present. But there are many ways to do this subtly so that it does not dominate the ceremony.

- **Have your favorite readings in different languages.** If the family of the bride or groom speaks different languages you can translate your favorite reading or scripture into their native tongue and have a family member read it. At Stephanie and Javier's wedding, one of the bride's family members read I Corinthians in English; to honor the groom's Costa Rican family, the groom's brother was invited to read the Spanish version.
- **Include blessings from both faiths and languages.** When Jean Paul and Sandra married, they had Catholic prayers in the groom's family's native French and a Jewish blessing in Hebrew to honor the bride's family, and some were spoken by family members.
- **Translate the wedding script.** Kyoko and Helmut opted for a nondenominational, English-language ceremony, but they had the wedding script translated into Japanese and German for the non-English-speaking relatives on both their sides.
- **Blending in traditional elements.** Don and Deb wanted a nonreligious ceremony, but Deb's parents were devout Buddhists from Vietnam concerned that family members would be insulted if there was not at least a bit of Buddhist tradition. The bride's mom was invited to step up to the altar and ring a Buddhist chime three times to create a sacred space for the wedding, and the bride's Dad wrote a prayer that the officiant read. Also, a friend read a poem by Vietnamese monk Thich Nhat Hanh.
- **Special blessings from parents.** It is always quite beautiful if parents or grandparents offer a special blessing and if symbols of family tradition are woven into the wedding. Just before Sophia and Zvonko's ceremony, the mother and father of the bride offered the couple a traditional Ukrainian blessing, with a holy icon of Mary and baby Jesus that belonged to Sophia's paternal grandmother. Several ritual cloths, embroidered by Sophia's relatives in the Ukraine, were used to decorate the altar. The bride and groom stood on one through the ceremony and used another for a handwrapping ritual.

10. **Including children.** If you or your beloved come to your new marriage with children in tow, it is important to acknowledge the new family that is formed on your wedding day. If you have all been together for a while, you might already feel like a family—which is great—so your ceremony can reinforce that. If there are tricky issues with being a stepparent, the ceremony can serve to begin to soften them.

- **Candle lighting.** When Tina married Jim, his two children from his first marriage were going to be living with them part of the time and with their mom the other part of the time. The bride's sons, though older, also still had a relationship with their dad. So Tina and Jim sought to mention the new blended family, without negating the kids' relationship to the other parents. They opted for a family unity candle ceremony with a special candelabra.

Officiant: Ordinarily, we have three candles—one for each partner and the one they light together. On this occasion, as a gesture of family unity, we have five candles. The top candle represents the bright light of Tina and Jim's love. The four candles around it represent their children and the new family that they form on this day.

We ask Janie to please, on behalf of herself and her brother Ryan, light two candles. We now ask Kevin, on behalf of himself and his brother Paul, to please light two candles.

It is important to mention here that people who are meant to be together do not always *begin* as blood relatives, but they share a common bond that helps them grow into a family. May the lighting of these candles represent the kindling of the divine light within each of you and the joining of a loving family.

- **Family medallion.** Mary Ann and Barry sought to include his daughter Cassidy in many ways, including with the gift of a family medallion. This involved presenting her with a piece of jewelry as part of the ceremony.

Officiant: Barry and Mary Ann, you have made a special place in one another's hearts, and your love for one another now creates a circle of love that gathers in the whole family, especially Cassidy.

Just as your wedding rings are the gifts you give one another on this day, the family medallion is a special gift you give to your daughter, to show her how much you love her and how happy you are to be a family—together. (Bride and groom give Cassidy the medallion.)

Please look at Cassidy and repeat after me:

With this medallion,
    We pledge to you,
    Our love and support.

- **Vows to the children.** For Patti and Orlander's wedding, it was all about kids—his two daughters and the bride and groom's baby son. The groom's daughters each read poems such as "The Owl and the Pussy Cat." And Patti made special efforts to offer her love and commitment to the girls as well as asking them to pledge to nurture their family life together. She did this through vows to which they each agreed.

Officiant: In this ceremony, we are joining more than just a man and a woman. We are bringing together a family. So we have some very special vows for Patti and the girls.

Patti's Vows to the Girls

Patti, do you promise . . .
To accept Meagan and Zaena as your own,
To love and support them,
To be patient and understanding,
To watch after their well-being,
To nurture their growth,
and to be there for them always?

Patti answers: I do.

Girls' Vows to Patti

And now, Meagan and Zaena,
Do you promise to love and respect your dad's new wife?
Do you promise to support their marriage and your new family?
Do you promise to accept the responsibility of being their children?
And to encourage them and support them in your new life together?

The girls answer: We do.

Officiant: May you all keep the sacred promises that have been spoken today.

- **Special offerings.** When Jocelyn married Daniel, the well-being and happiness of their kids was foremost in their minds. They created a unique ceremony that gave starring roles to Daniel's eight-year-old twins and Jocelyn's nine-year-old daughter. The kids were the only members of the bridal party. They walked down the aisle, they stood at the altar the whole time, and they all danced back up the aisle together when the ceremony was over. During the ceremony, they lit candles, and also Jocelyn's daughter read two very special poems she had written for the bride and groom. It was a truly unique moment.

11. **Honoring those no longer with us.** There are many poignant ways to do this. You can ask the officiant to call for a moment of silence. Have family members (siblings or surviving parent) come up and light a

remembrance candle, or light one yourself. Keep flowers on your wedding altar to represent the ones who have passed on. Create a memorial table or some physical remembrance. (At Ally and Jim's wedding, the groom placed the folded American flag from his dad's coffin on the front row seat next to his mother; another bride had the wedding picture of her deceased parents on a nearby table.) You can make the remembrance just a moment or two and move on quickly to a more uplifting part of the ceremony, or you can memorialize someone more extensively.

- **Personalized remembrance.** At Deborah and Steven's wedding, the groom honored his mother—who had never met his bride—by coming down the aisle with his two brothers, to a piece of music his brother had written for his mom, followed by the three of them lighting a candle for her. The officiant paid tribute to his mother immediately following the opening prayer and shared what she was like, how much she was loved. From then on, the ceremony was quite upbeat and funny, so the remembrance did not create sadness . . . just reflection.
- **General remembrance.** You can also choose a more general remembrance. Here's something your officiant can include at the start of the ceremony:

Officiant: None of us comes to an important moment like this without the love, support, and nurturing of the special people who help shape us and prepare us for love. We begin with a moment of silence for the souls that have touched this bride and groom and have brought them to this moment in time.

Let us remember: [speak the names]

Hold a moment of silence.

In loving memory, let us all light a candle in our hearts and our minds. We know on this joyful day that their love continues to live on in our hearts.

And let us also include in our circle of love those who could not physically be here today. Amen.

12. **Including those who cannot be present.** Many brides and grooms these days have to face the reality that some friends and relatives just cannot make it to the wedding. In Summer and Tony's wedding, there was an acknowledgment of the bride's grandparents, who were unable to travel. Since Monica and Simon came from England to New York to marry, they had only their best friend, along with the bride's sister and father, at their wedding; a candle was lit for all the folks back home

who wished them well. One bride and groom made a point of holding a moment of remembrance and prayer for a military friend who had just shipped out to Iraq for active duty. The idea is to just take a moment at the start of the ceremony in which you symbolically "invite" these loved ones to be part of the ceremony by acknowledging them. When Katerina married Xingman, her family in the Republic of Yugoslavia and his family in China could not be there, so they arranged for everyone to "tune in" at the time of their wedding. Here's one way to include loved ones from afar:

Officiant: The bride and groom would like to begin the ceremony by taking a moment to include those loved ones who could not physically be here. They have asked their families to send good wishes at the hour of their wedding. We light this candle to represent the light and love of their families. Symbolically, the light of the fire acts as "witness" and brings illumination to the ceremony. *Hold moment of silence.*

- **Other ways to honor loved ones who are far away.** Warren's dad couldn't make it to Warren and Kathy's wedding due to illness, so Warren's sister read a prayer his dad had written for the couple. Orlander's mom sent along a scriptural verse. Although the wedding was not religious, the couple asked their officiant to read the verse to honor the groom's mom; they sent her a videotape of the wedding to show her. Sunee and Christopher eloped but set up a computer remote of their ceremony for friends and family in Sri Lanka and Australia to see.

THOUGHTS TO PONDER: WHAT WORKS BEST WHEN IT COMES TO FAMILY INVOLVEMENT?

- As you go through the wedding-planning process, get a sense of where your family stands and how involved they might like to be.
- Look at any areas your family needs to be united, or healed, and seek to address those issues where possible through family involvement.
- Decide who you would like to include and how you'd like the ceremony organized before you approach your family.
- If you have a big family or extended family, make a project chart of how they can participate in your wedding ceremony.

11

Celebrating Your Love Story

What made our wedding so special was how our minister told the story of our relationship, including how we met, our time together and what we love about each other. It was special for us and our guests also enjoyed it. It reminded us how special our relationship is and the fun times we had together.

—Jessica

One of the most extraordinary ways to honor your love is to celebrate it in words in the ceremony. Every couple has a story to share. Perhaps it is the tale of how you met. Or maybe it is the revelation that you broke up in high school only to rediscover each other in your thirties or forties. It could even be the amazing way one of you secretly smuggled an engagement ring on vacation and proposed. Or the chance meeting that brought you together—in another country, in a bar, at school, at a wedding, during a vacation, or at a time when you least expected it.

Sharing the details of how love found you reminds everyone in the room that what you have together transcends religion and cultures, and it certainly rises high above prejudice and intolerant ideas. It makes your love seem even more fabulous!

HOW TO MAKE YOUR LOVE THE CENTRAL THEME OF YOUR WEDDING

There are a number of poignant and fun ways to add this special touch to your ceremony. I have had couples share the story of how they fought cancer together when one was sick, and couples who married 10, 20, and even 35 years after first meeting. There are stories of brides and grooms who resisted each other at first or could not make it work. Here are some excerpts from the personal stories and affirmations of love written especially for these couples and blended into the officiant's message in their ceremonies.

Soul Mates: Rachelle and Justin
(Bride Is Australian and Groom Is American)

Rachelle and Justin, you are two romantics who searched for love and found your soul mate in one another. Though you come from across the continents, it was no accident that you found one another. This is a relationship that is meant to be.

You share a strong spiritual connection to each other, and even though you hail from different parts of the world, you are so in tune with one another. You both believe that regardless of country, race, background, or culture, people who are meant for each other will find one another. Somehow, they recognize one another through the eyes of love, and they let no distance come between them. Rachelle and Justin, you have demonstrated that time and again by refusing to let an ocean—or immigration challenges—interfere with your love for one another.

Rachelle, I asked Justin what he loves about you, and he said: I love Rachelle's support and trust in me. I love her femininity and determination in life. She makes the best of any situation and is always strong. I love her instinct to care and look after people and ability to always see the best in them. I love her spirituality, creativeness, and elegance.

And Justin, I asked Rachelle what she loves about you, and she said: I love the romantic man that Justin is. He inspires me, makes me feel I have passion in my life, respects me, and is a true gentleman. I love the way he always supports me and is strong. He knows how to celebrate the important things in life. I love his creativity and determination, and his devotion and understanding.

Marriage, to you, means making your union as soul mates official. It means being allowed to live, work, and build a life together. It means promising to honor and respect each other and be able to express that in a recognized way. It means working as a team to achieve your goals and dreams in life.

You are already blessed with a wonderful relationship: you share the same ideals in life. You have the same wants for the future and understand each other fully. You have the ability to support and trust each other and communicate fully to work through anything that might stand in your way in life. When you look into one another's eyes, you see only love. You are, for each other, the perfect yin and yang, masculine and feminine, always balancing each other perfectly.

Today, as you agree to be steadfast in your commitment to love one another through all things, you also agree to a partnership of equals where you support one another and work together toward common goals. This marriage is an opportunity to include the world—and all its challenges—in your love.

Meant to Be: Traci and Partha (Bride Is Christian and Groom Is Hindu)

Traci and Partha, you are two people who have been blessed with one another's love for six years, and you know you are meant to be together.

From the Christian tradition, the world began with soul mates, Adam and Eve, set forth on this earth to explore the world together. From the Hindu tradition, when we think of soulful love, we think of Krishna and his beloved Radha, and the deep love between God and mortal, Man and Woman, giving strength and love to one another in their own unique ways.

You two met the old-fashioned way. You ran into each other in a New York hot spot—otherwise known as a bar. As it turns out, Traci was fulfilling the family prophecy that she was destined to meet the man she'd marry in a place that serves cocktails.

Traci, who lived in Dallas at the time, was ordering a cosmopolitan. Partha noticed her and remarked that she had beautiful eyes. They chatted. They danced. They talked some more. And although she was reluctant about giving out her number, Traci left that night with Partha's number scribbled on a napkin.

Fortunately, that cocktail napkin led to the start of their relationship. She called him on a drive to Philly. They talked through the whole trip.

When she came to town again for her best friend Heather's graduation party, Traci and Partha met up again, and their New York love story began. They both recall a lot of chemistry and clicking on all cylinders. They talked all night and shared their first kiss.

Five years later, Partha asked Traci to marry him, but not before completing Project Engagement. This included asking her parents for her hand and specially designing a ring based on the subtle—and not so subtle—hints Traci has dropped in the preceding years. It also involved a vacation and an elaborate proposal plan created with the help of the resort where they were staying.

Partha was able to arrange for a dinner on a private island. When they arrived, a beautiful table was laid out with a feast—a bonfire crackled and the evergreen trees swayed. Everything around them— the lake, the mountains behind them, and the breeze—was so calm. Except for Partha, who was so overcome with emotion that when he got down on one knee, he found himself at a loss for words.

Somehow, he managed to open the ring box, and Traci was able to figure it out from there. Everything he wanted to say in that moment was spoken through his eyes. When they came back to the main boathouse after their time on the private island, all the resort staff and other guests cheered the newly engaged couple. As they say, the rest is history!

Partha, I asked Traci what made her fall in love with you, and she said: There are so many things I love about Partha that words aren't really enough. I am incredibly blessed to have Partha in my life. His outlook and passion for life is something I immediately fell in love with. I've never met a man that has such a heart of gold. He has this innate ability to make me feel like I'm the most special person in the world every day. He's exceptionally kind, gentle, affectionate, encouraging, charitable, and loyal—not to mention incredibly handsome and vastly intelligent. I admire his brilliance and passion for his career, and he's one of the most generous people I know, next to my father. It's an extraordinary feeling to find someone in life that loves you unconditionally, and Partha has exuded his unconditional love for me since day one.

And Traci, I asked Partha what he loves about you, and he said: The things that I love about Traci are many. Her amazing confidence, her uncanny intelligence, her personality, her passion for everything she does in life, her strong sense of values, and her striking beauty on the outside—which always takes my breath away—but more important the beauty that she exudes from the inside, which makes me want to believe in the inherently good in the world. Getting married to Traci for me will be the start of a wonderful journey filled with love, respect, commitment, passion, laughter, and sharing in all of life's experiences...much like the journey we have been a part of over the last six years. She is the one that adds "any meaning" to all of it for me.

Laughter and Love: Jona and Henry
(Bride Is Christian and Groom Is Chinese)

Jona and Henry, this marriage to you means that you have found your ever-lasting soul mate, best friend, and lover. That you have someone to share your most intimate thoughts with and most intimate moments with. That you have a partner to enjoy life's adventures with. And that you have a dear one who will never judge you and always accept you as you are.

Henry, for Jona, the journey of falling in love has been learning to trust and to open her heart...and discovering it is OK to rest her head on your shoulder and relax from time to time. Today, she gives her heart to you even more completely, knowing that you will love and cherish that heart for all of your days. And that you will always offer your shoulder to lean on, in good times and in challenging times.

And Jona, for Henry, falling for you was immediate, yet he patiently embarked on a gentle journey with you, giving you a chance to fall for him. Like the famous tradition of the man who feeds his beloved pomegranate seeds one by one, to attest she is worth waiting for, he has lovingly offered you one seed at a time. Today, he offers you the whole pomegranate, knowing that you will always welcome his love and affection. And that you will continue to be the one person in the world who can always put a smile on his face!

Jona, I asked Henry to share one of his fondest memories of your time together, and he recalled the time when he made Chinese BBQ ribs for you the first time.

"It took me about two hours to make dinner," he recalled, "and about two minutes for her to devour the entire rack of ribs. I have never seen such a petite person move so fast. It was a blur, all I saw was teeth and limbs. When it was all done and said, I looked down at my plate, and I had one rib (uneaten); I then looked over at her plate, and there was nothing but a pile of bones.

She came out of her euphoric stupor and gave me the 'What? Why are you looking at me that way?' look. There was carnage everywhere—BBQ sauce on her, the table, me, the walls. We won't mention her face and fingers. Glad she likes my cooking."

He adds, affectionately, "She has the most adorable snort when she laughs hard. It is the cutest thing. My goal in life is to make her happy and try to make her laugh as much as possible to the point that she snorts, cries, and pees in her pants. Laughter is the best medicine."

Henry, I asked Jona to share one of her fondest memories, and she recalled that the first date was predicated on her now-famous Jona's 10 Commandments of Male Behavior, and she said that you didn't do so badly. It may have taken a while for her to catch on, but the real predictor of your future together was when her two dogs, Duncan, the six and a half pound Chihuahua, and Kayla, a 25 pound mixed breed, fell in love with you first.

The minute you walked through the door of her house the first time, it was pure puppy love. "These were dogs that didn't like *any* guy that came through those doors," she recalled. "Suddenly, they were jumping all over him." Soon enough, Jona was too!

She added, "From the very beginning of our friendship I have laughed and laughed. I have laughed more in these past few years than I ever have before. Even the sad or not so good times tend not to be so bad. First, because he's around, and second, because we both have learned that a sense of humor can get you through some of the worst times in life."

Jona and Henry, your life together began as a friendship and then caught on fire. You come to this day as partners in life, already united in so many ways. May your marriage become your new home. May it be the home you always find your way back to, no matter where life leads you.

Sharing the Ride Together: Howie and Barry
(Bride Is Christian and Groom Is Jewish)

Barrie and Howie, you have been blessed with the gift of one another's love. You knew early on this was *beschert*, meant to be, that you had found the "real deal." Today, you celebrate your sacred commitment to love one another through all things, as you look toward a life filled with fun and adventure.

This is a very special relationship. You share the passion for the open road and the wind against your skin, and you have found endless joys and adventures on the back of your Harley. It is one of many things that make this union so unique.

Howie, in Barrie you have found a partner who adores you. She loves your big heart, and says it is always in the right place, and she loves your complete honesty. She revels in your devotion, the way you make her feel so special, how you make her laugh all the time, the way you two have so much fun. You are her best friend, the person she trusts and can depend on. She says when she looks at you and sees the love in your eyes that she knows you are meant to be together.

Barrie, in Howie you have found a mate who has been enchanted and enamored by you from the moment he set eyes on you. He loves the way you both seemed to plop from the sky and into the crossroads of one another's lives at just the right moment, and how you just kept going on together. He tried to make his move slowly so as not to scare you away, so he refrained from proposing on the first date. But he was so crazy about you he could barely wait a month before asking you to marry him. "From the moment I met this little curly red-haired hippie chick," he says, "I knew we'd be together forever."

And here you are, poised and ready for the biggest ride of your lives—marriage! On this day you tell the world that you know your union is strong enough to last a lifetime and that you look forward to endless days that begin and end together, to always having a partner to laugh with and cry with and do everything in between with, to knowing that the most important person in your life is by your side, to giving all your love and devotion to the one person who makes you so incredibly happy.

Howie and Barrie, the love you radiate for one another speaks for itself. May it carry you through the years as you ride off into the wind, together, forever.

The Animal Lovers: Elizabeth and Nick (Nondenominational Couple)

Elizabeth and Nick, yours is a true New York love story. Where else can a devout vegetarian find love with a professional meat inspector and build a life that includes nurturing a menagerie of resident cats as well a countless transient felines?

Nick, I asked Elizabeth what she loves about you, and she offered a long list: I love Nick's sense of humor: he can always make me laugh no matter what kind of mood I am in. I love his morals. He is the most trustworthy, honest, and compassionate person I have ever met. I love the fact that he is an awesome chef; the man can find anything in the cupboard and refrigerator and make a gourmet dinner! Love his eyes, his smile, his legs (he really has great legs!). I love that he thinks the world of me and that even though we disagree on things, he still has utmost respect for my beliefs. I love how he takes care of me. He truly is the most amazing man I have ever met. And I am a very lucky woman.

Elizabeth, I also asked Nick what he loves about you! He may have less words to share but I know he makes up for it with 4:00 A.M. kisses before heading off to work and all the yummy vegetarian meals he whips up for you. He said: I love Elizabeth for her love of life and dedication toward the humane treatment, safety, and health of animals, especially cats. I love Elizabeth for the way she keeps me grounded and focused. I love Elizabeth because more often than not, she smiles; and when she does, it warms my heart and reminds me of how beautiful she is, inside and out.

To you, marriage means no matter what happens in this world, you are in it together. That you will still have your independence yet will stick by each other and be there for each other. It's a lifelong commitment to each other's health, happiness, safety, and security. I know you both dream of having children and experiencing all of life together (with children or not), starting an animal rescue sanctuary, growing old, happy, and content in each other's arms.

Elizabeth and Nick, may you remain each other's staunchest supporters through the best and the most challenging of times. And may you always relish the fact that you both agree: if you saw a hungry dog sitting patiently by a hot dog truck, you would buy it a hot dog!

Love Down Under: Keren and Darby

Your trip down the aisle brings you to beautiful Central Park in New York City, but it began in a small place in New South Wales called Nimbin. It was a weekend away at a cottage in the middle of the bush, surrounded by kangaroos and wallabies, when Darby proposed.

As Keren tells me, as they sat on the deck to watch the sun go down, Darby suddenly seemed a little nervous. He handed Keren a *huge* glass of wine and, as he passed it to her, said, "Before we get too drunk…will you marry me?"

There was quite a bit of laughter, and then eventually, she gave him a huge yes. And here we all are!

Keren and Darby, we rejoice with you that, out of all the world, you have found each other. And that in finding one another, you have both discovered a deeper meaning and fuller richness to life.

Sharing the journey of love with another human being is one of the greatest gifts any one of us can hope for. In this ceremony, you dedicate yourselves to the happiness and well-being of each other…and to the continued nurturing of your relationship.

Darby, I asked Keren what she loves about you, and she said: I know it sounds cliché, but the moment I laid eyes on Darby, that very first night of working together, I knew he was someone special and I felt an immediate connection. I love that he makes me laugh, that he is even tempered, kindhearted, and that he treats me with respect even when he's mad at me. He has a huge heart…and I am glad I have a place in it.

Keren, I asked Darby what he loves about you, and he said: I love Keren's passion and motivation in everything she does. The way she keeps me enthralled and guessing from day-to-day activities to the next perpetual holiday or day trip. I love her patience and support for me in whatever we may be doing. Keren is the proton to my electron.

As you pledge yourselves to one another as husband and wife, you make the commitment to spend the rest of your lives falling in love, over and over again…with one another.

Longtime Loves: Emily and Tim

You come to this day with the gift of wisdom, having already spent seven years of your lives building the relationship you share. You two have been through a lot together. And you have an intimate understanding of the *real* meaning of "for better or for worse."

You've grown up together. You've made separate accomplishments in your lives and accomplishments as a couple. It's taken compromises along the way, but you've always stuck together and gone through each challenge together, taking responsibility for each obstacle you've faced.

When I asked what you love about one another, you said: We are best friends, we are each other's support systems, critics, and counselors, and mentors—we reinspire and challenge each other every day as well as comfort and nurture each other. We connect through humor and insight and share similar life goals and visions.

Even though you come to this day as best friends and partners in life, united in so many ways, on this day, the journey of nourishing your love through all of life's cycles will take on new dimensions as you become husband and wife.

Marriage to you means making official something that you have known to be true for a long time. It means bringing loved ones together to celebrate friendships and commemorate the experiences that join us all. And it means looking forward toward the changes in your future and asking those same people to join you as you try to continue carving out the most fulfilling life possible.

You will discover that marriage is the deeper merging of two families and two life stories. And it is an opportunity to build an even stronger foundation for your family life.

You share a love that exists in the past, the present, the future. And you come to this day knowing that you are marrying your best friend and biggest ally, the person who knows you best and loves you most.

In your life as husband and wife, we wish for you that you enjoy the life you share to the fullest and that you always appreciate and honor what you have together. May you continue to keep falling in love with each other over and over again.

Reunited and It Feels So Good: Michelle and Joe

It has been said that "from every human being there rises a light that reaches straight to heaven. When two souls that are destined for each other find one another, their streams of light flow together and a single brighter light goes forth from their united being."

This marriage represents the coming together of two people who are clearly bright, beautiful lights unto themselves...yet who, together, radiate an even more extraordinary light.

Joe and Michelle, you have been blessed with the gift of one another's love. There is nothing holier than two people uniting in the spirit of committed love. It increases the love that exists in your families and circle of friends. And it brings healing to our world.

You come to this day as best friends and partners in life, united in so many ways. Yet, on this day, the journey of nourishing your love through *all* of life's cycles takes on a new dimension as you become husband and wife.

As many of you know, this relationship has been a *long* time in the making. Joe and Michelle met the first week of college but did not start dating until she graduated. Of course, that's about when she moved three hours away. They stayed together in a long-distance romance, and then the dance of love seemed to end. They said good-bye. And it would be nine years before they would speak again.

Thank God for Google, because that is how Joe reconnected with his true love.

As Joe tells it, "I knew Michelle had moved to New York, and I'd been thinking about her for a while. I wondered what she was up to…and how much she hated me! I called my sister and she said I should call Michelle up—'give it a chance!' Kathy said. I Googled Michelle and found about four different company e-mail addresses for her. I sent e-mails to each one…and I lucked out. We made plans to meet after work that day."

After Michelle made a mad dash home to wash her hair and "change into a cute outfit," they had their first date…as mature adults.

Joe said she looked the same. Michelle said, "He did too, except he didn't have any hair!"

They stayed out at the Russian Vodka Room until 2:00 A.M. on a Monday night. Joe called Michelle at 8:00 A.M. the next morning, and they haven't stopped talking since.

They began falling (back) in love; Joe began making plans to move here. One day he suggested they go to Michelle's favorite place, the Brooklyn Heights Promenade. A major snowstorm detoured them, but three weeks later, when the snow thawed, Joe proposed.

Their unique love story brings to mind the Chinese myth "The String of Fate." It tells us that at birth, the gods tie an invisible red string around the ankles of men and women who are destined to be soul mates and one day marry each other. As they grow, the string gets shorter and brings them closer. It is believed that they will find each other, "regardless of time, place, or circumstance.…The thread may stretch or tangle,…but it will never break."

It is believed it might take time for the man and woman to mature and ready themselves for a serious relationship. And it can take a while for them to recognize true love in one another's eyes.

As Michelle sums it up, "Joe and I were meant for each other…it just took us half our lives to figure it out!"

That's the thing about soul mates: it may take time and effort to bring them together, but once they recognize one another, they fall deeply in love and become inseparable—like Michelle and Joe!

Michelle, I asked Joe what he loves about you, and he said: That she likes me! Seriously, I like that she is smart and talented and that she laughs at my stupid jokes…but I've always liked that about her. To have a helpmate and have someone in my corner. To have a partner to build a life with. I see myself being happy with Michelle forever.

Joe, I asked Michelle what made her fall in love with you, and she said: I can't help it—I find his stupid jokes funny…most of the time. And I think he's the kindest, cutest, craftiest guy I know. I love doing everyday things with Joe like making dinner and riding the subway in the morning. And I love that he's handy enough to literally build our life together…he redid our bathroom and is already at work on our kitchen. I foresee a lifetime of handyman assistantship in my future, and that's A-OK with me.

Joe and Michelle, we congratulate you on the journey of your lives that has brought you to this moment. Today you make the commitment to love one another through all the seasons of life. Your marriage is now the common thread that joins your lives as one. You are ready to embrace a very powerful love. Our wish for you is that you share a married life filled with prosperity and good fortune and that you look back on your relationship every year, grateful for what a good year it has been.

Destined to Be: Jackie and Rob

Jackie and Rob, today we witness your commitment to one another, and you declare to the world that you will be there for one another through all things.

You met in a bar in London, and it was like Kismet. Within about an hour, you both felt you had met your soul mate. In fact, it was rather startling to you both at the time to feel so certain.

There was a moment that evening that changed the course of your lives. As Jackie recalls, you were all sitting around in Rob's favorite club sharing drinks. Jackie suddenly looked up and caught Rob's eye. You both were overcome with a sense of knowing.

Rob remembers that *in that moment*, he thought, "I could marry this girl."

Of course, you tried to be sensible during your courtship and take things slowly, but talk of marriage came up very early on. It was what you'd planned all along. As Jackie puts it, "I think we are both very pleased with ourselves that our immediate instincts turned out to be so right."

You've already bonded as a family. I hear Rory, Felix, and Rob all share the same schoolboy sense of humor, so it's fun to be part of the same family.

Rob, I asked Jackie what she loves about you, and she said: He is very handsome. He makes me feel safe. He makes me laugh a lot, mainly when he doesn't mean to. He's a great singer. He is very serious and passionate.

And Jackie, I asked Rob what he loves about you, and he said: He loves your home cooking, your creative mind, and the fact that you have a wonderful relationship with your children. He loves that you are a wise old owl and beautiful as well. He says you are the sober ying to his raging yang!

You come to this day as best friends and partners in life, already united in so many ways, yet on this day the journey of nourishing your love through *all* of life's cycles takes on a new dimension as you become husband and wife.

Jackie and Rob, your marriage is your new home. May this new home encourage you both to grow and evolve, to find success together and in your work in the world. May it offer a strong base of love and support for Felix and Rory. May you remain each other's staunchest supporters, through the best and the worst of times. And may you be given the vision to always behold one another with the eyes of love.

Absolute Comfort: Melissa and Roger

Melissa and Roger, you have been blessed with the vision to behold one another through the loving eyes of the soul. Although you come to this day as soul mates, best friends, and partners in life, already united in so many ways, on this day the journey of nourishing your love through *all* of life's cycles takes on a new dimension as you become husband and wife.

You will discover that marriage is even more than the joining of two lives. It is the merging of two families, two life stories, and two traditions. It is the spiritual, physical, and emotional union of two human beings. It is the fuller opening of two hearts and the ripening of two souls.

Roger, I asked Melissa what she loves about you, and she said: When Roger and I were first dating, I felt so comfortable and free to be myself. We made a strong connection, quickly. We just "fit." I now realize that Roger is like a part of me that was missing. I fell in love with Roger because of his sweet, caring, sensitive, goofy, funny self. I fell in love with him because he makes me laugh every single day. Ever since I was a little girl, I have imagined the man I would marry. Amazingly, he had brown hair and hazel or green eyes, just like Roger. Roger is like a part of my soul…a part I would never want to live without.

Melissa, I asked Roger what he loves about you, and he said that he, too, remembers the sparks between you on your first date. "I knew from the moment I saw her she was the one I was going to marry. Melissa is so genuinely caring for people that it immediately made me fall in love with her. Not only is she caring for people that are virtual strangers, but she shows such caring, love, and devotion to her friends and family. We are both unconditionally bound to our families; it is a perfect fit, although I expect it will make holiday choices tough! I am so grateful to Melissa for introducing me to so many new things in life—from food to the arts to diversity in cultures. Portuguese Manor is now my favorite restaurant, but maybe I shouldn't be thanking her for all the pounds I have put on since we met!"

Roger and Melissa, you come to this day knowing that you are marrying your soul mate, the person who knows you best and loves you most. Marriage, to you, is a way to further sanctify your love for each other and a way to plan the journey of life together. It means an affirmation of your love and respect, a way of showing the world how deeply committed you are and creating a strong foundation for a loving family life.

In your life as husband and wife, we pray that you continue to have a wonderful life together; explore each other on all levels, discovering new depths to one another; enjoy life to the fullest, appreciating what you have and sharing even more adventures together as a couple; grow together as individuals as you attain your aspirations and goals with one another's support; and find deeper spirituality and creativity together.

Melissa and Roger, may this marriage become your new home. May your home be filled with love, laughter, joy, and bliss.

Settling Down in the Same Country: Brad and Karin

Karin and Brad, you have been blessed with the gift of one another. Today, you tell one another—and the world—that you are ready to embrace a very serious commitment and responsibility.

All those gathered here who know you already know that you both live very stable, somewhat boring lives, always stuck in one place [smile], so it is doubtful that anyone here is surprised that you are both ready to settle down and live in the same country together!

Seriously, your marriage ceremony today punctuates a challenging year. With Brad being in the United States and Karin in the Netherlands, you had to cope with phone lines breaking up, calling cards running out, and the six hour time difference. It was hard just to say hello, yet this made you more determined, creative, and clever in your efforts to connect and communicate. Amazingly, only a few days ever passed when you did not speak to one another. Having to make these efforts to stay in touch has only strengthened the relationship!

You come to this day as best friends and partners in life, united in so many ways. It's important to acknowledge that you both have come a long way in the past five years and together have endured some very challenging moments. You have both undergone tremendous life changes, and you've had to rise above complexity and work through difficulties.

To you, this marriage means sharing dreams and direction, building a new home and harmony, and helping each other through challenging times. It means creating common ground and at the same time celebrating your differences, nurturing love and affection, and allowing it grow and evolve yet remain electric; holding hands every day you are together; sharing a tender touch; and having your favorite travel mate join you on life's journey!

Brad, I asked Karin what she loves about you, and she said: Brad has a great sense of humor, is very loving and caring, has a wonderful sense of adventure, and is very forgiving and compassionate. Besides that, Brad has a very versatile personality so that he continues to surprise me. He is a great storyteller, passionate about everything and everybody he cares about, and is the most loving person I've ever met. We complement each other in a lot of ways, which feels great when being together, just like a glove that fits perfectly.

And Karin, I asked Brad what he loves about you, and he said: Karin has a passionate sense of adventure and exploration in all things. Her convictions, even when we disagree, encourage me to see things in a new light, at a different angle. Karin has a strong devotion and loyalty to those she loves and a warm and steady glowing affection that makes me feel wonderful and alive. She is intelligent and possesses a keen sense of direction in many things. She is athletic, brave, and has a strength of body and mind. I love her clear blue eyes and easy laughter. When we are together, it all simply fits.

Karin and Brad, it is clear to see that you are two people deeply in love—your love for one another radiates all around you. You've had a long road to travel to get to this day. So let your marriage be your new home, and know that this special home is in your heart wherever you go!

Rising above the Challenges: Dean and Liz

Elizabeth and Dean, you have long been blessed with the gift of one another's love. You come to this day as best friends and partners in life, already united in your hearts and souls. Yet on this day you stand before family and friends to formally acknowledge your love for each other. You are both blessed to have found the one you can love, trust, and share your hopes with—the person who is your complement and equal.

As Liz says, "I have found someone who complements me exquisitely." And as Dean says, "I have found the woman of my dreams." Together, you share the motto: "The greatest thing you'll ever learn is just to love and be loved in return."

Marriage for both of you means embracing the opportunity to realize your greatest dreams and intentions—together and with each other's support. It is the beginning of what will be a journey that will take you farther and deeper into yourselves as individuals and as a couple. It means taking on the world as a team.

It would be putting it mildly to say your relationship has been tried and tested in many ways. It's not been easy for you or your families, and yet you have risen above the challenges and fears that filled the early days of your relationship...you have taken on the challenge of looking deeply into difficulties and exploring possibilities. And you have made it to this special day where, before loving friends and family, you come to pledge your love.

We congratulate you on the courage is has taken to make your way to this place. For any couple, this is a great achievement. For you two, it is especially poignant because there were so many hurdles for you to jump. Luckily, you have a theme song: *Come What May.*

Neither of you realized that a union like yours was possible until you gave it a chance. You were wary of deepening your relationship, yet the strength of your love gave you the power to say—*and sing*—"come what may." You have committed to stepping up to the plate to face life's challenges together, and no couple could ask for a stronger start!

Together, you are the perfect complements: Liz is a word person and Dean is a number person; Dean looks at the best case scenario and Liz looks at the worst case scenario in situations; Liz is ultraprepared and Dean flies by the seat of his pants. While you both tend toward extremes on your own, together you have found a way to meet on middle ground.

Obviously, you share many values and delights and have weathered many of life's storms together. Yet on this day, the journey of nourishing your love through all of life's cycles takes on a new dimension as you become husband and wife. You will discover that marriage is an even more complete joining of two lives. It's the spiritual, physical, and emotional union of two human beings. It is the fuller opening of two hearts and the ripening of two souls. It is the opportunity for both of you to become even more of whom you are meant to be.

Dean and Liz, may your marriage be your new home, and may you share a long and happy life together in the warmth of that home and on the journeys that life beckons you to.

THOUGHTS TO PONDER

- Some couples are shy and don't feel comfortable sharing personal stories. Are you one of them?
- Some couples love to tell their stories and engagement tales. Are you one of them?
- If you are open to sharing personal stories, which stories would you like to share?
- Would you like that part of the ceremony to be serious and solemn? Or are you happy to let it be humorous and fun?

12

Seal Your Relationship in a Love Contract

We sat down one night and wrote out a "wish list" for our married life. We put it into a beautiful scroll and had it blessed in our wedding ceremony.

—Liz

In the United States, the marriage license is the paperwork that will make your union legal. Your officiant must adhere to the laws of the state and city in which the marriage takes place, but the state- or city-issued license is not typically related to spiritual, religious, or cultural customs.

In addition to the legal license, some traditions have their own documents that celebrate the emotional and spiritual bond of your union as well as your responsibilities as marriage partners. In Judaism they call it a *ketubah.* Muslims have a similar contract given as part of the traditional *nikah* ceremony, and Quakers have a traditional marriage document the whole congregation signs.

Whether you include a contract from your faith tradition or create your own, it is important you invest some time focusing on what marriage truly means to you. Each marriage is unique, and so are the goals, desires, and hopes of each bride and groom. Before the ceremony it will be a blessing on your marriage if you both sit down and create your own personal wedding contract or agreement, or at least outline your intentions for married life.

Creating a personal marriage contract of your own is a beautiful way to clarify what you both anticipate and would like to experience and create in your marriage. It can include everything from being kind and thoughtful every day to having children to building a dream house and growing old together. This is not your legally binding document; rather it is a spiritually binding document. It can be adapted from a traditional format or can be created in a very nontraditional format, as long as it suits your needs. You can both sign this document, in the same spirit of commitment with which you sign your marriage license, and if you choose, you can have loved ones sign in witness. Many of the following ideas are suitable for framing. Here are some ways you can both express the spirit of the relationship you want to create.

1. Create an interfaith ketubah or a nondenominational marriage contract. In the Jewish custom, the *ketubah* is considered a marriage contract that binds husband and wife together in common goals and intentions for marriage. It begins with filling in the dates from the Jewish calendar as well as the name of the bride and groom and the location. It is signed by the bride and groom, two witnesses, and the rabbi or designated officiant:

> **HESHVAN,** in the year **5765,** corresponding to the **7th** day of **November,** in the year **2004,** a mutual On the **FIRST** day of the week, **the 23rd** day of covenant of marriage was entered in **The Rainbow Room at 30 Rockefeller Plaza,** between the groom, **John Jacobs,** and the bride, **Tina Fellows.**

Dana and Rob edited the language from a modern *ketubah* to suit their relationship. You can adapt this in a nondenominational or nonreligious marriage contract by filling in the standard dates. You can mention the blending of faiths or focus only on the language of love and commitment:

> On the _____ day in the month of _____ in the year _____, a mutual covenant of marriage was entered in [venue and city] between the groom, _____, and the bride, _____. (Today, this couple blends their lives and traditions as they promise to build a marriage based on love and mutual affection.)
>
> We promise to be ever-accepting of one another, while treasuring each other's individuality; to comfort and support each other through life's disappointments and sorrows; to revel and share in each other's joys and accomplishments; to share our hopes and dreams; to strive for an intimacy that will allow us to accomplish this promise and permit us to become the persons we are yet to be.

We vow to establish a home open to all of life's potential; a home filled with respect for all people; a home based on love and understanding. May we live each day as the first, the last, the only day we will have with each other.

2. Be inspired by the Quaker marriage contract or craft your own. Quaker marriages are among the simplest ceremonies. They typically take place as part of the worship service in reverent silence. The couple stands when they are ready and speaks their vows (traditional or personal), and the marriage agreement typically culminates with the signing of a document witnessed by all attending members of the Friends community. You can choose to incorporate this lovely language into your own wedding contract or write something that is most fitting to you both. Perhaps you would like to adapt the custom of having your love contract signed by the community and ask guests to sign in lieu of signing a guest book:

On this the [day], [month], in the year of our Lord, [year]
[bride] and [groom], appeared together,
and [groom] taking [bride]
by the hand, did, on this solemn and joyous occasion,
declare that he took
[bride] to be his wife, promising with Divine assistance
to be unto her a loving and faithful husband; and then,
in the same assembly, [bride], did in like manner declare that
she took [groom] to be her husband,
promising with Divine assistance, to be unto him
a loving and faithful wife.
And moreover they, [groom] and [bride],
did, as further confirmation thereof, then and there,
to this certificate set their hands.

3. Put your wedding vows in a document and sign them. You can select classic vows from your faith such as these classic Quaker vows:

In the presence of God and these our Friends,
I take thee to be my husband,
promising with Divine assistance to be unto thee
a loving and faithful wife
as long as we both shall live.
    In the presence of God and these our Friends,
I take thee to be my wife,

promising with Divine assistance to be unto thee
a loving and faithful husband
as long as we both shall live.

Or you can type up your personal vows, sign them, and have them
witnessed and signed by loved ones. Another approach is to select one
vow or sentiment on which you both agree:

We promise to love and honor one another for all our days.
We promise to stand by each other's side, partners in all things.
We promise to share responsibilities, chores, and childrearing.
We promise to help each other in daily life and works.
We promise to be loving to each other through dark and light times.
We promise to hold each other gently and give each other strength in
    the most difficult times.
We promise to always strive to see one another through the eyes
    of love.

4. Expand and elaborate on your vows. The vows you speak at your
wedding may be on the short side, or they may tend to be romantic.
There may have been some things you felt were too personal or too
practical to add. Privately, see if there are additional sentiments you
would like to add to your vows. These can be very personal statements
the two of you come up with together. You can add them to your actual
wedding vows and make them one document or just keep them separate in a sacred place such a holy book or even in a frame behind your
wedding photo, symbolically making them the foundation beneath
your marriage. Jan and Peter discovered there were a few more agree-
ments they needed to make with one another beyond their six line
wedding vows, so they expanded them to include these promises:

• We treat our love as sacred, and we are responsible for managing our
  relationship—we do not let others interfere.
• While we include others in our circle of love, we never take our issues
  outside the relationship or talk negatively about each other to relatives
  because this dissipates our sacred bond.
• We consult each other on all major life issues, purchases, and plans and
  yet give one another freedom and space to be individual and do our
  own thing.
• We make each other's well-being a priority!

5. Create a mission statement for your marriage. The first step of
any new enterprise is to create a mission statement. This can apply to

your marriage, as well. Brainstorm, discuss, process, and bat around ideas until you come up with a marriage mission statement. This is your mutual intention for marriage; it is what you want to *be* and *build* together. It can have one sentence or reflect a number of ideas:

> Our union gives us strength, power, and fortitude to deal with all of life's ups and downs, and it empowers us to contribute to others and the world. We are best friends, confidantes, and partners, and we have many close relationships with people we consider "spiritual family." We are a couple who inspire others with our love and who model what it is to be in a great relationship.

6. Craft wedding scrolls. Together, create a list that spells out your intentions, aspirations, goals, hopes, and dreams for your wedded life. Turn it into your official "wedding scroll." Write neatly or type. It can be on pretty parchment-like paper or any attractive paper. Consider having it written in calligraphy and framed, or simply roll it up and tie it with a gold ribbon. No one need see it but you two. Take it to your ceremony and keep it at the altar so it is blessed by the expressions of love and commitment shared at your ceremony and energized by the vows you exchange. It can be a list of loving but also practical intentions such as this sample list of 18 intentions:

1. Our relationship is the foundation of our lives.
2. When we disagree, we do so gently and lovingly.
3. We make each other number one in our lives.
4. We share the chores.
5. We blend our finances and financial life.
6. We share expenses, but whoever makes more pays more.
7. We never let a family member have undo influence in our lives.
8. We take at least one vacation each year.
9. We support each other in fulfilling dreams.
10. We each pursue individual passions.
11. We run errands together on Saturdays and leave Sundays for time alone.
12. We share the care of our dog and share dog walking.
13. We spend 10 minutes each day to connect, even when super busy.
14. We spend Christmas with John's family.
15. We spend Hanukah with Emily's family.
16. We will find an interfaith worship service we both agree on and enjoy.
17. We will never allow religion to disempower us and come between us.
18. We will learn more about what we love about our faiths and how we want to impart that to children, before we start a family.

7. Write love letters to one another. You can each take the time to craft a beautiful letter stating what you love about each other and what your promises for married life are, and place them in a sacred spot in your home or even include them in the ceremony. Rev. Victor Fuhrman, MSC, RM, an interfaith minister, regularly asks couples he marries to write love letters to each other to be exchanged on their wedding day. These become a contract of sorts that reminds them what they truly love about each other. During the ceremony, the bride and groom are handed the letters and he explains, "I know you two are utterly in love right now, but take my word for it, there will come a time, be it 10 months or 10 years from now, when you will have a fight. That's when you will open these letters and remember the spirit of the commitment you made here today."

8. Select a favorite wedding reading as your love contract. Sometimes the most profound and meaningful language already exists and can be adapted in some way to represent a contract for your married life. Eric Kent, cofounder of NJWeddings.com, created the "Art of Marriage" photo frame as a way of honoring marriage with a classic reading and favorite wedding photo. You can take that a step further and actually cosign a copy of the "Art of Marriage" or any favorite reading and agree that it represents the agreement between you two in your relationship.

9. Define what you bring to the relationship through your names. In the Kabbalistic tradition, as taught by Rabbi Joseph Gelberman, author of *Kabbalah as I See It* and founder of the New Synagogue, you can imbue a new meaning into a name or word if you take each letter and embellish it with a fuller definition. Write both your names vertically, and take each letter and use it to explain a quality that you intend to bring to your relationship:

L Love
A Affection
U Unity
R Renewal
I Inspiration
E Excitement

and

V Valor
I Insight

C Compassion
T Tenacity
O Openheartedness
R Responsibility and romance

THOUGHTS TO PONDER

1. What are your hopes and dreams for marriage?
2. What promises would you like to make in writing?
3. Knowing that putting things in writing can help make them happen, what intentions for marriage would you like to map out on paper for your wedding day?

Part Three

Resources I: A Multifaith View of Weddings

When planning your interfaith or mixed-culture ceremony—and life—it is helpful to know some of the rules of engagement of other faiths. This section is designed to give you a quick, overall view of how both your faiths look on interfaith marriage as well as some tips on aspects of each faith that you can adapt into a ceremony that honors more than one tradition.

The Jewish Wedding

We had a nontraditional Jewish wedding but honored my parent's traditions.

—Janine

Holy book(s): Torah, Talmud, Zohar

Who typically officiates: The ceremony is performed by one or more rabbis and a cantor (who is versed in Hebrew chants and sings them during the ceremony). Some cantors are ordained and can also perform the ceremony.

Where it takes place: It can take place in a synagogue, but this is not required. Usually, it takes place in the same venue as the celebration. In Israel, where there are often 300–600 guests, it is often in a wedding hall.

Belief about marriage: Marriage is called *kiddushin*, which translates as "sanctification" or "dedication." It is not just a social or contractual agreement; rather it is meant to be a spiritual bonding and fulfillment of a *mitzvah* (act of divine goodwill). A couple meant to be together is called *beschert*. The Kabbalah sees bride and groom as "one soul in two bodies."

View on intermarriage: Orthodox Judaism strictly forbids it. Conservative Judaism sees it as causing "demographic harm to the Jewish People," and Conservative rabbis are not permitted to officiate. Reform and Reconstructionist Judaism (Progress Judaism) do not *prohibit* intermarriage, but it is still very controversial. By Jewish law, children of a Jewish mother are considered Jewish.

Practice and ritual: There are many rituals before and during the wedding ceremony, depending on whether it is an Orthodox, Conservative, or Reform wedding. The wedding day is considered holy and seen as a day the bride and groom are forgiven their past shortcomings and sins as they merge into a new being. They are also considered very close to God on this day and are encouraged to offer blessings and advice to others.

What the couple wears: The groom typically wears a yarmulke (skullcap), and the bride wears a traditional white wedding dress. In an Orthodox wedding, the bride wears white to symbolize her purity and that she has been to the *mikvah* bath, and the groom wears a *kittel* (a short white linen robe) over his suit to indicate his spiritual readiness for marriage.

Preparation and supplies: Red wine and two kiddush cups (silver wine chalices); clear wine glass enclosed in a special cloth bag for the breaking of the glass (or wine glass or lightbulb tied in a linen napkin). The ceremony takes place under a huppah, which can be built to stand on its own or held by four huppah holders.

Elements from the traditional Jewish ceremony that you can adapt:

- Getting married under a huppah
- Bride circling the groom seven times
- Hebrew prayers and chants
- Seven blessings over the wine
- Stepping on the glass
- Signing of the *ketubah*

The Muslim Wedding

We had a nondenominational ceremony with an interfaith minister and, at my mother-in-law's request, a nikah *at a local mosque later that afternoon.*

—Janice

Holy book(s): Quran, specifically verse 4:21: *mithaqun Ghalithun* (a strong covenant).

Who officiates: Traditionally, an appointed Muslim judge (*qadi*) or any responsible adult Muslim who understands Islamic law can officiate. In the United States, it is more common to seek an imam (Muslim clergyperson) affiliated with a mosque.

Where it takes place: Traditionally, a mosque is preferred, but in most instances, it may be held in a location convenient to both bride and groom. Location is usually based on the customs of the nation where it is held.

Belief about marriage: In Islam, marriage is considered both a social relationship and a legal contract. It is not considered a "holy sacrament" and may be dissolved by legal divorce.

View on intermarriage: Muslim men are discouraged from marrying non-Muslim women, but it is not forbidden. Intermarriage with observant Jews and Christians, referred to as "People of the Book," is more acceptable than intermarriage with other faiths. Muslim women are prohibited from marrying non-Muslim men.

Practice and ritual: The marriage ceremony is most commonly called the *nikah* (meaning "marriage contract"). Traditionally, the marriage protocol consists of the proposal (*ijab*), in which both bride and groom must consent to the marriage both verbally and in writing; the *mahr*, a wedding gift (dowry) paid to the bride by the groom that remains her property as a form of security; and the *nikah*, in which the marriage contract is signed in front of two adult Muslim witnesses in the presence of the officiate. Next comes the *walimah*, a wedding celebration among family and friends. In some traditions, a *wali* (older male relative) may be present to speak on the bride's behalf and represent her interests.

What the couple wears: Muslim wedding clothing is linked to local custom and culture. Among Middle Eastern couples, the bride wears a white or off white *abaya,* a multilayered "modest" garment that conforms to Islamic tradition. The groom will wear a dishdasha, a one-piece, long, flowing shirt-dress. Among couples from South Asia, the bride will wear a red dress with golden ornaments with a comparable head covering, and the groom may wear a *sherwani* (shirt-dress) with a long *dupatta* (scarf). In Western societies, many Muslim couples will wear traditional but modest Western wedding clothing as long as they conform to Islamic tradition. In South Asian nations like India and Pakistan, there is a tradition to decorate the bride's hands and feet with henna.

Preparation and supplies: *Mahr* (dowry), *nikah* (contract), witnesses, and officiate are the necessary elements of the wedding. In some traditions, a *wali* (older male relative representing the bride) may also participate in the ceremony.

Elements from the traditional Muslim ceremony that you can adapt:

- Scriptural readings from the Quran
- Depending on the nationality of families, a reading from Rumi, the Persian poet
- Decorating the bride's hands with henna

The Hindu Wedding

I am Hindu and my husband-to-be is Christian. Both our parents are very traditional, but we only want one ceremony. I am choosing my favorite customs from the Hindu ceremony.

—Aloki

Holy book(s): Vedas (oral tradition), Upanishads (written commentaries on the Vedas)

Who officiates: It is the role of the Hindu priest or *pandit* to lead a couple and their families through the ceremony of marriage.

Where it takes place: Sometimes (in India) the whole community is invited to a Hindu wedding, so it rarely takes place in a temple and is more likely to be held outdoors, under a tent, in a wedding hall, or at the home of the bride's family. In the West, it may take place in an auditorium or huge room attached to a Hindu temple or at the venue where the reception will be held.

Belief about marriage: The Hindu wedding is called *samskara* and is one of 16 *samskaras*—"sacraments"—Hindus are expected to experience in life. Marriage is celebrated as a rite of passage in which two people elevate their physical journey into a spiritual journey when they become husband and wife.

View on intermarriage: Hindu people who still believe in the caste system reject intercaste marriages and frown on Hindu–non-Hindu unions. The faith itself is more open minded and does not restrict interfaith unions or turn people away if they choose to marry into a different caste.

Practice and ritual: During the wedding ceremony, there are typically 13 different rituals. A scared fire is always lit with ghee and woolen wicks to evoke the god of fire, Agni, to bear witness to the ceremony. There are many mantras and prayers to Hindu deities spoken. It always opens with a prayer to the god of obstacles, Ganesha, to remove all obstacles from a couple's marital path.

What the couple wears: The groom typically wears a kurta (also called kurta pajamas, made from thin material with a long top that flows to below the knees) or a *sherwanis* or *Jodhpuri* suit. These often are accessorized with elaborate waistbands and ornate turbans. Customary Indian shoes, *mojris,* are the traditional footwear worn. The bride typically wears a special sari given to her by her mother and is bedecked and jeweled like a goddess. Red is a very popular color, often with metallic gold or silver or bronze trim. Her eyes will be made up to the hilt, and there will typically be a lovely diamond post on the side of the nose (or perhaps an ornate piece of jewelry that connects from an earring to a nose piercing and covers one cheek). Lots of gold jewelry, lavish necklaces, and ornate dangling earrings are worn.

Preparation and supplies: Bride and groom are expected to gather and often prepare or help prepare the multiple *puja* supplies needed for the wedding. The Hindu temple or priest typically supplies them with a list that includes ghee, milk, yogurt, cum-cum, honey, flowers, nuts, assorted brass *puja* plates and bowls, rice, and so on. They are also expected to feed the priest and give him an offering. The temple charges usually start at $201 for a wedding. It is also a custom to give the priest a love offering of at least $101 (In the Hindu tradition, prices never end on zero).

Elements from the traditional Hindu ceremony that you can adapt:

- Exchanging of gifts between families
- Bowing at the feet of the Hindu parents for a blessing before the ceremony
- Gifts for the bride
- Sari for the bride
- Prayer to Ganesha
- Lighting of the sacred fire, Agni
- Exchange of garlands to welcome one another to each other's families
- Saptapadi (seven steps), considered the most important part of the ceremony, sealing the union forever
- Throwing of flower petals, sometimes mixed with blessed rice

The Buddhist Wedding

My mother chanted traditional chants, quietly, but she made sure they were uttered.

—Dee

Holy book(s): Sutras (Suttas): words of the Buddha

Who officiates: Buddhist weddings are simple, self-officiated ceremonies, but for purposes of legal requirements, they may be witnessed and officiated by ordained Buddhist monks.

Where it takes place: The ceremony may take place at a temple or any other designated place.

Belief about marriage: Marriage must be undertaken according to the basic tenets of Buddhism including mutual love and respect and an extension of the couple's compassion to the community and world.

View on intermarriage: As Buddhist marriage is not governed by religious tenets, marriage between a Buddhist and a member of another faith is widely accepted.

Practice and ritual: The Buddhist wedding ceremony is meant to be simple and involves a simple altar with candles and flowers, sometimes set before a representation of the Buddha. The ceremony includes the recitation of Buddhist Sutras and an exchange of vows, followed by an exchange of rings and a blessing.

What the couple wears: Clothing usually follows local customs, with an emphasis on simplicity and softness.

Preparation and supplies: An altar with candles, incense, and a tray containing the rings and offerings of fruit, flowers, cakes, and sweets are present.

The traditional Buddhist ceremony: The families of the bride and groom arrive early in the morning with the tray containing the candles, incense, rings, and offerings. They place the tray on the altar. The bride and groom then face the image of the Buddha and separately ask for blessings. The couple then chants three Sutras and devotional prayers. After the recitation, the couple lights the candles as a symbol of family unity and then lights the incense. The flowers are than presented as an offering to the image of the Buddha. The couple exchanges vows of mutual love, respect, devotion, and compassion. This is followed by the exchange of rings. The ceremony is concluded with the families and guests chanting the Mangala Sutra, a blessing of protection, and the Jayamangala Gatha, a prayer thanking the Buddha for his teachings and blessings. Following the ceremony, the couple and family may have a celebratory meal.

Elements from the traditional Buddhist ceremony that you can adapt:

- The tray with candles and incense and other items significant to your lives
- Various sutras and devotionals
- The Mangala Sutra blessing of protection
- Buddha icon on your wedding altar
- Any English translation of wisdom of the Buddha

The Catholic Wedding

I was divorced from my first husband and did not want an annulment because of my kids, so I could not marry in my church. We had a ceremony with Catholic elements but a woman officiated.

—Patricia

Holy book(s): New Testament

Who officiates: Traditionally, it is the role of a Catholic priest or deacon to officiate the wedding. Traditionally, that person is always male.

Where it takes place: It typically takes place in a Catholic church. The church frowns on weddings outside its walls, but in the case of an agreed on interfaith wedding, the priest *may* agree to do it at a venue or home.

Belief about marriage: The coming together of a couple in marriage is a sacrament of the Church, and it is believed that the marriage merges not only the couple and their families but the couple with God and the Church. A wedding performed by a Catholic priest is considered an official sacrament. The church will not let priests perform weddings for people who have been divorced—unless the marriage was annulled. They also want to make sure that every Catholic who is married is up to date with his or her sacraments.

View on intermarriage: The Church has become more open minded about it in recent years, generously allowing people of other Christian denominations to marry Catholics because it has become so much more common. The issue of intermarriage outside of interfaith Christianity is still frowned on but is not forbidden. However, it is not easy to find a priest who will preside or agree to co-officiate with another clergyperson, especially outside of the church walls.

Practice and ritual: The wedding ceremony is often celebrated with a full mass, choir, organist, and marriage ceremony that has specific language that weds the bride and groom to the Church and asks them to vow to raise their children Catholic.

What the couple wears: Bride and groom wear Western wedding clothes of white dress and tux.

Preparation and supplies: The Church has seven sacraments—Baptism, Eucharist, Reconciliation, Confirmation, Marriage, Holy Orders, and Anointing of the Sick—and Catholics must have satisfied the first four before marriage. They also must attend pre-Cana counseling and courses, without exception.

Elements from the traditional Catholic ceremony that you can adapt:

- Unity candles lit by mothers and brides and groom
- Reading of I Corinthians
- Scriptural references
- Passing of the Peace, where everyone stands and shakes hands and says, "The peace of God be with you"
- Icons of Jesus and/or Mary at your wedding altar

The Christian Wedding

My wedding will not be in a church, but we will have traditional Christian vows and prayers in addition to modern readings and family participation.

—Joan

Holy book(s): Old and New Testaments, Book of Common Prayer

Who officiates: Minister or pastor

Where it takes place: Depending on the denomination, the wedding may be celebrated in church or at a venue of the couple's choosing.

Belief about marriage: Marriage is a sacred covenant between the couple and God, ordained by God to exemplify his love in the world.

View on intermarriage: This is a question that must be answered by each denomination. Traditional, Bible-based churches will point to scripture dissuading Christians from marrying nonbelievers. Liberal churches may be more open to interfaith marriage. The best advice is to contact the pastor or minister of the church you attend or are contemplating for your wedding and have an open and frank discussion about your plans.

Practice and ritual: Much of the Christian wedding ritual is steeped in the tradition of God's covenant with Abraham. The covenant, from the Hebrew word *b'rith* (cutting), comes from the cutting of sacrificial animals in half and creating holy space between the halves. Those who would engage in the covenant (as the wedding couple does) walk this holy space (aisle) and come together at the altar. The division of the bride's and groom's families and friends on either side of the aisle is symbolic of this. In the biblical covenant, those making it would cut their right hands and join their "blood." The exchange of wedding rings emulates this sacred act. The idea behind the covenant is the equal sharing of all that both the groom and bride bring together in marriage as witnessed by God as a holy promise.

What the couple wears: The bride traditionally wears a white dress, symbolic of purity. The groom will wear a tuxedo or suit.

Preparation and supplies: Depending on the denomination, the couple should plan on contacting and meeting with the minister or pastor several months before the wedding. Unity candles are popular at Christian and Christian interfaith weddings, representing the two lives and two families joined as one.

The traditional Christian ceremony: Traditionally, the groom enters first, from the right, either on his own or accompanied by the groomsmen. The remaining wedding party, including the parents of the groom and the bride's mother, enter and are seated. The bridesmaids then enter, followed by the flower girl and, finally, the ring bearer. The bride's father will then accompany her to the altar and "give her away" to the groom. Other elements are usually dependent on the denomination.

Elements from the traditional Christian ceremony that you can adapt:

- Call to Worship
- Opening prayer
- Musical solo (or hymn)
- The Charge to the Bride and Groom
- Wedding vows
- Exchanging of rings
- Lighting of the unity candle
- Communion
- Pronouncement
- First kiss
- Closing prayer and recessional

The Greek Orthodox Wedding

Although we got married in an outdoor park, I loved wearing garlands as wedding crowns.

—Ana

Holy book(s): Greek version of the Old and New Testaments

Who officiates: Greek Orthodox priest

Where it takes place: Greek Orthodox church

Belief about marriage: Marriage is a sacrament reflecting love, mutual respect, equality, and sacrifice.

View on intermarriage: The Church prefers intra-Orthodox marriages but allows marriage of Orthodox to other Christians who believe in the Holy Trinity, provided the marriage is performed in an Orthodox church by an Orthodox priest and that the couple agree to baptize and raise their children in the Orthodox church.

Practice and ritual: The wedding consists of two parts, the Service or Betrothal and the Sacrament of Marriage. Each act in the service is repeated three times to mystically invoke the presence of the Holy Trinity. The bride and groom do not exchange vows because it is believed their presence in church for the ceremony already signifies their promise to "love, honor, and cherish" each other. Candy-coated almonds (*koufeta*) from the wedding altar are served to the guests after the ceremony, symbolizing the sweetness and durability of marriage as well as fertility and new life.

What the couple wears: Modern Greek couples wear traditional Western gowns and tuxedos. They will be given special crowns to wear during the ceremony.

Preparation and supplies: The altar is prepared with a special plate holding woven marriage crowns and candy-coated almonds (*koufeta*).

The traditional Greek Orthodox ceremony: The Service of Betrothal begins with those in attendance praying for the spiritual well-being of the couple. This is followed by the exchange of rings. The priest first blesses the rings, holding them in his right hand, and then makes the sign of the cross over the bride and groom's heads, betrothing them as servants of God. He then places the rings in their right hands, symbolic of the "right hand of God" bestowing blessings. The couple's religious sponsor, the *koumbaro*, then exchanges the rings three times, symbolizing the Holy Trinity, that each partner will strengthen and uplift the other and that, as betrothed, they become "perfected."

The second part of the ceremony is the Sacrament of Marriage. The ceremony begins with petitions and prayers and scriptural readings. The priest then joins the couple's hands, which remain joined until the conclusion of the ceremony. The crowning is the high point of the ceremony, where the bride and groom are crowned with *stefana*, thin, woven crowns that are joined together with a white silk ribbon. The priest blesses the crowns and then places them on the bride and groom. The *koumbaro* then exchanges the crowns between their heads three times. This is followed by the reading of Jesus' first miracle at the wedding in Cana. In remembrance of this, the couple is given a "common cup" of wine to drink from as recognition of how they will share their joys and burdens. The couple is then led by the priest in a circle around the altar containing the Gospels and the cross, symbolic of the Word and redemption being at the center of the new life together. After the walk, the priest removes the crowns, lifts the Gospels, and then separates their hands, with a prayer that from that point forward, only God may separate them.

Elements from the traditional Greek Orthodox ceremony that you can adapt:

- The wedding crown tradition
- The walk around the altar
- Sharing of the candied almonds
- Sharing from the "common cup"

The Sikh Wedding

My mother wants a traditional Sikh ceremony, but I would like to blend it with my future husband's Christian faith.

—Anika

Holy book(s): Guru Granth Sahib (Scripture Regarded as Living Guru)

Who officiates: The ceremony may be officiated by any adult Sikh man or woman but is often led by the *Granthi,* the temple keeper of the Guru Granth Sahib.

Where it takes place: This is dependent on local custom and culture but is most often held at the *gurdawara* (temple). The requirement is that the Guru Granth Sahib be present.

Belief about marriage: Marriage is an egalitarian partnership and a holy communion of two souls.

View on intermarriage: Both the bride and groom must be Sikh to be married in *gurdawara* in the presence of Guru Granth Sahib.

Practice and ritual: Both bride and groom are prepared for the day by their families, who will later rendezvous at the temple. The day is both joyous and prayerful. The families read Guru Granth Sahib before preparing for the day and also recite *ardas* (Sikh prayers). The groom is often given a ceremonial sword by his uncle, and his mother feeds him some sweets. Close family and friends often gather at the bride's and groom's homes for tea and sweets before traveling together to the *gurdawara.* The bridal party first travels to the temple and waits for the arrival of the groom's party. When possible, the groom rides on a horse for the final portion of the trip to the temple. The families greet each other outside the temple and recite prayers. This is followed by the exchange of gifts and sharing tea and sweets. They then enter the temple accompanied by the chanting of *kirtan* (hymns). All attending pay their respects before Guru Granth Sahib, and the ceremony then begins.

What the couple wears: The bride will wear a traditional, brightly colored but modest blouse with pants or a long skirt and a gold-embroidered shawl. The groom will wear traditional trousers and a shirt along with a long scarf and a red or pink turban.

The traditional Sikh ceremony: Also called the *Anand Karaj* (Bliss-ful Ceremony), the ceremony consists of *kirtan* (hymns) and prayer by the bride, groom, and their parents. The bride's father will then take the end of the groom's sash and hand it to the bride. The groom will then lead the bride around the Guru Granth Sahib four times while the celebrant reads one of four special prayers, accompanied by music and chanting. All in attendance say closing prayers, followed by the parents of the bride and groom blessing the couple. They are then given gifts by family and friends. The religious ceremony concludes with the serving of a blessed sweet pudding.

Elements from the traditional Sikh ceremony that you can adapt:

- Prayers
- *Kirtan*
- Sweet pudding

The Wiccan Wedding

We had a "Cathwic" wedding because I am Wiccan but our families are Catholic.

—Anne Marie

Holy book(s): Oral traditions and Wiccan redes (principles)

Who officiates: Traditionally, it is the role of a high priestess and priest to co-officiate the wedding, to have balance between the masculine and feminine.

Where it takes place: It can take place anywhere, but outdoors in nature is favored to bring bride and groom into the natural splendor of the Goddess. It typically takes place in a circle.

Belief about marriage: The coming together of a couple in marriage is considered a sacred act, a merging of God and Goddess in human form.

View on intermarriage: Technically, many Wiccans are in some form interfaith couples because many begin life in another faith tradition and adopt the Wiccan path along the way. In general, Wiccans and other pagans are open minded about marriage to people of other belief systems.

Practice and ritual: The wedding ceremony is typically called a handfasting, although some Wiccan couples opt for a nondenominational wedding ceremony that includes earth-based traditions. During the handfasting, the couple's hands are literally tied together by silk ribbons in multiple colors, with each color carrying a meaning for the couple. In a traditional handfasting each ribbon is tied separately with a blessing; couples sometimes use a braid of different color ribbons.

What the couple wears: At a traditional handfasting, velvet is popular in white, black, purples, and deep reds. Long and flowing or Renaissance-type wear is also popular.

Preparation and supplies: There are a lot of ritual elements in the ceremony, so brides and grooms often bring their own, have friends contribute spiritual supplies, and/or the priestess and priest likely have altar items.

Elements from the traditional Wiccan ceremony that you can adapt:

- Celebrated in a circle
- Opens with the Calling in of the Directions
- Closes by acknowledging and thanking the directions and ancestors
- Tying of the hands with different-colored ribbons
- Prayers to the Goddess or specific goddesses and gods
- Handfasting vows, which are often a series of questions rather than one question of intent

The Unitarian Universalist Wedding

I got married in a Unitarian church with their male minister and my female interfaith minister co-officiating. This is how I brought in the balance of the male-female from my pagan tradition without scaring my husband's 85-year-old Italian grandfather.

—Carol

Holy book(s): The holy books and wisdom of all traditions

Who officiates: A Unitarian Universalist minister

Where it takes place: The ceremony may take place at a Unitarian Universalist church or at any venue of the couple's choosing.

Belief about marriage: Marriage is a unique relationship for each couple, based on love, mutual respect, and the desire to grow together in spirit and truth.

View on intermarriage: Love is without boundary. Unitarian Universalists are open to marriages between people of all faiths and also will celebrate same-sex unions.

Sacraments: Love, respect, truth, and universal understanding are the sacraments, embracing the beliefs of all religions and faiths.

Practice and ritual: These are as varied as the people who make up the church. The minister will work with each couple to create the spiritual and romantic ceremony they desire.

What the couple wears: The couple may wear western wedding attire of tuxedo and white dress, or dress in any clothing that reflects their culture, passion, or needs.

Preparation and supplies: It is suggested that the couple meet with the minister two months before the planned wedding to discuss their spiritual and romantic requirements. The actual preparation and supplies will be as varied as the people who are drawn to Unitarian Universalism and can include everything from candle lighting to the reading of Buddhist scripture.

Elements from the traditional Unitarian Universalist ceremony that you can adapt: Since the tradition is no tradition other than the love between the couple and how they want that love expressed, you can blend in elements of any faith or culture.

Part Four

Resources II:
Ceremonies to Inspire You

Each interfaith and blended-culture union is as unique as the couple it honors. We all love weddings and peeking into the way other brides and grooms honor their love, families, faiths, and traditions. Be inspired by these real weddings of couples who came before you, and see if there is anything you would like to adapt for your own wedding.

More Christian than Jewish

Courtney and Ray

Supplies and logistics:
Sand
Two small, thin, clear containers for individual sand
one large, clear container into which to pour the sand
Votive candle
Lightbulb in a napkin or wine glass in a napkin
Vows
Music: *I'll Cover You* from *Rent*

GREETING

Welcome, family and friends. Love gathers us here today. On behalf of Courtney and Ray, thank you for being part of this joyous occasion. Today, we celebrate their relationship as we joyously witness the sacred vows that will express their commitment to one another. Let us offer them our blessings and best wishes for a marriage that is all they would choose it to be!

THE PRAYER/INVOCATION

Let's begin by sharing a moment of prayer. Dear God, we thank you for the gift of marriage. May you give Courtney and Ray the ability to rejoice always in their love. May you fulfill every wish of their hearts. May you open their eyes to the beauty and mystery of the love they have for each other, every day, as today.

And may their life together embrace and nurture the promise of this moment. As we open our hearts in celebration, may we all be surrounded and embraced by the light of love. Amen.

WEDDING READING 1

Love is the sacred, invisible force that brings people together and leads them to their wedding day. Yet it is also a tangible, living energy that has character and great substance...it draws us in...and guides our lives. Paul's letter to the Corinthians is a testament of true and abiding love that reminds us not only of what is important in marriage but of what is truly important in life!

> If I speak in the tongues of men and of angels,
> but have not love,
> I am nothing more than a noisy gong
> or a clanging cymbal.
> And if I have the gift of prophesy,
> and understand all mysteries,
> and have all knowledge,
> and a faith that can move mountains,
> but have not love,
> I am nothing ...
> Love is patient; love is kind.
> It is never jealous,
> nor boastful, proud or rude.
> It is never selfish, resentful, or quick-tempered.
> It keeps no records of wrongs.
> Love *rejoices* with truth.
> Love bears all things, believes all things, hopes all things,
>   endures all things.
> Love never fails.
> And love never ends.
> Faith, Hope and Love...abide in these three.
> But the greatest of these...is love.
> May love always be your aim. Amen.

MINISTER'S MESSAGE

Courtney and Ray, you have been blessed with the gift of love, friendship, and partnership. Today we joyfully celebrate your sacred agreement to love one another and care for one another through all things. You come to your wedding day already united in your hearts and souls.

You two were destined to be together, although you didn't know it at first! Back in 1998, you met on a blind date. You both went your separate ways after one meeting…but in the new millennium found one another again and have been living in the embrace of one another's love since June 2000.

Ray, in Courtney you have found a partner who loves your smile, your patience, your gentle nature. She adores your big heart, the way you share your love so willingly, the fact that your presence brings her peace and that you have the ability to help her calm down—most of the time. She admires the way you dedicate yourself to your own growth and to those you care for and the ways in which you challenge her. In her eyes, you are a beautiful man and a beautiful soul. She loves the way you love her, and she feels lucky and blessed.

Courtney, in Ray you have found a mate who sees in you a woman of substance and beauty, a woman who possesses a wonderful heart and great compassion for others. He loves the way you embrace him and accept him for who he is, that you never try to change him yet gently ask him to make changes. He appreciates that you are direct, honest, open minded, caring, and sincere. He is awed by your drive to succeed at whatever the task at hand and rise above any obstacles in your way. In his eyes, you are the person he can most depend on, the one who will always be there for him and the one who sees him for who he truly is.

Although you have each come to rely on the strength of your partnership, on this day, the journey of nourishing your love through *all* of life's cycles takes on a new dimension as you become husband and wife. Marriage is the more than the complete joining of two lives. It is the merging of two families and two life stories. It is the mystical, physical, and emotional union of two human beings. It is the fuller opening of two hearts and the ripening of two souls.

As you know, it is not a clergyperson standing before you who makes marriage real but rather the honesty and sincerity of your love for one another. I am sure you know it is up to you both to continue to nurture the impending possibilities that lie within your relationship.

The commitment you make today will give you an even stronger foundation upon which to build—*and live*—your lives. The challenge of marriage is to continue to expand and grow and to always honor one another's individual needs and positions within the framework of your partnership.

Welcome the changes to come. Change assures us love is alive. It tells us we are evolving, not stagnated, and that we always have the ability to grow even more.

Always give your relationship the room to grow; let it continually give way to the freshness of what follows. This will nourish you individually as it feeds the soul of your relationship. Enjoy the quiet times, the peace and the natural ways in which love will empower you both to pursue your dreams in life.

SAND CEREMONY

We are all made up of millions of molecules, facets, possibilities, points of view, experiences, desires, hopes, dreams...our very beings are as vast as a beach that stretches on forever and our makeup as complex and complete as the many tiny particles of sand that, when joined together, make that beach such a stunning sight.

In the modern tradition of the sand ceremony, a couple acknowledges their individuality and their desire to merge their lives in marriage by pouring two separate containers of different sand into one empty vessel. This joining of sand symbolically unites the many aspects of their individual selves and also brings together the families that are united by marriage.

Point to the two individual containers of sand. Courtney and Ray, you come to this day as individuals, whole and complete unto yourselves. Bringing the many tiny aspects that represent the two of you together into one vessel represents a joint venture that is a stronger, fuller, more powerful expression of your love.

These two containers of sand represent the two of you as well as your families, your ancestors, the source of who you are. These two distinct containers represent your lives...up until this moment.

Ask them to pour sand simultaneously. As you pour the sand from your individual containers, make the choice to leave behind anything that will not serve your marriage, and choose to bring into your marriage that which will help you grow, blossom, and expand.

After they pour both containers into one. The flowing together of this sand is symbolic of your unique union. Your newly formed union is represented by the intertwined pattern of sand you have created together. It represents all that you both are, all that you both bring into your marriage, and all that you will become together. May this union be blessed in all ways.

CONSECRATION

George Elliot summed up marriage eloquently: "What greater thing is there for two human souls to feel that they are joined for life, to strengthen each other in all labor, to rest on each other in all sorrow, to minister to each other in all pain, and to be one with each other for all time."

Ray and Courtney, as you have come here today of your own free will in the presence of witnesses to declare your love for each other, we ask that you both be honored and expanded by the promises you are about to make, by the expressions of love you are about to share, by the marriage you are about to create.

EXPRESSION OF INTENT

Officiant: Please face each other.

> Do you, Courtney, take Ray to be your husband,
> To have and to hold from this day forward
> In good times and bad times,
> In sickness and in health,
> To love, honor, and cherish forever?

Courtney answers: I do.

> And do you, Ray, take Courtney to be your wife,
> To have and to hold from this day forward
> In good times and bad times,
> In sickness and in health,
> To love, honor, and cherish forever?

Ray answers: I do.

VOWS

Officiant: You have some beautiful vows to share with one another.

Ray: Courtney, we are standing here today in front of the people who matter most to us in our lives, and yet they seem to have faded into the sunset that surrounds us now. You fill up all the space that would otherwise be empty in my eyes and my arms and my heart. You are the light ahead of me that puts all the shadows behind. I feel that with you by my side, the world will forever forget to spin on its axis and that the glow of the sky will surround us for all of our days.

I want to promise so many things to you, but all I can promise you is the following: I promise that you will always be the first person that I think of when I wake up and the last person I think of when I go to bed at night. You are the impossible dream that I never thought I'd achieve, and I promise that you will always be my most valuable possession.

We don't know what our road ahead is paved with. It may be gold, or it may be hard, cutting stones. But I *do* know that if we travel this road together, the gold will shine brighter, and the stones will not hurt our feet as much as they would if we traveled our roads separately.

My angel, I love you so much, and I vow to be the only one who is with you when you need someone to love, and I vow to be the only one there when you want someone to yell at. I promise you my heart, I promise you my soul, and I promise you our unknown future together.

Courtney: I, Courtney, take you, Ray, to be my husband, my friend, and my partner in life. I promise to love you, care for you, and cherish you for all of my days. When you are happy or sad, healthy or ill, I will be there for you and with you, holding your hand and loving you. Together, we will journey through life, and our love will fuel us, protect us, hold us, and grow deeper with each passing day. I cannot wait to grow old with you, laughing and crying at life's unexpected turns and wondering how it is that the time we spend together goes so quickly. Ray, I promise to work to keep our marriage and our friendship strong, communicative, and loving. I vow to honor the faith and trust you put in me. I will celebrate in your successes and respect your failures. I commit myself fully and happily to you and to us. You are my precious diamond. I thank God for you, I give my heart to you, and I love you forevermore.

Officiant: Courtney and Ray, may you always observe the sacred vows and declarations that have been spoken today.

BLESSING AND EXCHANGING OF RINGS

Officiant: And now we come to the exchanging of the rings. The wedding ring is a sacred gift that the bride and groom give to one another on their wedding day. A circle is the symbol of completeness—it has no beginning and it has no end. It represents wholeness, oneness, eternity. These rings are made of metal that will not tarnish. They are symbolic of a union that will endure. May I have the rings, please?

PRAYER, WEDDING READING 2, AND BLESSING OVER THE RINGS

I ask you all to join me, each in your own way, in blessing these rings so that our good wishes may be carried with Ray and Courtney each day of their lives. Let's all take this moment to fill our hearts and minds with good wishes and hopes for this couple—as I read Ray Croft's poem, "Love," which reflects the sentiments of this bride and groom.

Reads poem.

Ray, please take Courtney's hand. Slip the ring on her finger. And repeat after me: with this ring, I promise my love and affection.

Courtney, please take Ray's hand. Slip the ring on his finger. And repeat after me: with this ring, I promise my love and affection.

Pause for a moment.

May these rings serve as a constant reminder of the vows set forth here today.

THE PRONOUNCEMENT/HAND BLESSING

Please face each other and hold hands, so you may feel the gift that you are to one another. If you join your right palms together, and then your left, your hands will form a figure eight or infinity symbol. This represents a love that will go on forever.

These are the hands of your best friend, young and strong and full of love for you. They are holding yours on your wedding day as you promise to love each other today, tomorrow, and forever.

These are the hands that will work alongside yours as together you build your future.

These are the hands that will passionately love you and cherish you through the years and with the slightest touch will comfort you like no other.

These are the hands that will hold you when fear or grief wracks your mind.

These are the hands that will countless times wipe the tears from your eyes, tears of sorrow and tears of joy.

These are the hands that will tenderly hold your children and will help you to hold your family as one.

These are the hands that will give you strength when you need it.

And lastly, these are the hands that even when wrinkled and old will still be reaching for yours, still giving you the same unspoken tenderness with just a touch.

May these hands always reach out with love, tenderness, and respect. May these hands continue to build a loving relationship that lasts a lifetime.

Courtney and Ray, it is my honor to now pronounce you husband and wife.

THE KISS

You may share your first kiss as a married couple!

THE BREAKING OF THE GLASS

We conclude the ceremony with the Hebrew custom of the breaking of the glass. Traditionally, it symbolizes a breaking with childhood and the beginning of the wedding celebration. But it also suggests the frailty of human relationships. Even a strong love can be vulnerable to disruption. The glass, then, is broken to protect the marriage with an implied prayer: "as this glass shatters, so may our marriage never break." The man generally breaks the glass with one stomp of the right foot. So Ray...

We all yell: Mazel tov!

THE BRIDE AND GROOM GREET THE COMMUNITY

Please greet for the first time as a married couple Courtney and Ray!

OFFICIANT'S PARTING WORDS

Go in peace. Congratulations.
  Ceremony ends.

More Jewish than Christian

Jodi and Dennis

Officiating: male-female officiants; one does Hebrew.

Supplies and logistics:
Remembrance candle
One Light votive candle
Unity candle, individual candles, and holder
Wine glass and wine or grape juice
Lightbulb wrapped in a strong linen napkin
Copies of wedding readings

GREETING

Female officiant: Please stand. Welcome family and friends. We are gathered here to celebrate the love shared by Jodi and Dennis. Today we joyously witness the sacred vows that will join them in holy matrimony.

First, the bride and groom have asked that we light a candle in honor of those loved ones who are no longer with us. Let us all light a candle for them, in our hearts and minds, as we remember them with a moment of silence. *Candle is lit.*

And now, let us focus our good wishes and blessings on this bride and this groom as they join their lives as partners in marriage.

THE PRAYER/INVOCATION

Male officiant: Let us pray. Dear God, Eternal Source of Energy and Light, we pray that you shower your unconditional love and blessings

upon those gathered here today in the joy and celebration of the fulfillment of this union.

Your children, Jodi and Dennis, stand before your divine presence,
and the love of their friends and family, as they embark on this journey
that will interweave the threads of their souls in a new garment laced
through with tenderness, mutual respect, and partnership.

May their love serve as a shining example for all to witness. Please
fill us with your grace and surround us in your holy white light of
sanctity and peace as we all say amen.

And from the Hebrew tradition we say thanks: *Ba-ruch a-tah Ah-do-
nai Eh-lo-hay-nu Meh-lech Ha-oh-lahm, sheh-heh-key-ah-nu v'key-y'ma-nu
v'hi-gi-ah-nu la-z'man ha-zeh. Amein.*

Blessed are You, Lord, our God, King of the Universe,

who has kept us alive, sustained us, and brought us to this joyous
season. Amen.

And so it is! Please be seated.

WINE CEREMONY

Have wine chalice and wine/juice ready

Male officiant: And now, we offer the bride and groom a sip of wine
to celebrate their holy union.

And from the Hebrew we say: *Ba-ruch a-tah Ah-do-nai Eh-lo-hay-nu
Meh-lech Ha-oh-lahm, bo-ray p'ree hah-gahfen. Amein*

Blessed are You, Lord, our God, King of the Universe, who creates
the fruit of the vine. Amen.

Officiant fills the cup and hands it to Jodi first.

This cup is symbolic of the pledges you will make to one another
to share together the fullness of life. As you drink from this cup, you
acknowledge that your lives, until this moment separate, have become one vessel into which all your sorrows and joys, all your hopes
and fears, will be poured, and from which you will receive mutual
sustenance.

Please share a sip of wine.

WEDDING READING 1

"The Music of Love," by Amy Barth.

MINISTERS' ADDRESS

Female officiant: Jodi and Dennis, you have been blessed with the gift of one another's love. On this day, the journey of nourishing your love through *all* of life's cycles takes on a new dimension as you become husband and wife.

You will discover that marriage is more than the joining of two lives. It is the merging of two families, two life stories, two traditions. It's the mystical, physical, and emotional union of two human beings. It is the fuller opening of two hearts and the ripening of two souls.

On this day, we joyfully celebrate a sacred agreement between the two of you...an agreement to be steadfast in your intention to love one another through *all* things.

Male officiant: As you live your marriage, you will find that your relationship has moods and seasons, wonderful times as well as challenges. You will have opportunities to make the decision to reach for something deeper within yourselves, a compassion, a caring, a love that is stronger. These are the qualities that will carry you through any challenges.

From this point forward, the energies of your lives shall blend into harmony and oneness.

May you find in each other's love profound acceptance and total release.

May you be given the vision to behold one another with the eyes of love.

May you experience the endless generosity of spirit with which to nurture one another's soul and sweetly keep the promises you make here today. *Pause.*

THE LIGHTING OF THE UNITY CANDLE

Female officiant: It has been said that "from every human being there rises a light that reaches straight to heaven. When two souls that are destined for each other find one another, their streams of light flow together and a single brighter light goes forth from their united being."

Male officiant: The lighting of the unity candle symbolizes the light of two individuals coming together as one brighter light. It also symbolizes the merging of two families, two traditions, and two lives as one.

Female officiant: As a gesture of unity between the two families that are united on this day, and as an acknowledgment of the loving beings who brought Jodi and Dennis into this world, we ask the mother of the bride and the mother and father of the groom to light the individual candles. They will light the individual candles from the one light that already burns on the altar—a light that represents the light of God that shines within us all.

Instruct them to light the tapers.

Now, please pass the light to your children. Thanks. Please return to your seats.

Male officiant to the bride and groom: These two lighted candles represent the bride and the groom as well as their families, their ancestors, the source of who they are. These two distinct flames represent their lives, up until this moment, separate.

We now ask Jodi and Dennis to bring these two separate candles together to light the unity candle.

May the loving light of God, of family, community, and good friends always bless this marriage.

WEDDING READING 2

"When I Come to You," a poem by Carol Fitchett that captures the heart and soul of modern marriage.

THE CONSECRATION

Female officiant: Jodi and Dennis, as you have come here today of your own free will in the presence of witnesses to declare your love for each other, we ask that you both be honored and expanded by the promises you are about to make, by the expressions of love you are about to share, and by the marriage you are about to create. May love be always in your midst!

EXPRESSION OF INTENT AND CONSENT

Male officiant: Please face each other.

Jodi, do you come here freely and without reservation to give yourself in marriage to Dennis? And do you promise to love and honor him as your husband for the rest of your life?

Jodi answers: I do.

Dennis, do you come here freely and without reservation to give yourself in marriage to Jodi? And do you promise to love and honor her as your wife for the rest of your life?

Dennis answers: I do.

VOWS

Female officiant: Since it is your intention to enter into marriage, we ask that you declare your consent before the Divine Spirit and these witnesses. Please look into each other's eyes as you repeat after me.

Jodi:

> I, Jodi, take you, Dennis, to be my husband.
> I promise to be true to you
> in good times and in bad,
> in sickness and in health.
> I will love you and honor you
> all the days of my life.

Dennis:

> I, Dennis, take you, Jodi, to be my wife.
> I promise to be true to you
> in good times and in bad,
> in sickness and in health.
> I will love you and honor you
> all the days of my life.

Officiant: Jodi and Dennis, may you always observe the sacred vows and declarations that have been spoken today. Amen.

BLESSING AND EXCHANGING OF RINGS

Male officiant: Your wedding rings are the gifts you give one another today. The wedding ring has long been a symbol of love and devotion that, like a circle, is unbroken. It has no beginning and no end. It represents unity, wholeness, oneness, and eternity. The rings that Jodi and Dennis are exchanging are made of metal that will not tarnish, metal that is enduring. These rings are symbolic of a union that will endure.

PRAYER OVER THE RINGS

Female officiant: May I have the rings ... I ask everyone here to please silently join us in this prayer over the rings:

> Dear God, spirit of divine love, please bless the giving of these rings so that they who wear them may go on living in your peace and continue in your grace. May these rings be a lifelong symbol of the unity and love between Jodi and Dennis. May these rings serve as a constant reminder of the vows set forth here today. Amen.

RING VOWS

Jodi, please take Dennis's hand, slip the ring on his finger, and repeat after me: with this ring, I pledge my love.

Dennis, please take Jodi's hand, slip the ring on her finger, and repeat after me: with this ring, I pledge my love.

SACRED VOWS FROM SONG OF SOLOMON

Male officiant: And now, the bride and groom will express a sacred vow to each other in English and Hebrew from the Song of Solomon. Dennis and Jodi, please repeat after me simultaneously:

> I am my beloved's
> and my beloved is mine.
> *Ani L'Dodi V'Dodi Li.*

THE PRONOUNCEMENT

Female officiant: Please look at each other. Your two lives are now joined in one unbroken circle.

Male officiant: Wherever you go, may you return to one another ... in togetherness.

Female officiant: May you dare to dream, and plan, and create together.

Male officiant: May you greet each other's sorrow with compassion and fulfill each other's need with the sureness of love.

Female officiant: May the years bring you joy and contentment.

Male officiant: May you share a life of affection and devotion.

Female officiant: May you have happiness.

Male officiant: May you have peace.

Both officiants: Jodi and Dennis, it is our honor to now pronounce you husband and wife.

THE KISS

Dennis, you may now kiss your bride!

THE BREAKING OF THE GLASS

Male officiant: We conclude the ceremony with the breaking of the glass. It is traditional for the man to break the glass with one stomp of the right foot. So Dennis ...

Officiants/all call out: Mazel tov! Salute!
    And now, for the first time as a married couple, please greet Jodi and Dennis!
    Ceremony ends.

Mystical Catholic, Multicultural, Costa Rican

Annie and Arturo

Supplies and logistics:

Altar table
Special incense to burn during procession
Two candle(s) floating in water
Two hurricane candle glasses to keep candles from blowing out
White peacock feather
Sacred Native American stone
Vatican holy water bottle and bowl
Rings in tiny box
Singing bowl
Bindis

WELCOME

Officiant comes to altar with church incense burner, leaving the scent and smoke in the aisle for the bride.

Officiant: Welcome, friends and family. Love gathers us here today, and on behalf of Arturo and Annie, I welcome you to this very special moment.

Annie and Arturo, today we celebrate the place you have made in each other's hearts, and we witness the sacred vows that will join your lives as partners in marriage.

May the promises you make here become the foundation of the life you build together. And now, we share a special opening blessing.

SPECIAL PRAYER AND ANOINTING/UNCTION

Vatican holy water on altar in bowl. After prayer, bride and groom anoint themselves with the sign of the cross.

Officiant: We begin this ceremony with a prayer from Annie's childhood, which was spoken at mealtimes at the camp she attended in New Mexico. We use holy water blessed at the Vatican to bless the bride and groom.

> Divine Spirit
> help us to live as honestly
> and as gently
> and as joyously,
> under these blue skies,
> and among these beautiful trees,
> as God has created us.

Allow the couple to dip their fingers in holy water and cross themselves.
We ask this in the name of the Father, the Son, and the Holy Spirit. *Couple does the sign of the cross during this last line.*
Amen.

INVOCATION

Officiant: Now, an invocation from the Native American tradition.
Divine Spirit of all there is, we honor all you have created. We rejoice in all that is beautiful in the world.
Gesture toward the stone on the altar.
We honor mother earth and ask that this marriage be abundant and grow stronger with each season.
Gesture toward the feather on the altar.
We honor wind and ask that this couple sail through life safely and calmly.
Gesture toward the candles on the altar.
We honor fire and ask that this union be warm and glowing and that their hearts are always filled.
Gesture toward the bowls around the candles on the altar.
We honor water and ask that it cleanse this couple for marriage and soothe them so that they may never thirst for love.

We honor heaven and the power within. With all the forces of the universe, we pray for harmony and joy as this couple grows forever young with one another. Please surround us all in a circle of light. Amen.

PEACE OFFERING

Gregorian chant CD plays in the background "Pax Aeterna."

Officiant: Now, let's all create the spirit of love and community by partaking in the rite of the peace. Please stand and just shake hands—or hug!—people around you, and say, "Peace be with you."

Let them shake until it feels done.

HONORING LOVED ONES

Not only will two people be joined today, but two families will become one. The light of love that illuminates this marriage is inspired by the support of the parents and grandparents of this bride and groom as well as many other loved ones.

Let us extend our hearts to those who could not be here today and also take a moment to remember specific loved ones who no longer reside on earth. These angels surely smile upon us this evening. *More or less five seconds of silence for each, so guests can picture their faces.*

1. Pablo
   Five seconds of silence.
2. Walter
   Five seconds of silence.
3. Inza
   Five seconds of silence.
4. David
   Five seconds of silence.
5. Elouise
   Five seconds of silence.
6. Jane
   Five seconds of silence.
7. Vernon
   Five seconds of silence.
8. Hugh
   Five seconds of silence.

9. David
   Five seconds of silence.
10. Lisa
   Five seconds of silence.
11. Helen
   Five seconds of silence.
12. Ian
   Five seconds of silence.

WEDDING READING 1

And now the mothers of the groom and bride offer a reading, in Spanish and English, of the classic "Marriage Blessing," by the Persian poet Jalalludin Rumi.

Maria:

Bendiciones para una boda, del poeta persa Jalalludin Rumi
Que estos votos y esta unión sean bendecidos
Que la dulzura cunda
Como el vino y la miel
Que esta unión ofrezca fruta y sombra, como el dátil de la palma.
Que traiga dicha y sea cada día un paraíso.
Que fomente la compasión
E irradie felicidad aquí y más allá.
Que su rostro sea claro y su nombre recto,
Una promesa venturosa
Como una luna en medio de un cielo azul.
Me faltan palabras para decir
de que modo fulgura el espíritu en esta unión.

Lucy:

May these vows and this marriage be blessed.
May it be sweet milk,
this marriage, like wine and *halvah.*
May this marriage offer fruit and shade, like the date palm.
May this marriage be full of laughter,
our every day a paradise.
May this marriage be a sign of compassion,
a seal of happiness here and hereafter.

> May this marriage have a fair face and a good name,
> an omen as welcome
> as the moon in a clear blue sky.
> I am out of words to describe
> how spirit mingles in this marriage.

MINISTER'S MESSAGE

Annie and Arturo cultivated their love here at Sarah Lawrence College and consider this campus sacred ground. On April 3, 2003, 19-year-old Annie and 21-year-old Arturo met in the library, just a few yards from this space. *Gesture to the left.*

Arturo offered Annie the use of his copy pass, and she introduced herself. After a dinner together in the dining hall, Arturo was smitten. Separated by the summer, the two got to know each other through romantic e-mail letters, and on September 3, 2003, they reunited for their first date. Just 11 days later, the two began talking of marriage. They knew they would have to see how things went, but they just felt right together.

Annie and Arturo, you are two people who have been blessed with the discovery of one another's love.

Annie, I asked Arturo what he loves about you, and he said: Annie encapsulates everything that's good about humanity. I love her because when I'm with her, I can stay out of the future. She is the most loving woman I have ever met. I love her because all her thoughts and actions arise from a place of love and peace. She loves herself just as she is, and I'm a sucker for her integrity.

And Arturo, I asked Annie what she loves about you, and she said: Arturo is the only person with whom I can be completely myself. I was drawn to Arturo by his boyish soft-spokenness and by his eyes, which are filled with a pure, childlike joy. I love his buttery skin and his precious head. Arturo is as loyal as a puppy. From the beginning I have seen Arturo as a role model, and he has taught me that all of my needs will be taken care of as long as I follow my higher path.

Arturo and Annie, we rejoice with you that, out of all the world, you have found each other.

In this ceremony, you dedicate yourselves to the continued nurturing of your relationship. You are already married in your hearts, and today, you marry each other for all time. May your partnership embody the values inspired by Jesus Christ: love of all people, service, healing, and peace. No matter where life leads you, may this marriage always be your home.

FREE WILL QUESTION

Officiant: Annie and Arturo, in the presence of these witnesses I ask you to declare your intentions. Do you come here today of your own free will to be married to one another?
Annie and Arturo answer: We do.

VOWS

Officiant: You have some beautiful vows to share. And now, Annie and Arturo, please face each other, and together take a deep breath. Arturo will speak the vows first in English, and Annie will repeat them in Spanish. Now speak what is in your heart. *They say one line each at a time, reading from cue cards.*

Arturo (English):

> Annie, you are what I love most about life, and I am ready to marry you.
> First, I vow to you that I will nurture our union by becoming a diplomatic communicator.
> I will treat you with respect and have realistic expectations of you.
> I will meet you halfway, be fair to you, and be responsible for my behavior.
> I promise to be faithful to you, and trust in you.
> I will protect and comfort you, and give you the space you need.
> I will be grateful for our challenges and work with you to overcome them.
> I vow to heal you by bathing you in praise, openness, and affection.
> I will strengthen your very being with nourishing foods.
> I will take the best possible care of myself so that I may live a long, full life by your side.
> And I will honor the pure divinity in you and walk with you on our spiritual journey.
> Lastly, I will be your partner all the days of my life.

Annie (Spanish):

> Arturo, Sos lo que más quiero en la vida, y estoy lista para nos casemos.

Juro hacía vos que alimentaré nuestra unidad convirtiendome en una comunicadora diplomática.

Te trataré con respeto y tendré expectativas realistas.

Estaré dispuesta, seré justa contigo, y seré responsible por mi comportamiento.

Seré fiel contigo y confiaré en ti.

Te protejeré y mimaré, y daré el espacio que necesites.

Estaré agradecida por nuestros desafios, y trabajaré contigo para superarlos.

Te curaré y te bañaré con elogios y afecto.

Fortaleceré tu ser con comida sana.

Me cuidaré de la mejor forma posible así puedo vivir una vida larga y sana, junto a tu lado.

Honraré la divinidad pura en ti y caminaremos juntos en nuestro viaje espiritual.

Finalmente, seré tu compañera todos los dias de mi vida.

BLESSING OF RINGS (AND HANDS)

And now we come to the presentation of your rings. These rings are a symbol of your commitment and devotion to one another. Before you exchange them, I would like to ask everyone here to help me bless these rings by visualizing, with this bride and groom, the delightful, rich, and balanced life that they will share.

VISUALIZATION AND BLESSING OVER THE RINGS

Officiant clinks singing bowl with each line of the following visualization.

Annie and Arturo, please face each other and press your palms against the heart of your partner and see if you can hear each other's hearts beating. Using the healing vibrations of the sound of this chime, we will uplift the energy all around us and together create a clear and sacred moment for this visualization. I ask everyone to:

Ring chime a total of seven times, one for each of the seven visualizations.

1. Visualize Annie and Arturo living in harmony with the earth and feeling the comfort, stability, and safety of each other's arms. *Pause five seconds.*
2. Picture Annie and Arturo connected to their inner children, using their creative energy to serve others, and bringing new life into the world. *Pause five seconds.*

3. Envision Annie and Arturo having the self-respect, confidence, and drive to fulfill their dreams. *Pause five seconds.*
4. See Annie and Arturo feeling compassion for themselves, each other, and everyone they meet. *Pause five seconds.*
5. Visualize Annie and Arturo freely and clearly expressing their thoughts and feelings. *Pause five seconds.*
6. Picture Annie and Arturo growing wiser each day and trusting life as it unfolds. *Pause five seconds.*
7. Envision Annie and Arturo closely connected to Spirit and their higher selves, living out their life's purpose.

Thank you.

EXCHANGE OF RINGS

Couple replaces ring vows with hand kisses.

Officiant: Annie, please kiss Arturo's hand and give her this sign of your devotion. *Annie kisses Arturo's hand and puts on the ring.*

Arturo, please kiss Annie's hand and give her this sign of your devotion. *Arturo kisses Annie's hand and puts on the ring.*

May the loving energy held in these rings be with you every day from now on.

TILIK/TIKKI

Couple gives each other bindis, a Hindu tradition.

Officiant: The bride and groom will now offer one another *tilik* and *tikki* in the form of a *bindi.* This Hindu tradition symbolizes they have become spiritually joined in marriage.
   Annie kisses Arturo's forehead and puts the bindi *on Arturo.*
   Arturo kisses Annie's forehead and puts the bindi *on Annie.*

BLESSING OF THE HANDS

Officiant: The hands have been a channel of healing in many religions and cultures throughout history. Some celebrate weddings and other joyous occasions with *mendhi,* the decorating of the hands with dye from the henna plant. This bride and groom honor the 9,000-year-old tradition today to show their belief of the sacredness and healing power of the hands.

To couple: For this blessing, please face each other, joining your right palms together, and then your left, forming a figure eight or infinity symbol representing your eternal love in the Celtic tradition. Because of the veins that run from the left hand to the heart, bringing your hands together is like merging your beating hearts. Feel the gift that you are to one another! I offer this blessing to your hands and to the power of touch between you.

> Take my hand,
> And walk with me into our new life,
> You and me,
> Together,
> Blending our lives.
> Building our dreams,
> Enhancing our passion,
> Exploring the world,
> Improving ourselves,
> Preparing for a Family,
> Embracing the ones we care for,
> Sharing our love,
> Leaving our mark,
> Creating our legacy of love.
> Marriage means we will grow,
> and grow older, together.
> We will support each other,
> And be there for each other,
> Through the good,
> and not so great times.
> We are a pair now,
> Partners in the game of life,
> And we are meant to stick together,
> No matter what,
> You and me,
> Together,
> Holding on to each other,
> And living the journey of our new life.

FINAL PRAYER/LEAD TO PRONOUNCEMENT

Father of bride reads final blessing.

Officiant: I'd like to ask the bride and groom to please face each other. And I would like to ask all those who are able to stand to please rise and gather around the bride and groom, forming a circle of love. They would like their loved ones to totally surround them.

Officiant to couple: Your lives are now joined in one unbroken circle. On behalf of all those here today witnessing your commitment to each other, we wish you a long, healthy, and happy life together.

WEDDING READING 2

Officiant: For the closing prayer, the father of the bride will read "An Apache Blessing":

> May the sun bring you new energy by day.
> May the moon softly restore you by night.
> May the rain wash away your worries.
> May the breeze blow new strength into your being.
> May you walk gently through the world and know its beauty all the days of your life.

PRONOUNCEMENT

Officiant: Annie and Arturo, as we have all witnessed your pledge to be life partners, it is my honor to now pronounce you wife and husband.

THE KISS

Please share your first kiss—and hug—as a married couple.

MINISTER'S PARTING WORDS

Congratulations!
Ceremony ends.

Catholic, Mormon

Suzanne and Jake

WELCOME

Welcome, family and friends. We are gathered here by love...the love between Suzanne and Jake, who come before God, family, and community today to be joined in holy matrimony. Here amidst God's creation, we will joyously witness the rituals of marriage and the sacred wedding vows that will confirm their commitment to one another. Today, we celebrate the love they share in an especially meaningful and auspicious way. It is Easter Sunday, a time of holy renewal. It is also the 37th wedding anniversary of the bride's parents. This date was chosen because it represents a legacy of enduring love that is an inspiration to this couple. Let us offer our blessings and our good wishes to these two as they prepare to join their lives as partners in marriage.

OPENING PRAYER

Let us begin by sharing a moment of prayer. God of all creation, as we open our hearts in prayer on behalf of Jake and Suzanne, please surround and embrace us *all* in your light. Please fill this beautiful place with your holy presence and bring your divine grace to these two who stand before you in the name of love.

In happiness and joy we thank you for the gift of marriage. May you give Jake and Suzanne the ability to rejoice always in their love. May you fulfill every wish of their hearts. May you open their eyes to the beauty and mystery of the love they have for each other, every day, as today. May their life together embrace and nurture the promise of this moment. And may the promises they make inspire and instruct us all. Amen. So be it and so it is.

WEDDING READING 1

We now call on the bride's friend Susan to say a few words and to offer a special reading and tribute to the bride and groom from Song of Solomon 2:10–13:

> My lover spoke and said to me, "Arise, my darling,
> my beautiful one, and come with me.
> See! The winter is past; the rains are over and gone.
> Flowers appear on the earth; the season of singing has come,
> the cooing of doves is heard in our land.
> The fig tree forms its early fruit; the blossoming vines spread their fragrance.
> Arise, come, my darling; my beautiful one, come with me."

MINISTER'S MESSAGE

Suzanne and Jake, I know you both agree that it is by the grace of God that you stand here today. Life has brought you together and you took on the challenge of making it work. You choose love over all the reasons not to love, and eventually, through all your efforts and determination, you allowed love to grow beyond fear.

You come here today with great joy in your hearts and with the full appreciation that the love you share is a blessing, a gift. And you arrive at this moment with the experience, wisdom, and gratitude that will allow you to build a strong, loving, and truly sacred union.

On this day, you lovingly step into the future, together. And the journey of nourishing your love through *all* of life's cycles takes on a new dimension as you become husband and wife. You will discover that marriage is an even more complete joining two lives. It's the mystical, physical, and emotional union of two human beings. It is the merging of two families and two life stories. It is the fuller opening of two hearts and the ripening of two souls.

Jake and Suzanne, the love you radiate for one another speaks for itself. I have heard you refer to one another as "a gift from God." May you always cherish the gift you've been given. And may your love for one another be an eternal light, a star that shines and can always show you your way home...to each other.

INCLUSION OF THE PARENTS

Officiant asks: Who brings Suzanne to this day of union, partnership, love, and marriage with Jake? And who brings Jake to this day of union, partnership, love, and marriage with Suzanne?
Both sets of parents are asked to stand.

They answer simultaneously: We do.

Officiant: Do you give your blessing upon the marriage of these two? Will you honor the covenant into which your children enter on this day? Will you give them both your loving support?

They answer simultaneously: We do.

Officiant: Thank you. I ask the mother of the bride and the mother of the groom to please come forward. *Dad can sit.*

THE LIGHTING OF THE UNITY CANDLE

It has been said that "from every human being there rises a light that reaches straight to heaven. When two souls that are destined for each other find one another, their streams of light flow together and a single brighter light goes forth from their united being."

The lighting of the unity candle symbolizes the light of two individuals coming together as one brighter light. It also symbolizes God's promise to merge two lives as one. And it represents the promise to honor the greatest commandment of all, "Love one another, as I have loved you."

As a gesture of unity between the two families that are united on this day, and as an acknowledgment of the loving beings who brought Suzanne and Jake into this world, we ask the mother of the bride and the mother of the groom to step forward and light the solo candles from the one light that already burns on the altar. This light represents the all-mighty source of all that is, the oneness of us all.

Bride and groom step aside.

First, the bride's mother lights the candle. And now, the groom's mother. Thank you...please be seated. *Suzanne and Jake step back into place.*

To the bride and groom: These two lighted candles represent the bride and the groom as well as their families, their ancestors, the source of who they are. These two distinct flames represent their lives, up until this moment. We now ask Jake and Suzanne to bring these two separate candles together to light the unity candle.

Know that as you do this you are kindling the divine light in one another. Make a promise in this moment to always see the light in one another, to nurture and tend to that divine flame in your partner every day, especially in times when it is hardest to see.

May the loving light of God and of family, community, and good friends always bless this marriage. May this light now illuminate the ceremony of your vows and your rings—and illuminate your entire marriage! Amen.

THE CONSECRATION

Suzanne and Jake, as you have come here today of your own free will in the presence of witnesses to declare your love for each other, we ask God to bless your marriage in all ways.

EXPRESSION OF INTENT

Please face each other.

> Do you, Suzanne, take Jake to be your husband,
> To have and to hold from this day forward
> In good times and bad times,
> In sickness and in health,
> To love, honor, and cherish forever?

Suzanne answers: I do.

> And do you, Jake, take Suzanne to be your wife,
> To have and to hold from this day forward
> In good times and bad times,
> In sickness and in health,
> To love, honor, and cherish forever?

Jake answers: I do.

VOWS

The bride and groom have written beautiful vows to share. Suzanne, please turn to Jake and share your vows. *She shares.* Now Jake. *He shares.*

Officiant: Jake and Suzanne, with the help of divine grace, may you observe the sacred vows and declarations that have been spoken today. Amen.

BLESSING AND EXCHANGING OF RINGS

The wedding ring has long been a symbol of commitment and devotion that represents an unbroken circle of love. Like a circle, love given freely has no beginning and no end. These rings represent unity, wholeness, oneness, and eternity. They are made of metal that does not tarnish, metal that is enduring. They are symbolic of a union that will endure.

PRAYER OVER THE RINGS

I ask everyone here to please silently join me in this prayer over the rings: Dear God, creator of all that is, please bless the giving of these rings so that they who wear them may go on living in your peace and continue in your grace. May these rings be a lifelong symbol of the unity and love between Suzanne and Jake. May they always call to mind the freedom and the power of the love they share. May these rings serve as a constant reminder of the vows set forth here today Amen.

Minister asks the bride and groom to prepare to exchange rings.

Jake, please take Suzanne's hand, slip the ring on her finger, and repeat after me:

> You are a blessing in my life.
> With this ring,
> as a sign of my love and fidelity,
> I pledge my devotion forever.

Suzanne, please take Jake's hand, slip the ring on his finger, and repeat after me:

You are a blessing in my life.
With this ring,
as a sign of my love and fidelity,
I pledge my devotion forever.

THE PRONOUNCEMENT

Officiant: Your two lives are now joined in one unbroken circle. Wherever you go, may you return to one another in togetherness.

> May you dare to dream, plan, and create together.
> May you always have a special sense of mission together in life and never tire of the endless possibilities of exploring your shared existence.
> May the winds that blow bring warmth that makes you happy, but may they never blow you apart.
> May you greet each other's sorrow with compassion and enter each other's need with the sureness of love.
> May the years bring you joy and contentment as well as wisdom and spiritual evolution.
> May you share a life of affection and devotion and honor the gift of love that God has given you—forever more.
> Suzanne and Jake, it is my honor to now pronounce you husband and wife.

THE KISS

You may kiss the bride.
Give them a few moments to smooch.

FIRST ACT AS A MARRIED COUPLE

I'd like to now open the ceremony to the participation of all of Suzanne and Jake's loved ones. It is a lovely tradition in some cultures to shower the newlyweds with candy, flowers or rice. We will instead take this moment to shower them with your blessings and good wishes. Please stand, or simply call out, whatever is in your heart. *People shout out blessings.*

THE BRIDE AND GROOM GREET THE COMMUNITY

For the first time as a married couple, please greet Suzanne and Jake!

MINSTER'S PARTING WORDS

Go in peace. Congratulations. You're married!
  Ceremony ends.

Buddhist, Sri Lankan, Christian

Rachel and Sanith

Supplies and logistics
Readings
String for ceremony
Water and water urn
Hurricane candle holder
Family lamp and oil

WELCOME

Officiant: Welcome, family and friends. Love gathers us here today. On behalf of Rachel and Sanith, thank you for being part of this joyous occasion. You are all very special to this bride and groom, and they are so grateful that you can be here to share in this very special moment in their lives. Today we celebrate the place that Sanith and Rachel have made in each other's hearts, as we joyously witness the sacred vows that will join their lives as partners in marriage.

OPENING BLESSING

Let us begin this ceremony by sharing a moment of peaceful silence as we allow our hearts to open to fill this beautiful place with harmony and joy.
Hold the silence for a moment.
In happiness and joy, we are thankful for the gift of this marriage.

May Sanith and Rachel have the ability, always, to rejoice in their love.

May every wish of their hearts be fulfilled.

May they open their eyes to the beauty and mystery of the love they have for each other, every day, as today.

May their life together embrace and nurture the promise of this moment.

May their marriage be a strong foundation for their family life.

May this bride and groom, and all those who have come to witness their joining, be uplifted and embraced by God's love.

MUSICAL INTERLUDE

Now the bride's sister and cousin offer a prayer in song. "Evening Prayer" from *Hansel and Gretel* by Engelbert Humperdinck (sung by two sopranos).

LIGHT SRI LANKAN FAMILY LAMP

Light six-wick deepa lamp. Both sets of parents with brides and groom. Bride and groom first. Light two candles and extra seventh for all family.

Officiant: The light of love that illuminates this marriage would not be possible without the love passed on to Sanith by his parents and to Rachel by hers. Both bride and groom are blessed with extraordinary examples of love and marriage as their parents have been wed almost 40 years.

So before we go on, let us thank the bride's parents and the groom's parents and invite them all to step up to light the traditional Sri Lankan oil lamp, or family lamp, which symbolizes the light of love and the joining of two families today as well as symbolizing the light of hope and success.

First the parents will light using a long candle. Then the bride and groom.

To parents: You have all brought forth love. And this bride and groom are a living example of two people who carry that love in their hearts. Today they make the choice to share that love for all of their days. It is most appropriate on this day, that we thank you for all you have given. *Pause.*

Before we go on, the bride and groom would like acknowledge the bride's grandmother, who is here today.

And they would like to take a moment to honor the memories of the beautiful souls who've touched their lives but are no longer with us, especially [name them]. Let us light a candle for these loved ones in our hearts and minds. We know that their love, and their spirits, live on.

Parents, please be seated, except for the bride's mom.

WEDDING READING 1

Officiant: *The bride's mother reads "Thoughts on Marriage," by Kahlil Gibran, from* The Prophet.

MINISTER'S MESSAGE

Sanith and Rachel, yours is a true love story between soul mates, a tale of two people meant to be together.

I congratulate you both on the journey of your lives...and on the strength and the courage it has taken for each of you to make your way to this place. You both hail from different worlds and backgrounds, you were living such different lives in different cities, and yet you have found a common ground in the love and respect you have for one another. You have found a way to work through differences and embrace a very powerful love.

Sanith, I asked Rachel what she loves about you, and she said: I love Sanith's constancy, his sensitivity and his intellect. In the middle of complete chaos, Sanith stays completely calm. I love that he hates football, doesn't care how much I talk during a movie, and that he truly appreciates me, idiosyncrasies and all. He takes as much care in listening to others as he does in choosing his own words. He has accomplished so much in his career and he is one of the most humble people I know. Above all else, he is kind, patient, and loving.

Rachel, I also asked Sanith what he loves about you, and he said: I love Rachel's wonderful smile, great voice, engaging charm, and sensitive soul. Rachel is one of the most warmhearted and sincere people I know. She is always considerate of others and goes out of her way to help those in need. She cares immensely about her family and friends (and pets!), is compassionate, and gives unselfishly. It is wonderful that I have met someone as kind—even more so that she will be my wife.

Today, as you agree to be steadfast in your commitment to love one another through all things, you also agree to a partnership of equals, where you support one another and work together toward common goals. This marriage is an opportunity to include the world—and all its challenges—in your love. By loving one another, you play a part in the healing of the world.

Rachel and Sanith, may this marriage be your home and sanctuary, a place to grow your dreams and a family of your own.

May you remain each other's greatest supporters and help each other succeed in all ways.

May you be blessed with the essential power of dialogue and always be able to communicate openly and honestly.

May you stand strong together and let nothing and no one come between you.

When you have moments of differences or misunderstandings, may you both have the courage to face them together.

May you always treasure and appreciate the love you share, and may it be a great force in your lives and the lives of those you touch.

WEDDING READING 2/BUDDHIST BLESSING

Officiant: And now, the mother of the groom offers a blessing from the Buddhist scriptures, the Buddha's sermon at Raja-Gaha. She will read in Pali [the native language of Sri Lanka] first, followed by the English translation.

"Do not deceive, do not despise each other anywhere. Do not be angry nor bear secret resentments; for as a mother will risk her life and watches over her child, so boundless be your love to all, so tender, kind and mild."

"Cherish good will right and left, early and late, and without hindrance, without stint, be free of hate and envy, while standing and walking and sitting down, what ever you have in mind, the rule of life that is always best is to be loving-kind."

THE CONSECRATION

Rachel and Sanith, as you have come here today of your own free will in the presence of witnesses to declare your love for each other, we ask that you both be strengthened by the promises you are about to make.

EXPRESSION OF INTENT AND CONSENT

Please face each other.

Rachel, do you come here freely and without reservation to give yourself in marriage to Sanith?

Rachel answers: I do.

Sanith, do you come here freely and without reservation to give yourself in marriage to Rachel?

Sanith answers: I do.

VOWS

Please face one another to express your wedding vows. Rachel will read from *The Music of Love,* by Amy K. Barth, and Sanith will read the vows he wrote for his bride.

Bride reads from a beautiful Hallmark card.

Sanith:

My dearest Rachel,

Long ago you were just a dream and a prayer.

A ray of hope in an otherwise sea of despair.

But just when I had almost given up hope, my wishes were finally answered.

Your love came softly upon my heart.

It was easy from the very start.

This past year you have taught me how to love again and be loved in return. Thank you for bringing so much joy and happiness into my life.

Today I marry my friend, the one I will live with, dream with, and love.

I promise to encourage and inspire you, to laugh with you,

and to comfort you in times of sorrow and struggle.

I promise to love you in good times and in bad,

when life seems easy and when it seems hard,

when our love is simple, and when it is an effort.

I promise to cherish you and to always hold you in highest regard.

These things I give to you today and all the days of our life.

BLESSING AND EXCHANGING OF RINGS

Now we come to the presentation of the rings. These rings represent unity, wholeness, oneness, and they are symbolic of a union that will continue to endure.

PRAYER/BLESSING OVER THE RINGS

May I please have the rings. I ask everyone here to fill their minds and hearts with good wishes and blessings for this couple...and to please silently join me in blessing these rings.

Officiant to couple: Sanith, please take Rachel's hand. Slip the ring on her finger. And repeat after me: with this ring, I thee wed.

Rachel, please take Sanith's hand. Slip the ring on his finger. And repeat after me: with this ring, I thee wed.

May you sweetly keep the promises you made here today.

SRI LANKAN STRING CEREMONY

White string tied by groom's father to join bride's and groom's fingers—his right, her left. Groom's father recites a prayer in Pali. Officiant pours water on their fingers from an urn. Groom's sister holds a bowl beneath them.

Now, a traditional Sri Lankan string ceremony, whereby the bride's and groom's pinkies are tied together with blessed white thread to symbolize the bond of unity. Then water is poured over their fingers and is collected in a special bowl. This captures the blessings of all the gods.

The groom's dad will chant a traditional prayer in Pali as he ties their fingers together. His sister will hold the bowl to capture the blessings as I pour water over their joined fingers.

After the water is poured: Now here's the tricky part: Rachel and Sanith must now remove the string—they have to slip out of it without breaking it or untying the knot. This symbolized a bond that will last forever, a bond that cannot be broken. *Watch them do it. Hurray!*

Thank you to the groom's dad and sister. Please be seated.

CLOSING BLESSING (RESPONSIVE) AND PRONOUNCEMENT

Officiant: I ask the bride and groom to please take each other by the hand so they can feel the gift they are to one another and continue looking at each other. And I ask everyone here to join me in this blessing. Look in your programs for the insert titled "Closing Blessing." Let us begin together:

> May you be blessed by the sun and the moon,
> By the stability of earth and elements of our being,
> By music and laughter,
> By family and friends,
> By the love you have for each other,
> And by the love you share in the world.
> May you always be surrounded by love.
> Your lives are now joined. May you share a life time of kindness, happiness, and love.

Rachel and Sanith, as you have pledged your love devotion before these witnesses today, it is my honor to now pronounce you husband and wife.

KISS

You may kiss the bride.
Ceremony ends.

Celtic/Scottish

Elle and Eddie

Supplies and logistics:
Loving cup/chalice
Apple juice

GREETING

Officiant: Welcome, everyone. Love gathers us here today. You are all very special to this bride and groom, and they are so grateful that you can share in this very special moment in their lives. Elle and Eddie, today we celebrate the place you have made in each other's hearts as we joyously witness the sacred vows that will join your lives as partners in marriage. Let us all offer our good wishes and blessings as you become husband and wife.

And let us also celebrate this marriage as a beautiful circle of love that gathers in Jenni, Sarah, and Joanne and gives a formal start to your life as a family.

OPENING PRAYER

Let us begin by sharing a moment of prayer from the Book of Common Prayer.

Dear God, creator and preserver of all life,
and giver of all grace:

Look with favor upon the world you have made,
and especially upon Elle and Eddie,
whom you make one flesh in their love and commitment.
Give them wisdom and devotion in the ordering of their common life,
that each may be to the other
a strength in need...a counselor in perplexity,
a comfort in sorrow...and a companion in joy.
Grant that their wills may be so knit that they
may grow in love and peace with you, and one another,
all the days of their lives.
Give them grace and make their life together be such that their unity
may overcome estrangement, their forgiveness heal hurt, and their
joy may conquer any despair.
Give them such fulfillment of their mutual affection
that they may reach out in love and concern for others.
Make their marriage a strong foundation for their family life.
Please bless this bride and groom and all who have come to share in
this special day and surround us all in a circle of love. Amen.

WEDDING READING

Eddie and Elle, the love that has been created by your coming together
in marriage increases the love that exists in your families, in your circle
of dear friends, and in the world. Your love for one another adds a
dimension of strength and holiness that can only be brought about
when two people come together and join their energies in love. We
congratulate you on the journey of your lives that has brought you
to this moment. *Pause.* And now, Jenni, Sarah, and Joanne honor your
marriage with a reading of "With These Rings."

LOVING CUP CEREMONY

We now take a special moment for Eddie and Elle to toast their love,
devotion, and friendship.

On this, your wedding day, we celebrate the Celtic spirit of "soul
friend." By entering in a partnership with your soul friend, you are
joined in an ancient and eternal way with this person whom you most
cherish. I ask you to toast one another. First, may I say:

The bride and groom hold the loving cup as the officiant speaks.

Today you become a part of one another in sacred kinship.
Together…you have the greatest courage and strength.
Together…you share a rhythm of grace and faith.
Together…you love freely…and you are loved freely.
Love has reawakened you both to this new beginning.
With one another, you are home.
Now, please drink to the love you've shared in the past.
The couple take turns sipping from the loving cup.
Drink to your love in the present.
The couple take turns sipping from the loving cup.
Drink to your love in the future and forever more.
The couple take turns sipping from the loving cup.
And drink to the love shared by this newly formed family.
The couple take turns sipping from the loving cup.
May this marriage and this family be blessed in all ways.

MINISTER'S MESSAGE

Elle and Eddie, you come here with joy in your heart and with the full appreciation that the love you share is a blessing, a gift.

It has taken you a while to get to this day—it's been a decade in the making! Your love story is rooted in a friendship of six years that was very special to you both. Gradually, that friendship caught on fire and evolved into a deepening love. It was in New York City four years ago that you realized how much you truly meant to one another.

Having become engaged in Florida and having purchased your wedding rings in America, it seemed fitting to formalize your lifelong commitment to one another right here in New York—the city that brought you together.

What do you love about each other? When I posed that question, this is what you shared: "The way we continually make each other laugh and are able to enjoy each other's company. The feeling of looking forward to meeting up with each other when we are apart. When any problem arises, the other person can often help resolve it. The way in which we can accept each other's little faults and see the other person for what they truly are—a life partner."

Marriage is possibly the most serious commitment a person can make, and you both feel very lucky to have met each other. Marriage to you means a lifetime of contentment, love, and happiness; to be able to support each other in all of life's challenge; to grow together emotionally and to be there for each other as you enjoy a healthy, happy, and fulfilling life together.

While you come to this day as best friends, and partners in life, already a family in spirit, today the journey of nourishing your love through *all* of life's cycles takes on a new dimension as you become husband and wife.

And this marriage also marks the creation of a new family. While you are already close in heart and spirit, today all of you become a part of one another. You already have a strong foundation of love and commitment. May your devotion for one another always create a circle of love that gathers in the whole family. May your friendship and support of one another grow even stronger with each passing year. May you all share a lifetime of happiness and fulfillment!

THE CONSECRATION

Elle and Eddie, as you have come here today of your own free will in the presence of witnesses to declare your love for each other, we ask that you both be strengthened by the promises you are about to make and by the expressions of love you are about to share.

EXPRESSION OF INTENT

Please face each other.

> Do you, Elle, take Eddie to be your husband?
> To have and to hold from this day forward.
> In good times and bad times,
> In sickness and in health,
> To love, honor, and cherish
> For the rest of your days?

Elle answers: I do.

> And do you, Eddie, take Elle to be your wife?
> To have and to hold from this day forward.
> In good times and bad times,
> In sickness and in health,
> To love, honor, and cherish
> For the rest of your days?

Eddie answers: I do.

VOWS

You have some beautiful vows to share. Please face each other and repeat after me, simultaneously.

> I take you
> As my partner in life
> and my one true love.
>   I will cherish our union
> and love you more each day.
>   I will trust you and respect you,
> laugh with you
> and cry with you.
>   I will love you faithfully
> through good times and bad
>   I give you my hand,
> my heart,
> and my love,
> from this day forward
> for as long as we both shall live.

BLESSING AND EXCHANGING OF THE RINGS/READING

Officiant: Now we come to the presentation of the rings. Now, I ask everyone here to fill their minds and hearts with good wishes and blessings for this couple and please silently join me in blessing these rings.
Ask bride and groom to prepare to exchange rings.
Eddie, please take Elle's hand. Slip the ring on her finger. And repeat after me: with this ring, I thee wed.
Elle, please take Eddie's hand. Slip the ring on his finger. And repeat after me: with this ring, I thee wed.
May you lovingly keep the promises made here today.

HAND BLESSING

It is an ancient Celtic tradition to join two lives as one through the rite of handfasting. The couple's hands are literally tied together to symbolize their unity. Today we will use the more high-tech approach of hand-holding.
Eddie and Elle, please place your right palms together and then place your left palms over them. This creates a figure eight, or infinity

symbol, with your hands. It signifies hearts that will love forever. And now, a blessing over your hands:

These are the hands of your best friend, the one who will love you through all time.

These are the hands that will work alongside yours as together you build your future.

These are the hands that will passionately love you and cherish you through the years and with the slightest touch will comfort you like no other.

These are the hands that will hold you when you need strength.

These are the hands that will help you to hold your family as one.

May these hands always reach out with love, tenderness, and respect. May these hands continue to build a loving relationship that lasts a lifetime.

FINAL PRAYER

Officiant: Let us bring the ceremony to a close with a special blessing. I'd like to ask everyone here, in your own way, to join me in this prayer.

1. We bless this couple in the name of Love.
2. We bless this couple in the name of Friendship.
3. We bless this couple in the name of Health.
4. We bless this couple in the name of Wisdom.
5. We bless this couple in the name of Happiness.
6. We bless this couple in the name of Creativity.
7. We bless this couple in the name of Kindness.

Your two lives are now joined. May God bless this marriage in all ways.

Elle and Edward, it is my honor to now pronounce you husband and wife.

KISS

You may share your first kiss as a married couple!

MINISTER'S PARTING REMARK

Live from New York, we welcome Eddie, Ellie, Jennie, Sarah, and Joanne as a family! Congratulations!

Ceremony ends.

Nondenominational Filipino

Robert and Michelle

Supplies and logistics:
Wedding cup
Cord, veil, and coins
Wedding rings
Wedding license
Processional of sponsors
Seating of 20 sponsors

GREETING

Officiant: Welcome, family and friends. Love gathers us here today. On behalf of Michelle and Robert, thank you for being part of this joyous occasion. Today we celebrate the place that Robert and Michelle have made in each other's hearts as we joyously witness the sacred vows that will join their lives as partners in marriage. They have created a ceremony that reflects their family heritage as well as the spirit of their relationship. Let us all offer our good wishes and blessings as they formally begin their life as partners in marriage.

OPENING BLESSING

"A Blessing for a Marriage" by James Dillet Freeman.

COIN CEREMONY

In Filipino weddings, there is a special coin ceremony. Traditionally, the groom presents his bride with 13 coins, or *arrhea,* as a symbol of his promise to provide for the welfare of his new family.

As a contemporary twist, Robert and Michelle have chosen dear friends to present specially blessed coins the bride and groom have collected during their travels together. These 13 coin sponsors will come up to the altar in pairs and each bring up a coin and present it to the bride or groom.

Then, together, the bride and groom will pour the coins into the special wedding vessel, blending their coins and representing the embodiments of all these qualities into their union.

Sponsors bring up coins. The sound of the coins is a significant part of the ceremony and should be heard, so music lowers. After the coins are all poured, all the sponsors are seated.

MINISTER'S MESSAGE

Michelle and Robert, you have been blessed with the gift of one another's love. In the time you have been together, you have been strengthened by the many challenges you have faced together. So you come to this day not only best friends and partners in life in so many ways but as two people who have already come to understand the true meaning of "for better or for worse." You hearts and souls are already wedded to one another.

We congratulate you on the journey of your lives and on the strength and the courage it has taken for each of you to make your way to this place.

Today, as you agree to be steadfast in your commitment to continue to love one another through *all* things, you also agree to a partnership of equals where you support one another and work together toward common goals.

On this day, the journey of nourishing your love through *all* of life's cycles takes on a new dimension as you become husband and wife.

May you continue to laugh together, surprise each other, and challenge one another to be the best you can be.

May you both be blessed as you travel life's road ... together!

VEIL AND CORD CEREMONY

Veil and cord sponsors will bring veil and cord up with them. Maid of honor and best man bring chairs over so bride and groom can sit in them. Bride and groom are seated.

Officiant: Traditionally, two sponsors pin a veil from the groom's shoulders, extending it to cover the bride's head and shoulders. This is symbolic of the groom pledging his strength and protection to his bride and his promise to take care of her from that day forward. In this modern interpretation, the veil ceremony sponsors will be the parents of the bride and the parents of the groom.

The veil represents a shroud for health and protection during their married life, and it is a symbol of the unity of the two families blending into one.

Then, there are two cord sponsors, who will come and place a cord in the shape of a figure eight over the veils that are on the heads and shoulders of the bride and groom.

Officiant: This cord symbolizes unity and infinity—sharing a love together, forever!

Parents, please come forward and place the veil over your children.

Parents step up. Veil and cord ritual begins.

Officiant: Cord sponsors, please come and place the cord on the bride and groom.

Cord sponsors rise and tie cord. Bride and groom remain seated as all sponsors are asked an intent question.

SPONSORS' VOWS: ASKING FOR THE SUPPORT OF THE SPONSORS

Officiant: Will all the sponsors please stand. Sponsors, you were chosen by the bride and groom for the significant roles you have played in their lives, individually and as a couple. So I ask you: will you agree to support this couple in their journey through life together?

All agree: Yes.

Will you honor this marriage and welcome them into the community with love?

All agree: Yes.

Thank you ... please be seated.

Maid of honor and best man remove cord and veil and move chairs.

THE CONSECRATION

Officiant: Michelle and Robert, as you have come here today of your own free will, we celebrate with you as you prepare to pledge your love to one another.

EXPRESSION OF INTENT

Officiant: Please face each other.

> Do you, Michelle, take Robert to be your husband?
> To have and to hold from this day forward
> In good times and bad times
> Will you cherish him always?

Michelle answers: I do.

> And do you, Robert, take Michelle to be your wife?
> To have and to hold from this day forward
> In good times and bad times
> Will you cherish her always?

Robert answers: I do.

BLESSING AND EXCHANGING OF RINGS

Officiant: Now we come to the presentation of the rings.

PRAYER/BLESSING OVER THE RINGS

I ask everyone here to fill their minds and hearts with good wishes and blessings for this couple and to please silently join me in blessing these rings. May God bless these rings so that they who wear them may dwell in the grace and love of God.

Ask bride and groom to prepare to exchange rings.

Officiant:

> Robert, please take Michelle's hand. Slip the ring on her finger.
> Michelle, please take Robert's hand. Slip the ring on his finger.

Please hold each other's hands so you can feel the gift you are to one another, looking into each other's eyes, and simultaneously repeat after me:

I promise to love you,
Cherish you, respect you.
With this ring, I thee wed.

THE PRONOUNCEMENT

Your two lives are now joined. May you always be loving companions who treat each other with respect. May you have happiness. May you have peace. May God bless this marriage in all ways.

Michelle and Robert, it is my honor to now pronounce you husband and wife.

THE KISS

You may kiss the bride!

MINISTER'S PARTING REMARK

Please greet Michelle and Robert for the first time as a married couple! Congratulations!

Ceremony ends.

Hindu, Jewish

Shari and Sanjai

Supplies and logistics:

Altar table
Small alter table for sacred fire
Kiddush cup for libation ceremony
White wine libation
Ghee or candle for sacred fire
Puja plate for fire
Puffed rice, *laja,* for Agni
Lightbulb and linen napkin
Sandlewood ash
Puja plates
Indian wedding tablecloth for small altar
Huppah

GREETING

Female officiant: Welcome, family and friends. Love gathers us here today. We come together in great happiness to celebrate the love between Shari and Sanjai. This couple believes strongly in the sacred union they already share. Thus, with much care and tenderness, they've created a contemporary wedding ceremony that fully expresses their adoration for one another and that celebrates their families by blending traditions from both. Let us offer them our blessings and best wishes for a marriage that is all they would choose it to be!

THE PRAYER/INVOCATION

And let us begin by sharing a moment of prayer and invocation.

Female officiant: From the Hindu tradition, we ask first for the blessings of the Lord of Obstacles, Ganesha. May he remove all obstacles to this union. May he support this couple in overcoming the challenges of married life. May he pave the way for a good and happy life. May he bring peace and ease to this ceremony as we evoke him: *Om Ganesh. Om Ganesh. Om Ganesh.*
  Officiant rings bell three times.

Male officiant: And from the Jewish tradition, we say:
  Ba-ruch a-tah Ah-do-nai Eh-lo-hay-nu
  Meh-lech Ha-oh-lahm, sheh-heh-key-ah-nu
  v'key-y'ma-nu v'hi-gi-ah-nu la-z'man ha-zeh.
  Amein.
  Blessed are You, Lord, Our God, King of the Universe, who has kept us alive, and sustained us, and brought us to this joyous season. Amen.
  We pray that all that is shared in this ceremony bring this couple closer together as they stand before us all in the name of love. And we ask that blessings be showered upon the families that are joined on this day...and all those gathered here today in the joy and celebration of the fulfillment of this union. May we all be surrounded and uplifted by the light of love. And so it is.

OFFICIANT'S MESSAGE

Female officiant: An old Jewish legend tells us that when two certain souls are created in heaven, an angel cries out, "This man is made for this woman!" It is said that if these people meet on earth and recognize each other for who they truly are, they will fall in love and become as one, working together in unison. Then no hardship can alter the strength of their enduring love. Everything they do shall succeed.
  Shari and Sanjai, you are two people who have been blessed with the discovery of one another's love. In Hebrew we call this *beschert*, "meant to be." From the Hindu tradition, there is a prayer that sums it up this way: "We are word and meaning, united. You are thought and I am sound."
  The groom remembers it this way: "We met the old-fashioned way, fortuitously. There was no setup, no knowledge of each other. Her

style attracted me and I decided to chat her up when I saw her at a party I hosted on my roof deck. It was a night when neither of us had any intentions of finding someone, at least not consciously. To the contrary, we were both a little exasperated at the thought of dating. It was a warm, beautiful night for a party on a roof deck in Manhattan, and there she was: that hip, artistic type from Brooklyn—*what was she doing at my party?*"

Even Shari was wondering that! As she remembers, "A friend was headed to a party held on a roof deck, one that happened to belong to Sanjai. I was tagging along, not really interested in going out, tired from training for a triathlon...but I did go, and that changed my life."

Perhaps one of the most amazing parts of the story is that they learned soon after that they actually grew up just 10 minutes away from each other in New Jersey! Perhaps God was waiting to introduce them at the moment when they could see each other clearly through spiritual eyes.

Male officiant: Sanjai, I asked Shari what made her fall in love with you, and she said: I love Sanjai's enthusiasm and how he relishes life and all it has to offer. I love that he hugs me all the time, that he listens to what I say and remembers the details of my life. I love that when I picture him in my mind the vision of him that appears has a big smile. Always a smile. I love that he appreciates things I do for him and that he talks about me to his friends and family, that he wants me to meet everyone and share all of his life.

And Shari, I asked Sanjai what he loves about you, and he said: Her kindness, consideration, creativity, compassion. And that we are considerate with one another. Our marriage is the quintessence of a meaningful second part to my life, the first part being establishing myself as an adult. To go on without a wife who I adore and see as my best friend would be sad. I love that she is the woman I will create a family with...and that I have a lifetime to continue to learn from her.

We congratulate you both on the journey of your lives and on the strength and the courage it has taken for each of you to make your way to this place. You both hail from different worlds and backgrounds and you were living such different lives and have such different styles and careers, yet you have found a common ground in the love and respect you have for one another. You have found a way to work through differences and embrace a very powerful love.

Today, as you agree to be steadfast in your commitment to love one another through all things, you also agree to a partnership of equals where you support one another and work together toward common goals. This marriage is an opportunity to include the world—and all its challenges—in your love. By loving one another, you play a part in the healing of the world.

And remember that any difficulties you may encounter give you an opportunity to grow and love even more.

LIGHTING THE SACRED FIRE

Female officiant: And now, with the help of the groom's brother, we light and prepare the sacred fire to bear witness to the rites of marriage that will bring Sanjai and Shari together as husband and wife.

*Groom's brother pulls small table closer to altar and lights the sacred fire on the altar/*puja *table. He holds the bowl of rice for them.*

Jewish tradition tells us that life is like a flame. It has its own warmth, and its own brilliance. But it's in the union of two in which something brighter, warmer, and more wonderful takes place. When man and woman bring their two lights together, a brighter light goes forth from their united being.

In the Hindu faith, all solemn rites and ceremonies commence with the performance of *homa*, the sacred fire ceremony, to create an atmosphere of purity and spirituality. The fire evokes Agni, God of Fire, to witness the love and vows between this bride and groom and to bring them blessings.

Today this fire is also symbolic of the merging of cultures and the melting away of any barriers that will not serve this marriage.

WEDDING READING

"Privileged Lovers," a 13th-century ode by Jalalud'din Rumi, one of the world's most revered mystical poets.

CONSECRATION/CONSENT

Female officiant: As you two have come here today of your own free will to declare your love for one another, we ask you to declare your consent in the presence of God and all assembled.

Do you, Shari, take Sanjai as your husband?
Will you continue to love and cherish him,
Be honest and open with him,
And grow with him in mind and spirit?

Shari answers: I do.

And do you, Sanjai, take Shari as your wife?
Will you continue to love and cherish him,
Be honest and open with him,
And grow with him in mind and spirit?

Sanjai answers: I do.

BLESSING AND EXCHANGING OF RINGS

And now, we come to the presentation of rings. The wedding ring is a symbol of love and devotion in any culture. A circle is the symbol of the universe, it is a symbol of holiness and of perfection. In these rings it is the symbol of unity, in which your lives are now joined in one un-broken circle. These rings are made of metal and will not tarnish. They are symbolic of a union that will endure. *Pause.*

May I have the rings, please. Let's all take this moment to fill our hearts and minds with good wishes and hopes for this couple. I ask you all to join us, each in your own way, in blessing these rings so that our good wishes may be carried with them each day of their lives.

Sanjai, please take Shari's hand. Slip the ring on her finger. And, from the Song of Solomon, please repeat after me.

Ani L'Dodi V'Dodi Li.

I am my beloved's and my beloved is mine.

Shari, please take Sanjai's hand.

Slip the ring on his finger. And now, from the Hindi translation, please repeat after me:

Tum hamaare priya, hum tumhare priyatama.

[phonetic: thoom ha-mar-ay pree-ya, hum thoom-har-ay pree-ya-thama]

"You are my love, and I am your beloved."

SAPTAPADI (THE SEVEN STEPS, CIRCLING)

Bride and groom will step clockwise seven times and will drop small bits of rice into the fire and the plate beneath with each step.

Now, we symbolically blend two traditions of "sevens": the seven steps and circling seven times. Together, the bride and groom will take seven sacred steps to seal their marriage covenant.

In the Jewish tradition, the bride circles her beloved seven times, representing perfection and completion. In the Hindu tradition, the seven steps taken by the couple together mark the completion of the wedding ceremony, the moment in which bride and groom become husband and wife.

With each step, they will make an offering of puffed rice to the fire, a symbol of prosperity. These seven steps are also symbolic of seven marital vows.

With God as your guide, please take

1. The first step to ensure that together you will share the duties and responsibilities of your home by protecting and providing for your family
2. The second step to develop physical, mental, and spiritual health
3. The third step to increase wealth by righteous means for proper use
4. The fourth step to acquire knowledge, happiness, and harmony by mutual love and trust
5. The fifth step to be blessed with a healthy family
6. The sixth step to develop mutual respect
7. The seventh step so that you become true companions and remain lifelong partners through this wedlock, the perfect halves to make a perfect whole

Bride and groom come back in front of the altar.

And now, the bride and groom will come back under the huppah for the blessing over the wine.

BLESSING OVER THE WINE

Male officiant: This cup of wine represents your new relationship as husband and wife. Up until this moment, your lives were separate. Now you blend all you are, and all you will become, into this one union.

This represents all the celebrations to come...*and may there be many.* And all the challenges you will handle together...*may they be minimal.* It is symbolic of all the hopes and dreams, as well as disappointments, you will share together as a married couple. And now, we offer the seven blessings over the wine.

Chanted in Hebrew, except for the last line, which is also given in English translation.

1. *Baruch Ata Adonai Elokainu Melech HaOlam, SheHakol Barah Lichvodo*
2. *Baruch Ata Adonai Elokainu Melech HaOlam, Yotzer Ha'Adam*
3. *Baruch Ata Adonai Elokainu Melech HaOlam, Asher Yatzar Et Ha'Adam Betzalmo, b'Tzelem Dmut Tavnito, VeHitkon Lo Mimenu Binyan Adei Ad. Baruch Ata Adonai Yotzer Ha'Adam*
4. *Sos Tasis VeTagel HaAkarah, BeKibbutz Bane'ha Letocha BeSimchaa. Baruch Ata Adonai, Mesame'ach Tzion BeVaneha*
5. *Sameach TeSamach Re'im Ahuvim, KeSamechacha Yetzircha BeGan Eden MiKedem. Baruch Ata Adonai, MeSame'ach Chatan VeKalah*
6. *Baruch Ata Adonai Elokainu Melech HaOlam, Asher Barah Sasson VeSimcha, Chatan VeKalah, Gila Rina, Ditza VeChedva, Ahava VeAchava, VeShalom VeRe'ut. MeHera Adonai Elokeinu Yishama BeArei Yehudah U'Vchutzot Yerushalayim, Kol Sasson V'eKol Simcha, Kol Chatan V'eKol Kalah, Kol Mitzhalot Chatanim MeChupatam, U'Nearim Mimishte Neginatam. Baruch Ata Adonai MeSame'ach Chatan Im Hakalah*
7. *Baruch Ata Adonai Elokainu Melech HaOlam, Boreh Pri HaGafen* (Blessed are You, Lord, our God, King of the Universe, who creates the fruit of the vine. Amen.)

Officiant hands them a cup.

Share a drink now, together, to symbolize your willingness to share all of life. And may the cup of life be full to overflowing. *They sip!*

FINAL BLESSING/PRONOUNCEMENT

Female officiant: Your lives are now joined. On behalf of all those here today witnessing your commitment to each other, we wish you a long, healthy, and happy life together.

> May the earth be brought closer to heaven through this love.
> May all the world be blessed hereby.
> And May God bless this marriage in all ways.

And now, the bride and groom will offer one another *tilik* and *tikki* to symbolize they have become spiritually joined in marriage. *Sanjai gives Shari, Shari gives Sanjai.*

Shari and Sanjai, by the power vested in us by the state of New York, we now pronounce you husband and wife.

KISS

Please share your first kiss as husband and wife!

THE BREAKING OF THE GLASS

Male officiant: We conclude the ceremony with the breaking of the glass.

   I am going to ask the bride's sister to lay the glass down, and Sanjai, it is customary to give it a good stomp with your right foot. So Sanjai...

We all yell: Mazel tov!
   Ceremony ends.

Nondenominational Chinese

Betty and David

One family was Buddhist and one was Christian, and both bride and groom were Chinese. This focused on honoring the families and their relationship. No religion was involved.

GREETING

Welcome, family and friends. On behalf of David and Betty, thank you for being part of this joyous occasion. Many of you have traveled quite a distance to be here, and they are so grateful that you can share in this very special moment in their lives.

Today, we celebrate the place that David and Betty have made in each other's hearts as we also celebrate the joining of two wonderful families and extended families of loved ones and dear friends.

At this time, David and Betty would like to take a moment to honor *everyone* here today.

Bride and groom turn to the groom's mom and bow.

First, the bride and groom will bow to David's mother. They honor your love, hard work, and sacrifice in raising your son, which brought him to this day. Please accept their gratitude.

They turn to the bride's parents and bow.

Now, the bride and groom will bow to Betty's parents. They honor your love, hard work, and sacrifice in raising your daughter, which brought her to this day. Please accept their gratitude.

They turn to face the aisle and bow.

And last but not least, David and Betty will bow to all their family and friends who have come to celebrate this joyous occasion. They are honored to have the privilege of your attendance today. Please accept their gratitude.

Bride and groom turn back to the officiant.

OPENING BLESSING

Let us begin the ceremony by breathing in the beauty all around us, relaxing into a moment of silence and filling our hearts and minds with peace and joy. And now, a blessing:

In happiness and joy, we are thankful for the gift of this marriage.

May David and Betty have the ability to rejoice, always, in their love.

May every wish of their heart be fulfilled.

May they open their eyes to the beauty and wonder of the love they have for each other, every day, as today.

May their life together embrace and nurture the promise of this moment.

As we open our hearts in celebration, may this bride and groom, and all those who have come here to share in this joyous occasion, be uplifted and embraced by love.

HONORING FAMILY AND LOVE

The light of love that illuminates this marriage would not be possible without the love passed on to David and Betty by their parents and grandparents.

It is most appropriate on this day that we thank you, [name all the parents], and that we acknowledge the grandparents who were unable to make the trip. You have brought forth love, and Betty and David are a reflection of this.

They would also like to take a moment to remember the loved ones who are no longer with us, especially [list names]. We know they rejoice with us on this day.

This marriage brings together two unique families—and extended families—as one. It is Betty and David's intention for married life to create a circle of love that gathers all their loved ones together.

WEDDING READING

Betty and David, your love brought you to this day. May it guide you and nourish you in the years to come. Here is a reading about the simple things that make a marriage last, called "The Art of Marriage," by Wilfred Arlan Peterson.

> Happiness in marriage is not something that just happens.
> A good marriage must be created.
> In the art of marriage the little things are the big things ...
> It is never being too old to hold hands.
> It is remembering to say "I love you" at least once a day.
> It is never going to sleep angry.
> It is at no time taking the other for granted;
> the courtship should not end with the honeymoon,
> it should continue through all the years.
> It is having a mutual sense of values and common objectives.
> It is standing together facing the world.
> It is forming a circle of love that gathers in the whole family.
> It is doing things for each other, not in the attitude
> of duty or sacrifice, but in the spirit of joy.
> It is speaking words of appreciation
> and demonstrating gratitude in thoughtful ways.
> It is not looking for perfection in each other.
> It is cultivating flexibility, patience,
> understanding and a sense of humour.
> It is having the capacity to forgive and forget.
> It is giving each other an atmosphere in which each can grow.
> It is finding room for the things of the spirit.
> It is a common search for the good and the beautiful.
> It is establishing a relationship in which the independence is equal,
> dependence is mutual and the obligation is reciprocal.
> It is not only marrying the right partner, it is being the right partner.

MINISTER'S MESSAGE

An old legend tells us that soul mates, who are meant to be, are tied together at the ankle by an invisible red string. As they grow, the string gets shorter, until one day, they are standing before one another.

It is said that if these people meet on earth and recognize each other for who they truly are, they will fall in love and become as one, working together in unison. Then no hardship can alter the strength of their enduring love. Everything they do shall succeed.

Betty and David, you are two people who have been blessed with the discovery of one another's love.

Victor Hugo summed it up this way in a letter to his beloved:

> When two souls, which have sought each other for however long in the throng, have finally found each other, when they discover that they suit one another, that they understand one another, that they hear one another, in essence that they are one and the same, then a union is created between them, fiery and pure as they themselves are, a union that begins on earth and continues forever in heaven. This union is love, true love.

It may have taken Betty a little while to realize destiny was standing before her in the form of David, but David knew immediately that she would be his bride.

When they first met, he told his best friend, "I met the woman I am going to marry."

He responded, "Oh, really? Does she know yet?"

She found out, soon enough, when he proposed on Valentine's Day. By then, she, too, knew that they were meant to be together!

Marriage, to you, means making your union as soul mates official. It means building a life together. It means promising to honor and respect each other. It means working as a team to achieve your goals and dreams in life. It means creating wonderful memories together.

I congratulate you both on the journey of your lives. You have found a way to embrace a very powerful love—and to have fun along the way.

You are already blessed with a wonderful relationship: today, as you agree to be steadfast in your commitment to love one another through all things, you also agree to a partnership of equals, where you support one another and work together toward common goals.

You will discover that marriage is the deeper merging of two families and two life stories. And it is an opportunity to build an even stronger foundation for your family life.

In your life as husband and wife, we wish for you that you enjoy the life you share to the fullest and that you always appreciate and honor what you have together.

May you continue to keep falling in love with each other over and over again. And when you are 100 years old, may you still walk around holding hands, surrounded by your children, grandchildren, and great grandchildren.

THE CONSECRATION AND CONSENT

Betty and David, as you have come here today of your own free will in the presence of these witnesses to declare your love for each other, we ask that you both be strengthened by the expressions of love you are about to share. Please face each other.

> Do you, Betty, take David to be your husband?
> To have and to hold from this day forward.
> In good times and bad,
> In sickness and in health,
> To love, honor, and treasure,
> All the days of your lives?

Betty answers: I do.

> And do you, David, take Betty to be your wife?
> To have and to hold from this day forward.
> In good times and bad,
> In sickness and in health,
> To love, honor, and treasure,
> All the days of your lives?

David answers: I do.

BLESSING AND EXCHANGING OF THE RINGS

Now we come to the presentation of the rings. These rings represent unity, wholeness, oneness, eternity. They are made of material that is strong and enduring. They are symbolic of a union that will continue to endure. May I have the rings please.

Ask the couple to prepare to exchange rings.

David, please take Betty's hand. Slip the ring on her finger. Please repeat after me: with this ring, I pledge my love.

Betty, please take David's hand. Slip the ring on his finger. Please repeat after me: with this ring, I pledge my love.

Officiant: May you joyously keep the promises you make here today.

HAND BLESSING

Please hold each other's hands so you can feel the gift you truly are to one another. And now, a blessing over your hands.

Fill your hearts with hope for our future,
And be confident your love can see you through challenges.
　　On this day, as you pledge your love and devotion,
Trust your commitment is strong enough to last forever.
　　As you join your hands, hearts and souls for all of your days.
　　May you grow in love and respect for one another.
May you always reach out your hands in tenderness.
May this marriage be blessed in all ways.

THE PRONOUNCEMENT

Your two lives are now joined.

May the bond that unites you be ever strengthened.

May you be blessed with health, prosperity, a long life, a strong family—and the time to enjoy it all!

Betty and David, it is my honor to now pronounce you husband and wife.

THE KISS

Please seal it with a kiss!

Ceremony ends.

Japanese, Christian

Kiko and Yoshi

Supplies and logistics:
Red clergy stole
Red altar tablecloth
Altar table
Sake and sake cups

GREETING

Officiant: On behalf of Kiko and Yoshi, thank you for being part of this joyous occasion. They are so happy you could all make the trip to be here for their wedding.

Today we celebrate the place that Yoshi and Kiko have made in each other's hearts as we joyously witness the sacred vows that will join their lives as partners in marriage.

Let us all offer our blessings and good wishes.

INVOCATION

Officiant: Let us begin this ceremony with a blessing.

Dear God, we are thankful for the gift of this marriage.

May Kiko and Yoshi have the ability to rejoice always in their love.

May their eyes be open to the beauty and mystery of the love they have for each other, every day, as today.

May every wish of their hearts be fulfilled.

And may their life together embrace and nurture the promise of this moment.

As we open our hearts in celebration, may this bride and groom, and all those who have come here to share in this joyous occasion, be uplifted and embraced by love.

MINISTER'S MESSAGE

Officiant: Yoshi and Kiko, you have shared a bond of love and respect for many years. You come to this day with the gift of wisdom, having already spent more than five years of your lives building the relationship you share. Your love has flourished because you both dearly cherish one another and value your relationship.

This is your wedding day, an opportunity to stand before friends and family and proclaim your commitment to one another. This day is also a celebration and affirmation of your relationship. It is an affirmation of the life you have built together and the promise of an even stronger union in years to come.

Kiko, I asked Yoshi what he loves about you, and he said: I love her because she thinks a great deal about other people, and she always thinks about me.

Yoshi, I asked Kiko what she loves about you, and she said: I love him because he respects the values of others, and he is a very thoughtful person.

Though you come to this day already united in so many ways, the journey of nourishing your love through all of life's cycles will take on new dimensions as you become husband and wife before these witnesses.

You share a love that exists in the past, the present, the future. And you come to this day knowing that you are marrying your best friend...the person who knows you best and loves you most.

In your life as husband and wife, our wish for you is that you enjoy the life you share to the fullest and that you always appreciate and honor what you have together.

May your marriage become your new home. And may that home be filled with love, and joy, and promise. And may you still be happily holding hands when you are both 100 years old, surrounded by your children, grandchildren, and great grandchildren.

THE CONSECRATION

Officiant: Kiko and Yoshi, as you have come here today of your own free will in the presence of witnesses to declare your love for each other, we ask that you both be honored by the promises you make here today. Please face each other.

EXPRESSION OF INTENT

Officiant:

> Do you, Kiko, take Yoshi to be your husband?
> Do you promise to be a faithful mate?
> To share your hopes, dreams, and goals?
> Will you catch him if he falls …
> Comfort him when he cries …
> Laugh with him in times of joy, and
> Support him in times of challenge?
> Today in front of your friends and family,
> Do you promise to continue to love and respect him for the rest of your life?

Kiko answers: I do.

> And do you, Yoshi, take Kiko to be your wife?
> Do you promise to be a faithful mate?
> To share your hopes, dreams, and goals?
> Will you catch her if she falls …
> Comfort her when she cries …
> Laugh with her in times of joy, and
> Support her in times of challenge?
> Today in front of your friends and family,
> Do you promise to continue to love and respect her for the rest of your life?

Yoshi answers: I do.

Pause a moment.

BLESSING AND EXCHANGING OF THE RINGS AND VOWS

Officiant: And now we come to the presentation of the rings. The wedding ring has long been a symbol of commitment and devotion that represents unity, wholeness, oneness, and eternity. These rings are made of metal that does not tarnish, metal that is enduring. They are symbolic of a union that will endure.

I ask everyone here to silently join me in blessing these rings and those who wear them.

Hand rings to bride and groom and ask them to exchange rings.

Officiant:

Yoshi, please take Kiko's hand. Slip the ring on her finger.

Kiko, please take Yoshi's hand. Slip the ring on his finger.

And now, the bride and groom will exchange vows in Japanese, speaking them simultaneously to one another. *They exchange vows.*

English translation:

I marry this woman
I marry this man
I will love, console, and help this person
Until death.
Protecting fidelity.
To this I swear.

Officiant: May these rings serve as a constant reminder of the vows set forth here today.

SAKE CEREMONY

Officiant holds up cup and says: To celebrate your union, we call upon a Western version of a Japanese custom using only one cup of sake.

This cup of sake represents your new relationship as husband and wife. Today, you blend all you are, and all you will become, into this one union.

This represents all the celebrations to come and all the challenges you will handle together. It is symbolic of all the hopes and dreams, as well as disappointments, you will share during a long life together as a married couple.

Hand them the cup.

Share a drink now, together, to symbolize your willingness to share all of life. And may the cup of life be full to overflowing. *They sip.*

FINAL PRAYER

Officiant: Let us bring the ceremony to a close with a special blessing. I'd like to ask everyone here, in your own way, again, to join me.

Dear God, please bless this couple.

May their love be nurtured, always and forever.

May they live in peace and in happiness.

Yoshi and Kiko,

As you have pledged your love and devotion before these witnesses today, it is my honor to now pronounce you husband and wife.

THE KISS

You may seal it with a kiss!

Ceremony ends.

Pagan, Nondenominational

Amy and Joe

This wedding brought together a family that includes the bride's four boys. The overall theme is nondenominational, and it includes several pagan/earth-based traditions.

Supplies and logistics:

Small altar table
Seven clear containers for colored sand
Central container for sand
Colored sand

Altar items:

Air: small golden feather butterfly
Fire: special candle
Water: small bowl with flower floating in it
Earth: crystal or stone
Wedding rings
Wedding license
Vows, if the bride and groom are reading them

GREETING

Officiant: Welcome, family and friends. We come together in great happiness to celebrate the love between Amy and Joe and to witness the sacred rituals and vows that will unite them as partners in marriage.

This couple believes strongly in the sacred union of love that they already share. Thus, with much love and tenderness, they've created a contemporary wedding ceremony that fully expresses their adoration for one another, their personal beliefs, and their intentions for their marriage. They have taken care to represent both the masculine and the feminine as they understand this to be the true balance of life, love, and divinity.

Let us offer them our blessings and best wishes for a marriage that is all they would choose it to be!

STEP INTO WREATH/PRAYER

Officiant: Let us begin by asking the bride and groom to step into the beautiful wreath of flowers that they have designed for their wedding altar.

This wreath represents a circle of love. It is the circle of love they choose to live the rest of their lives in—the circle of love they will include the bride's children in. It is symbolic of the closeness, unity, and oneness of the relationship they share.

As they step inside, let us pray: God, Goddess, Divine Spirit of all that is, please bestow great blessings and grace upon this couple who stand before us in the name of love. And so it is.

INVOCATION/CALLING THE DIRECTIONS

Officiant: We now offer a special blessing culled from the Native American tradition. Our ancestors reveled in their connection to nature and to the elements of earth, air, fire, water, and spirit. They believed that great blessings are bestowed from all corners of the universe. Thus, for this bride and groom, we call to the spirits of the East, the South, the West, and the North to bless this union.

We call to the spirits of the East. We honor wind and ask that this couple sail through life safely and calmly.

We call to the spirits of the South. We honor fire and ask that this union be warm and glowing and that the hearts of this man and woman be always filled.

We call to the spirits of the West. We honor water and ask that it cleanse this couple for marriage and soothe them so that they may never thirst for love.

We call to spirits of the North. We honor mother earth and ask that this marriage be abundant and grow stronger with each season.

We call to the spirits of above, of below, and within.

With all the forces of the universe, we pray for harmony and joy as this couple grows forever young with one another.

May this couple be blessed in all ways…and may all who have come to share in this day be encircled and embraced by divine light, good spirits, and love.

And so it is. Please be seated.

WEDDING READING

Officiant: These "Thoughts on Marriage" from *The Prophet*, by Kahlil Gibran, reflect the sentiments of the bride and groom:

> Then Almitra spoke again and said,
> *And what of Marriage, Master?*
>
> And he answered, saying:
> You were born together,
> and together you shall be forevermore.
> You shall be together when the white wings of death scatter your days.
> You shall be together even in the silent memory of God.
> But let there be spaces in your togetherness,
> And let the winds of the heavens dance between you.
> Love one another, but make not a bond of love.
> Let it rather be a moving sea,
> between the shores of your souls.
> Fill each other's cup …
> but drink not from one cup.
> Give one another of your bread …
> but eat not from the same loaf.
> Sing and dance together and be joyous,
> but let each one of you be alone,
> Even as the strings of a lute are alone …
> though they quiver with the same music.
> Give your hearts, but not into each other's keeping.
> For only the hand of Life can contain your hearts.
> And stand together yet not too near
> together:

For the pillars of the temple stand apart,
And the oak tree and the cypress grow
not in each other's shadow.

MINISTER'S ADDRESS

Amy and Joe, you are soul mates who have found one another and have been blessed with the gift of one another's love. Today, we celebrate your sacred agreement of marriage, and we honor your commitment to be steadfast in your intention to love one another through all things.

You come to this day as partners in life, already united in your hearts and souls. Yet, on this day, the journey of nourishing your love through *all* of life's cycles takes on a new dimension as you become husband and wife.

You will discover that marriage is even more than the joining of two lives. It is the merging of two families and two life stories. It is the mystical, physical, and emotional union of two human beings. It is the fuller opening of two hearts and the ripening of two souls. And it is the creation of a new family...a family that includes the two of you as well as Stephen, Angelo, Mathew, and Frank.

As you live your marriage, you will find that your relationship has moods and seasons, wonderful times as well as challenges. Trust that even through the darkest night of your relationship, your love and commitment will be a guiding light, the northern star that can show you your way home to one another's hearts.

It is important that you release, at this time, any obstacles to your happiness. Please look at one another and in this moment may you forgive each other any past transgressions, and forgive transgressions of relationships past, that you might enter this marriage reborn. Allow the waters of forgiveness to wash you clean.

You are given the chance to begin your lives, again, as the Divine Spirit of all there is—by all names and images—grants you complete renewal through the power of the commitment you make here today.

Amy and Joe, may you find in each other's love profound acceptance and total release. May you be given the vision to behold one another with the eyes of love. And may you experience the endless generosity of spirit with which to nurture one another's soul and sweetly keep the promises you make here today.

SAND CEREMONY

Officiant: We are all made up of millions of molecules, facets, possibilities, points of views, experiences, desires, hopes, and dreams. Our very beings are as vast as a beach that stretches on forever and our makeup as complex and complete as the many tiny particles of sand that, when joined together, make that beach such a stunning sight.

In the modern tradition of the sand ceremony, a couple acknowledges their individuality—and their desire to merge their lives in marriage—by pouring two separate containers of different sand into one empty vessel.

This joining of sand symbolically unites the many aspects of their individual selves. It also brings together the families that are united by marriage.

Call up mom and the boys.

To honor the family ties that are created on this day, we ask the mother of the groom and the bride's four sons to step to the wedding altar.

To mom and the boys: There are seven containers of sand here. Two for the bride and groom and five for mom and the boys.

Representing the bride and groom's families and ancestors—the source of who they are—each of you will all add sand to the central container. Hence your love and support become an essential part, a foundation, of this marriage.

Officiant leads them through pouring the sand.

First the groom's mom pours. Now, guys, please pour your sand one at a time.

Once they've done it: Terrific. Now you can be seated. Thanks!

Point to the two individual containers of sand.

And now, the bride and groom will add themselves to the mix of love and family.

Amy and Joe, you come to this day as individuals, whole and complete unto yourselves. This ritual brings the many tiny aspects that represent the two of you and your families together into one vessel that is symbolic of a joint venture that is a stronger, fuller, more powerful expression of your love.

The two remaining containers of sand represent the two of you as individuals. These two distinct containers represent your lives...up until this moment.

Officiant asks them to pour sand simultaneously.

As you pour the sand from your individual containers, make the choice to leave behind anything that will not serve your marriage and choose to bring into your marriage that which will help you grow, and blossom, and expand.

After they pour both containers into one: The flowing together of this sand is symbolic of your unique union. Your newly formed family is represented by the intertwined pattern of sand you have all created together.

May this union and this family be blessed in all ways.

THE CONSECRATION/QUESTIONS

Officiant: Please look at each other.

Amy and Joe, have you come here today to give yourself freely to one another in marriage?

They both answer: We have. *They each answer yes for all the following questions.*

Do you love each other without reservation?
Do you have the will to argue, to air your problems, and then stand together against adversity?
Do you share your thoughts and ideas, your hopes and dreams, your fears and burdens?
Do you agree that you are soul mates, partners, and lovers for life?

After they answer yes to all: All challenges have been answered, and thus we shall proceed. May God and Goddess bless this rite.

HANDFASTING AND WRAPPING OF THE HANDS

Officiant: It is an ancient tradition to join two lives as one through the rite of handfasting. The couple joins hands and is literally tied together to symbolize their unity. Today we will use the slightly modern tradition of hand-*wrapping*.

Amy and Joe, if you choose to become one with each other, please place your right palms together and then place your left palms over them. This creates a figure eight, or infinity symbol, with your hands. It signifies hearts that will love forever.

I will wrap them with a sacred cloth, also in an infinity symbol. This will signify a relationship that lasts forever.

EXPRESSION OF INTENT

Hands still wrapped for I do's.

Amy, in the sight of God, Goddess, Divine Spirit of all there is, do you take this man, Joe, to be your lawful wedded husband?

Amy answers: I do.

Joe, in the sight of God, Goddess, Divine Spirit of all there is, do you take this woman, Amy, to be your lawful wedded wife?

Joe answers: I do.

HANDFASTING PRAYER/UNWRAPPING OF HANDS

Minister comes from around the altar to offer this prayer over their hands and unwraps the hands.

As your hands are bound together,
now so shall your lives and spirits
be joined in a union of love, trust, and mutual support. Heart to heart, soul to soul,
body to body…and so it is.

VOWS

Officiant: You've chosen some beautiful words to speak to each other today. Please prepare to speak what is in your heart.
They read.

BLESSING UPON THE VOWS

With these vows, you swear, by God and Goddess, to be full partners, each to the other.

BLESSING AND EXCHANGING OF RINGS

Officiant: From the earliest times, the circle has been a symbol of completeness. And the wedding ring has long been a symbol of love and devotion that, like a circle, is unbroken. The rings that are to be exchanged today are made of metal that does not tarnish, metal that is enduring. These rings are symbolic of a union that will endure.

To the best man and maid of honor: Please present the rings.

RING EXCHANGE

As a symbol of joining one to another, we will now ask the bride and groom to place the rings upon each others' fingers.

Joe, please take your lady's hand. Slip the ring on her finger. And repeat after me: now and forever, thou art my love.

Amy, please take your beloved's hand. Slip the ring on his finger. And repeat after me: now and forever, thou art my love.

BLESSING OF THE RINGS AND MARRIAGE

I ask all of you to help bless this marriage by taking a moment to fill your hearts and minds with joyous thoughts and good wishes for this couple. And now, join me in calling out a special prayer and blessing. It goes like this: Long live this marriage!

Now, we'll all say it together: *Long live this marriage!*

Everyone calls it out: Long live this marriage!

Officiant: So it is spoken, so it is done. May these rings be a life-long symbol for all to see that these two people have been joined in marriage.

CLOSING/FINAL PRAYER

Officiant: Please rise. Now, we lovingly open the sacred circle of love that we have created here today by expressing gratitude to God, Goddess, Divine Spirit of all that is.

We are thankful for the sacred space we have all shared together and thankful to the spirits of the East, South, West, North, Above, Below, and Within for blessing this ceremony of marriage.

We thank the elements for blessing this altar.

For the bride and groom, and their children, let us offer a closing blessing. I'd like to ask everyone here, in your own way, to silently join me in this prayer.

THE PRONOUNCEMENT

May the Highest Power bless you and keep you.

May the presence of Divine Grace shine down upon you and be gracious to you.

May the peace of God and Goddess be with you now, and all of your days.

Amy and Joe, it is my honor to now pronounce you husband and wife.

THE KISS

You may kiss!

THE BRIDE AND GROOM GREET THE COMMUNITY

Motion for the bride and groom to turn around and greet the community.

Nondenominational
Vow Renewal

Zak and Terry

OPENING

> What greater thing is there for two human souls
> than to feel that they are joined together
> to strengthen each other in all labor,
> to minister to each other in all sorrow,
> to share with each other in all gladness,
> and to be one with each other,
> in the silent, unspoken memories.

—George Eliot

GREETING

Officiant: Terry and Zak, today we joyfully celebrate your renewed commitment to your love and to your marriage. Today, before God and your community, you honor the place that you have made in one another's hearts as you deepen the bond that began at the wedding altar 10 years ago.

THE INVOCATION/BLESSING

Let us link hearts and begin with a blessing.
   We are grateful for this marriage.
   May your marriage continue to bring you joy and great delight.

May you have the ability to rejoice, always, in your love.

May you always see one another through the eyes of love.

May you continue to fall in love with each other, over and over again.

May this couple, and all those who have come here to share in this joyous occasion, be uplifted and embraced by love. Amen.

WEDDING READING

Love is the sacred, invisible force that brings people together and leads them to their wedding day. Yet it also is a tangible, living energy that has character and great substance. It draws us in, changes us, and ultimately, it guides our lives and intertwines our destinies. Here is a special recipe for keeping marriage fresh and vibrant:

> Give life to your love.
> Through small acts of kindness and caring
> Communicate clearly.
> Always tell one another what is on your minds.
> Listen to each other.
> Truly hear what your partner has to say.
> Have a shared mission.
> Know what you want your marriage to be.
> Follow dreams together.
> Decide on worthy goals that you can pursue together.
> Support each other's dreams.
> Be the wind beneath one another's wings.
> Be there in tough times.
> Conjure strength for each other in sorrow and disappointment.
> Cherish what you have.
> Always treasure your relationship and the one you love.
> Hold on to each other.
> Remember how valuable it is to love and be loved.
> Continue to make this marriage the foundation of your lives.
> Let it always be the home you return to,
> and the safe haven that the outside world cannot disturb.

MINISTER'S MESSAGE

Theodore Parker once said, "It takes years to marry completely two hearts. Even the most loving and well assorted. A happy wedlock is a falling in love. Young persons think love belongs to the brown-haired and crimson cheeked. So it does for its beginning. But the golden marriage is a part of love which the bridal day knows nothing of. Such a large and sweet fruit is marriage that is needs a long summer to ripen, and then a long winter to mellow and season it."

Terry and Zak, you have long been blessed with one another's love. And you come to this day united in your hearts and souls and united in all aspects of your lives.

Today is a celebration of a long-running romance and affirmation of the life you have built together—and the promise of a stronger union in years to come

You've shared a bond of love and respect for so long, you arrive at this day with the gift of true wisdom, having invested many years building the relationship you share.

Terry, in Zak you have a partner who loves and adores you. He admires your intelligence, inner strength, and determination. He revels in your integrity, honesty, and loyalty. He feels blessed for the support you have offered throughout your marriage. He says he loves to look into your beautiful eyes and see the love you have for him.

And Zak, in Terry you have a partner who considers you her closest and most valued friend...as well as the most fun to be with person she knows. She is so proud of you and all you have accomplished. Marrying you, she says, was the best decision she ever made...that's why she wanted to do it again!

You two have been through a lot together. And you have an intimate understanding of the real meaning of "for better or for worse."

You share a love that exists in the past, the present, the future. And you come to this day knowing that you married your best friend and biggest ally, the person who knows you best and loves you most—and that you'd do it again.

As you continue your life as husband and wife, our wish for you is that that you enjoy the life you share to the fullest and that you always appreciate and honor what you have together.

THE CONSECRATION

Your marriage is a precious gift, a lifelong dedication, and a daily challenge to love one another more fully and more freely. As you have come here today to re-declare your love for each other, we ask that you both be honored and expanded by the renewed expressions of love you are about to share. Let us celebrate because you still can think of no place you would rather be than at one another's side.

VOWS RENEWED

Officiant: At this time, we ask you to please look at one another and share the beautiful vows that will express and renew your commitment. Please repeat after me.

Zak:

> I bring myself to you this day to reaffirm my life with you.
> It is my honor to share and support your hopes, dreams, and goals.
> when you fall, I will catch you;
> when you cry, I will comfort you;
> when you laugh, I will share your joy;
> I vow to be there for you always.

Terry:

> I bring myself to you this day to reaffirm my life with you.
> I honor, trust, and respect you, and support your hopes and dreams
> And I will stand with you through all challenges.
> I will forever be your companion, your best friend, and your equal,
> as we continue this great journey, together.
> I promise to love you always.

Officiant: Terry and Zak, may you always observe the sacred vows and declarations that have been spoken today.

FINAL PRAYER

Officiant: We would like to offer you a final prayer.

> May the moon softly restore you by night.
> May the rain wash away your worries.
> May you live the days of your lives in peace, love, and happiness.
> May the sun bring you new energy by day.
> May you continue to share a beautiful family life of affection, devotion, and joy.

Having witnessed the love that radiates between you, I hereby reaffirm your vows, and we wish you the best as you continue on your journey together!

KISS

Please seal it with a kiss.

PARTING WORDS

Congratulations!
  Ceremony ends.

Highly Personalized

Claudine and Michael

The ceremony is highly personal and loving and often evokes God and Christian traditions as it blends this new family together.

Supplies and logistics:
Printed seven blessings for readers
Family unity jewelry for bride's daughter
Two unscented white memorial candles

GREETING

Welcome, family and friends. Love gathers us here today. On behalf of Claudine and Michael, thank you for being part of this joyous occasion. You are all very special to this bride and groom, and they are so grateful that you can share in this very special moment in their lives. Today we celebrate the commitment that Michael and Claudine are making to each other. Let us joyously witness the sacred vows that will join their lives as partners in marriage and that will officially begin their life as a family.

This is a marriage that has been 17 years in the making! So let us all offer our good wishes and blessings. I am sure you join me in saying, Hooray! They're finally getting married!

OPENING PRAYER

Please rise. Now, we share a moment of prayer from the Book of Common Prayer.

Dear God, creator of all life, and giver of all grace:
Look with favor upon the world you have made,
and especially upon Claudine and Michael,
who today pledge their love and commitment.

Give them wisdom and devotion in the ordering of their common life,
that each may be to the other
a strength in need, a counselor in perplexity,
a comfort in sorrow, and a companion in joy.
Give them grace when they hurt each other,
to recognize and acknowledge their fault,
and to seek each other's forgiveness.
Make their life together be such that their unity may overcome estrangement, their forgiveness heal hurt, and their joy may conquer any despair.
Give them such fulfillment of their mutual affection
that they may reach out in love and concern for others.
And may this marriage be a strong foundation and a safe haven for Veronica.
May this bride and groom, and all who have come to witness this joyous occasion, be embraced and uplifted by love. And we all say, Amen.

HONORING FAMILY

Claudine, Michael, and Veronica have linked hearts and lives to create a family. And at a wedding, we see firsthand how the lineage of love gets passed along from generation to generation. The light of love that illuminates this marriage would not be possible without the love passed on to Claudine and Michael by their families.

This family is united in a circle of love and strength.

Every joy shared adds more love.

Every obstacle faced together makes the circle stronger.

With every birth and every new union, the circle will grow.

At this time we would like to invite the groom's parents and bride's mother and father up to the altar.

First, we take a moment, together, to remember the loved ones who are no longer with us.

We ask the fathers of the groom and the bride to do the honors of lighting candles in their memory.

Dads light a candle and remembers loved ones.

These candles will stay alight, side by side during this ceremony, representing the joint history and ancestry that Claudine and Michael blend into their marriage.

This bride and groom suspect that some of their beloved grandparents offered a helping hand from heaven to bring these two together. On the bride's side, we lovingly remember Claudine's grandparents. From the groom's side, we remember loved ones as well. We believe they are celebrating with us on this special day!

THE LIGHTING OF THE UNITY CANDLE

And now, we ask the moms to help light the unity candle. It has been said that "from every human being there rises a light that reaches straight to the heavens. And when two souls that are destined for each other find one another, their streams of light flow together and a single brighter light goes forth from their united being."

The lighting of the unity candle symbolizes the light of two individuals coming together as one brighter light. It also symbolizes the merging of two families, and two lives, as one.

We ask the mom of the bride and the mom of the groom to step up and light the two tapers, representing each family. They will light it from the one light that burns on the altar that represents the light of God in us all.

They light the tapers from the one light (votive) that burns on the altar. Officiant leads them through.

Now, please pass the light to your children. *Bride and groom hold candles.* Parents, thank you all for being part of this special part of the ceremony. You may be seated.

To bride and groom: Hold your candles for a moment. These two candles represent the two of you as well as your families, your ancestors, the source of who you are. These two distinct flames represent your lives...up until this moment. Now, please bring these two separate candles together to light the unity candle. *Then they put the tapers back into the holder.* May the loving light of family, community, and good friends always bless and illuminate this marriage.

MINISTER'S MESSAGE

An old legend tells us that when two certain souls are created in heaven, an angel cries out, "These two are made for each other!" It is said that if these people meet on earth and recognize each other for who they truly are, they will fall in love and become as one, working together in unison. Then, even if they face hardships in their relationship, these will not alter the strength of their enduring love.

Claudine and Michael, you are certainly two people who have been blessed, and blessed, and blessed again with the discovery of one another's love. It is no secret that you were first engaged in July 2006. Love took a detour in December 2006. But you never let go of one another, and once you shook off the fear and doubts, you recommitted to your life together. Now you believe strongly that God brought you together. And you are so enormously grateful to be standing here today!

But what some people may not realize is that you originally met in 1990. Back then, Claudine remembers being *crazy* about Michael. For example, one night, while Claudine was out at a restaurant with friends, she saw Michael across the room and remembers becoming weak in the knees just seeing him! Michael, however, had *no clue* how much she liked him.

So we thought it would be fitting and fun to share some of Claudine's journal entries from the nineties. Now, just imagine her, with the nineties hair, sitting and making these entries into her diary:

> September 11, 1990: "Dear Diary: In a silly kind of way...I hope we stay together a very long time."
> October 23, 1990: "Dear Diary: I know we should be together. I truly believe we are good for each other. Oh, well, maybe in the future. Who knows?"
> And later that day: "Dear Diary: I wish Mike really loved me....He's a strange guy."
> October 29, 1990: "Dear Diary: Michael Thomas Gallo...what a beautiful name. Definitely attached to a beautiful man."

Well, after that, these two beautiful people drifted away from one another. But fast-forward to 2005. That's when Claudine and Michael rediscovered each other. By then, Michael was *really feeling it*. Claudine was more nonchalant.

Michael would text her really sweet messages all day long. He was so attentive. For example, during a Utah ski trip, Claudine and Michael and two guy friends were getting ready for the last run of the vacation. The men elected a more dangerous route, and they sent Claudine down a safer path. She and Michael planned to meet at the bottom. All of a sudden, she turns, and there he is.

He sacrificed the last run just to follow and make sure she was OK. It made her feel so cared for. True love bloomed…and then temporarily hit a slippery slope.

Fast-forward to 2007. That's when Claudine and Michael realized that their 17-year journey to love was truly no accident—that it was part of God's plan. They were ready to recommit and to embrace a very serious love and lifelong commitment. Now they are thrilled to be *equally* crazy about one another.

For this couple, three time's a charm! In the words of Peaches and Herb: "reunited and it feels so good!"

Michael and Claudine, we congratulate you on the courage it has taken to make your way to this place. And we rejoice with you!

Michael, I asked Claudine what she loves about you, and she gave me a huge list. I had to edit it because it would have run into your cocktail hour. Here are some of the highlights:

I love how caring and generous he is to his family, his friends, and to all human beings. He is easygoing and rarely says no if he can say yes. He is nonjudgmental. Michael is one of the smartest, most intuitive people I have ever met. He has great insight. He has a gentle, quiet way of knowing. He is very sensitive, and I adore this about him. Whenever we fight, he is always the first one to come to me and hug me, to let it go, and start resolving the issue at hand. He is so courageous in so many ways. I am in awe. Michael is so loving and genuine with Veronica, and she loves him. I am very grateful that Michael loves me so much. I appreciate that Michael is organized and efficient because that is not my strong point—to put it lightly—and in that way, I feel he really balances me out. Last, I love the love and attraction Michael and I feel for each other. I know how blessed we are. I know how very, very special our relationship is. I thank God for this relationship, and I am so excited to be his wife.

Claudine, I asked Michael what he loves about you, and he, in a very organized presentation, said: She is a very loving person, respectful and loyal. She is so thoughtful. I love that she cares about me in so many ways. She is not only beautiful on the outside, but most important, on the inside. I love that she cares about my feelings and my thoughts, that she wants to have kids and create a loving and caring home, that she wants to have a family and provide for our family in many ways. I love that she also wants to be a giving person to our family and also in giving back to the community. I love that she wants to grow together and have a life of love together and that we both feel spiritually connected in so many ways.

Marriage, to you, is about making a commitment to each other on a spiritual level, sharing a life fulfilled with joy, peace, and happiness. It's about being there for each other in good times and challenging times. It's about family—raising Veronica, adding to your family, and sharing a true family life. It's about creating and nurturing a safe, non-judgmental relationship in which you both know you are accepted and loved.

As you pledge yourselves to one another as husband and wife, you make the commitment to spend the rest of your lives together, growing emotionally and spiritually, sharing and experiencing life together. We wish you these things and more:

> May you create a home and a life together filled with joy and happiness. May you enjoy being devoted parents and partners. May your relationship deepen with each passing day, bringing you more love, appreciation, intimacy, friendship, and laughter. May you embrace the power of dialogue and always communicate clearly and lovingly to one another. May you be inspired and supported by the power and strength of your love to reach out and help others in a meaningful way. In your life as husband and wife, we wish for you that you enjoy the life you share to the fullest and that you always appreciate and honor what you have together.

THE CONSECRATION

Claudine and Michael, as you have come here today of your own free will in the presence of God, family, and friends to declare your love and commitment to each other, we ask that you both be strengthened by the promises you are about to make. Claudine has asked me to share her personal prayer she says each day to God:

> Lord God, please accept our gratitude for this day, for this love, for this community of friends and family. We are so grateful for Your favor upon us, for bringing us together, for being present in our lives and for the good health You have bestowed upon us and our loved ones. We pray that Your presence, Your blessings, and Your love are with us today and always. Amen.

EXPRESSION OF INTENT

Please face each other.

Do you, Claudine, take Michael to be your husband?
Do you promise to grow with him in mind and spirit,
To always be open and honest with him,
to cherish and respect him?
Do you agree to accept his faults,
as much as embrace his attributes?
Do you promise to be a partner to Michael,
in sickness and in health,
for all your days on earth?

Claudine answers: I do.

And do you, Michael, take Claudine to be your wife?
Do you promise to grow with her in mind and spirit,
To always be open and honest with her,
And cherish and respect her?
Do you agree to accept her faults,
as much as embrace her attributes?
Do you promise to be a partner to Claudine,
in sickness and in health,
for all your days on earth?

Michael answers: I do.

VOWS

Officiant: Vows are not just the hallmark of the wedding ceremony. They are the foundation of your married life. We speak wedding vows as a way of setting forth the intentions we want to *live from* in married life. We speak them knowing that while times may change, our vows are meant to be constants in our lives.

Claudine and Michael, please use this opportunity to express to each other what your intentions are for your married life. You have some beautiful vows to share. Please face each other and speak what is in your heart.

Claudine:
Michael, I can't believe this incredible day has come.
On this day, I become your wife, and we all become a family.
It is my priority to make you happy,
And take care of you, our family, and myself.
I want to always have the courage to communicate with you,
To have patience and understanding when you communicate with me,

To listen with love, understanding, and openness,

And to mean what I say, say what I mean, but never say it mean.

I will always encourage you because I believe so deeply in you.

I will prioritize our relationship because it is the foundation of our lives and the

Sacred and safe haven for our family.

And I will continue to build a community of friends and family.

I intend on loving, respecting, and honoring you, caring for and about you,

For the rest of my days on this earth.

These are my hopes and prayers for our marriage:

I pray that our love increases daily,

That our intimate connection becomes enhanced over the years,

That we continue to trust, connect, and like each other with each passing day,

That we handle difficulties with patience, understanding, tenaciousness, and utilize those

Moments to grow as a couple.

When I look in your eyes, I feel like I am home.

I am safe, loved, and cared for.

I am so in love with you and very

Grateful to God for deeply blessing me

With your love and this wonderful time in our life.

Michael:

Claudine, I love you for accepting me as I am. I love you for filling my life with joy, peace, and happiness. I love you not only for who you are but for who I am when I am with you. You have helped me see the dreams I have for life more clearly than ever before. I promise to grow with you in mind and spirit. I promise to trust and respect you. I promise to be patient and understanding, and I promise to share my thoughts, fears, and dreams with you. I promise to you today that I will forever fulfill my role as your partner in the life we build together. I will cherish you always. You are my one and only true love.

BLESSING AND EXCHANGING OF THE RINGS/VOWS

Now we come to the presentation of the rings. May I please have the rings.

PRAYER/BLESSING OVER THE RINGS

I ask everyone here to fill their minds and hearts with good wishes and blessings for this couple and to please silently join me in blessing these rings. May God bless these rings and the two who wear them. May this union be blessed in all ways. Amen.

Hold a moment of silence. Ask bride and groom to prepare to exchange rings.

Michael, please take Claudine's hand. Slip the ring on her finger. And repeat after me:

> May you wear this on your finger,
> for all of your days.
> May it represent our love and unity,
> And commitment.
> This ring symbolizes
> My faithfulness *to you,*
> my trust *in you,*
> and my belief in our relationship.
> With this ring I become your husband.
> May it serve as a constant reminder
> of the love we experienced today.

Claudine, please take Michael's hand. Slip the ring on his finger. And repeat after me:

> May you wear this on your finger,
> for all of your days.
> May it represent our love and unity,
> And commitment.
> This ring symbolizes
> My faithfulness *to you,*
> my trust *in you,*
> and my belief in our relationship.
> With this ring I become your wife.
> May it serve as a constant reminder
> of the love we experienced today.

FAMILY UNITY GIFT (FOR BRIDE'S DAUGHTER)

Officiant: We would like to request that Veronica please join us.

It is challenging to find the right person to spend the rest of your life with, so Michael is doubly blessed because he has found two! Veronica, since Mom and Mikey exchanged wedding rings, they would also like to give you a piece of sacred jewelry. There are six charms on this necklace, each representing something significant to this family.

Couple gives Veronica the gift. Michael puts the necklace on Veronica.

Veronica, Mommy was telling me that you shared some beautiful comments about her getting married. Can I share some of them with Mikey?

When Mommy asked how you feel about their marriage, you said, "Awesome! I think Mommy and Mikey are the best couple I ever knew. Mikey is really kind. He really loves me. I think he will be a good stepfather because I love him. I love him forever!"

Veronica, I know you have a special gift for Michael. Would you like to give it to him now? *She gives it to him with Claudine's help.*

Officiant: It's a bracelet…and it says, "I Love My Stepfather."

SEVEN BLESSINGS

And now, the bridal party will offer seven special blessings upon this marriage:

1. We bless this marriage in the name of Friendship.
   Amanda: May this couple prosper and share the strengthening bonds of two who know, trust, and savor each other.
2. We bless this marriage in the name of Intimacy.
   Jackie: May this couple always know the satisfaction of deep sharing.
3. We bless this marriage in the name of Balance.
   Roseanne: May this couple seek what is good and right…and flourish with love and respect.
4. We bless this marriage in the name of Wisdom.
   Leiann: May this couple write a new chapter in the book of experience…husband and wife learning from one another.
5. We bless this marriage in the name of Joy.
   Joe: May this couple hear the song of gladness…and may their love shine the light of happiness on others.
6. We bless this marriage in the name of Creativity.
   John: May this couple create special dreams…and revel in their fulfillment.
7. We bless this marriage in the name of Appreciation and Kindness.

Cousin Michael: May this marriage flourish as this couple keeps their hearts open to one another day and night, and may this marriage show that these two can treat each other, always, with generosity and goodwill.

FINAL BLESSING AND PRONOUNCEMENT

Officiant: Please hold each other's hands so you can feel the gift you truly are. Let us bring the ceremony to a close with a special blessing. I ask everyone here to join me in their own way.

In the Bible, Corinthians tells us

> If I speak in the tongues of men
> and of angels,
> but have not love,
> I am nothing more than a noisy gong
> or a clanging cymbal.
> And if I have the gift of prophecy,
> and understand all mysteries,
> and have all knowledge,
> and a faith that can move mountains,
> but have not love,
> I am nothing...

And John 4:7–8 tells us

> Beloved, let us love one another, because love is from God; everyone who loves is born of God and knows God.
> Whoever does not love does not know God, for God is love.

So Claudine and Michael, remember that anything beautiful you have came from God. And in the beginning, God gave us our free will and our identity to walk the earth.

Don't ever try to change each other. Because if you do, you will lose exactly *who* you fell in love with. So each day, give thanks to God for your partnership and remind yourself of how truly blessed you are. Remind yourself what it is you cherish most about your partner. Make the choice to uphold your vows.

Song of Solomon reminds us, "I am my beloved's and my beloved is mine." God made you for one another, and this is a very special gift. Your love is a gift to be honored and appreciated each day.

On behalf of all those here today and those with us in spirit witnessing your commitment to each other, I wish you a long and happy life together. And may it be filled with God's favor and blessings, love, peace, joy, passion, patience—yes, lots of patience—and happiness, always.

Your lives, hearts, and spirits are now officially joined. May God bless your marriage.

Claudine and Michael, it is my honor to now pronounce you husband and wife.

THE BREAKING OF THE GLASS

We conclude the ceremony with the breaking of the glass. The tradition teaches that even in moments of our greatest joy, we are to remember that we live in a broken world, and while we celebrate, suffering still exists in the world. It is our responsibility, as partners with God, to do the work of mending the brokenness that exists. The Hebrew term for this is *tikkun olam.* It means, literally, to repair the world. The glass that is broken serves as a reminder that through our efforts and our love, the world can be perfected.

Thus the union that you have formed today inherently serves to heal the world and to do the work of *tikkun olam.*

I am going to ask the best man to lay the glass down. Michael, it's customary to give it a good stomp with your right foot. So Michael...

We all yell: Mazel tov!

THE KISS

You may kiss the bride!

Singer begins singing on the kiss, and bride, groom, and Veronica walk out together.

Ceremony ends.

Part Five

Parting Words

ACKNOWLEDGING MY SOURCES OF INSPIRATION

Praise the bridge that carried you over.

—George Colman

I never dreamed I would become a minister and a wedding officiant. I was a journalist for 20 years before I got the call to ministry, and it was something I just hadn't planned on. I didn't know that I could even be considered for such a vocation. Yet when life's amazing road led me to the New Seminary in New York, I felt that I had found home.

The New Seminary, at the time, was the only one I had ever heard of that trained people to become interfaith ministers who would then go out into the community and serve people of all faiths. It mattered not the tradition into which you were born—everyone was welcome. There, Christians, Jews, Muslims, Wiccans, and people of faiths I had never heard of could study in the same seminary and learn to speak the same interfaith language. I was in awe. Soon, the sense of awe became a way of life that seemed perfectly natural.

It was in the spiritual cocoon of seminary school that I was able to make peace with my own religion and learn to celebrate and embrace so many others. And it was in seminary that I came to understand we are not really separated by religion and background and that there is one light that burns within us all—it is the divine light that connects us to one another and all that is. I realized that even though people come into the world representing this religion or that, the truest essence of us all has no specific religion, tradition, skin color, or ethnic background. This light is the light of our souls, and our souls are connected to something far larger than the label of Jewish or pagan or African American. That is why interfaith and intercultural weddings have become a special mission. I want to try to help couples respond to the highest calling of love rather than see them bogged down in the mundane issues of being a mixed couple. Every day, I think about what an honor and privilege it is to do this work.

As I was putting together this book, I thought of the amazing, generous people who have shared their knowledge and helped me develop my wisdom and skills as a wedding officiant. I wanted to share part of my journey and acknowledge the people who helped shape my approach to weddings. This book is filled with hundreds of ideas, prayers, blessings, expressions of love, and insights into interfaith marriage. I know I did not invent them all myself. They have been passed along through generations of ministers and wedding professionals, through spiritual wisdom and traditions, through family customs and through the couples themselves. I cannot attribute every word, phrase, or idea I got from the people I learned from. Let's just say their teaching has become a part of me and hence is a part of this book.

A CALL OUT TO MY MENTORS AND TEACHERS

- I was blessed to have studied directly with Rabbi Joseph Gelberman, pioneer of the concept of interfaith and all-faith ministry and founder of the New Seminary and the New Synagogue. He showed me how to see people through my "spiritual eyes" and how to serve others without ever making judgments. Without him, my work in this field would not have been possible. (I might add, he was also responsible for me meeting my husband, Rev. Victor Fuhrman, and was our wedding officiant!) At this writing, we are celebrating his 98th year and looking forward to his 99th birthday!
- The New Seminary was a place of rebirth for me. I traded one career for the great unknown, and the seminary sustained me during my studies and taught me life lessons I could not have hoped to find any place else. The motto was "never instead of, always in addition to." We were encouraged to honor people wherever they were in their religious journey and never negate it or sway anyone from their religion of birth (including ourselves!). We learned to celebrate all faiths and celebrate more

than one faith simultaneously, which is how I have come to specialize in blended marriages of all kinds.

- In seminary, I encountered many amazing female deans, professional clergywomen, and colleagues from all faiths and backgrounds, and they inspired me to believe in myself and be my best self as a minister. They helped me see what it could be like to be a strong female clergyperson, and to confidently help people and spiritually guide them. Some of these women truly took my breath away when they spoke—they were so clear, so congruent, and spoke with such richness. I came to understand that we had entered a new age for ministry. It looked to me like women were leading the call for a more healing, all-embracing, and accepting spirituality.

- Rev. Ann Gordon, who is also a psychotherapist and one of the most empowering people I know, was one of my first friends in seminary. Her friendship and encouragement are precious gifts. Even when I felt like a student taking small baby steps toward a goal, she treated me as if I had already arrived.

- Writing wedding ceremonies was part of my course work at the New Seminary, and Rev. Judith Marcus was my primary dean. She was a role model of grace and love. She also challenged me to step out of my comfort zone and spread my wings. She empowered me and offered guidance, feedback, and coaching on writing and delivering weddings even after I graduated. She was there, to answer questions and offer support, when I started officiating weddings.

- I learned more about how to help wedding couples, organize the wedding day, deal with the legalities, and craft a ceremony in a New Seminary class led by Rev. Diane Berke, Rev. Julie Omstead, and other deans who all shared their experiences as active wedding officiants. Diane has officiated more weddings than she could count and had perfected the art of the interfaith wedding ceremony. She had published a small booklet of wedding ceremonies with Rev. Ron Mundy and shared those with the class. I could listen to her speak for hours. Her voice and presentation of spiritual material inspired me to be a better communicator.

- Rev. Deb Steen Ross was one of the first friends I met in seminary when I came for my orientation night, and she became an important mentor. Today she is codirector of the New Seminary along with her husband, Rabbi Roger Ross (who is also a great inspiration to me). Back then, she was about to graduate from seminary, and once she did, she became one of the leading interfaith officiants in New York. Soon enough, she was balancing her new work as a dean at the New Seminary with a highly successful wedding ministry. She generously taught me some of the ropes of being a working wedding officiant in New York. She shared her ideas for organizing and researching a wedding ceremony and even asked me to be one of six officiants to co-officiate her wedding to Rabbi Roger. Once I was ordained and registered to perform weddings, she referred couples to me in that first year, and this helped me start my wedding ministry. She was there for me when I had my first panic over the first wedding license I signed, worried that I may not have done it correctly—she assured me I did! She also gifted me with a copy of *Weddings from the Heart,* by Daphne Rose Kingma, at my graduation, a book that became an important inspiration.

- Daphne Rose Kingma has been one of my greatest inspirations in understanding soul mates and what brings people together. She is a relationship counselor and best-selling author. I had read her book *The Future of Love* and interviewed her in 1998, before I was ordained. Her philosophy, that the soul knows no boundaries when it comes to love, has stuck with me and shaped my worldview on love and later on interfaith unions. She maintained that couples are led to find one another by the call of the soul—and not the color of their skin or religion of their birth. Her writings and teaching on this topic touched me deeply and helped me to understand that when we truly follow our hearts and souls, love will come to us, but not always in the package we might expect. I was awestruck when I discovered she had written a popular wedding book. When I graduated from seminary, it was one of the few books available that helped show how diverse, loving, and personal a wedding could be.

- Rev. Joyce Lichenstein, PhD, is an amazing dean with a strong background in psychotherapy and spiritual counseling. She once told me that "all relationships have a dragon to slay," and this has become one of my favorite ways to explain relationship issues that challenge us, especially ornery interfaith issues. I also fondly remember that the Monday after our Saturday graduation and ordination, she organized a trip to the Manhattan City Clerk's Office to assist a dozen or so new ministers in formally registering as wedding clergy in New York City. Since it is mandatory to be registered to perform weddings in New York City proper, this was a rite of passage I will never forget! Taking this step was one of the most exciting moments of my life. Rev. Joyce was there to guide us through all the paperwork.

- At the clerk's office, we met with the amazing Ms. Audrey Sparks (now Audrey Sparks Fussa), who was in charge of clergy registration. Back then, it was in the Municipal Building in lower Manhattan, and all registering clergy had to sign a huge ledger when they brought in their formal paperwork. She guided us in our responsibilities as wedding officiants and the rules and regulations governing the wedding license. I still have a photo of her showing me where to sign the book! Over time, she continued to be a wonderful resource on wedding laws and protocol and was also someone I worked with when I was a volunteer Chaplain for the Red Cross during the 9/11 recovery efforts.

- In my second year of ministry, I connected with the awesome Rev. Paul Michael, who became a friend and supporter as I was starting my ministry career. For those beginning years, I sometimes worked in conjunction with his WeddingOfficiants.com, which helped connect couples of all backgrounds with officiants around the United States. I was one of his New York clergy and learned so much from him about building a wedding ministry and serving couples of all backgrounds. He is a wise and generous wedding professional and was the one who first gave language to the idea of making *everyone* comfortable in a wedding. He called it serving "the greatest common denominator."

- One of the most amazing blessings in my life has been that I met my own soul mate in seminary in 1997. Two years later, Rev. Victor Fuhrman and I became a couple and partners in ministry. Although we have both pursued our individual ministry paths (his is healing), we have co-officiated many weddings and worked with many couples together. He brings a sense of healing to some of the darkest situations couples face, and he has taught me not to be afraid of serving people who are struggling or in pain. He shares brilliant ideas with me on a regular basis, and I can bet many of them end up in my books. He also brings a very special energy when we work together: balance and calm. He has worked with me on every book I have written since we began dating. The last book, *Pet Prayers and Blessings,* we wrote together in 2008. He wrote the resource section on different faiths for *Your Interfaith Wedding* as well as allowing me to use some of his wedding prayers and rituals.

- Long before I ever thought of attending seminary school, I learned about rituals from my friend Barbara Biziou, author of *The Joy of Everyday Ritual* and a longtime teacher and group leader. Her loving, compassionate celebrations showed me initially that there was another way to offer a ceremony other than in church or in a traditional manner. She was also part of all my major life moments: a blessing ritual for my son and me before I gave birth; leading a healing circle with my sisters and me at my dad's funeral; opening her home for a special engagement ritual when Vic and I decided to marry; creating the sacred space on our official wedding day with Rabbi Gelberman as a small group of family arrived; and renewing our vows at a family gathering so all could witness a few days later. When we had a Goddess group of media friends in the 1990s, she patiently let me learn the ropes of leading group rituals until I was finally skilled enough to do it on my own.

- Even before I ever knew I could or would become a wedding officiant, I was awed and inspired by the amazing Charolette Richards, proprietor of the Little White Chapel in Las Vegas. While on assignment for *Brides* magazine in 1991, I interviewed her and was invited to observe her perform a wedding. I'd come there thinking all Las Vegas wedding ministers were men, and kind of schmaltzy. I had no idea a wedding minister could be so beautiful, prayerful, and loving, or that the ceremonies in Las Vegas could be so meaningful. I thought she was one of the loveliest women I had ever met, with the coolest job on the planet—she spent all her time helping people get hitched in beautiful ceremonies. Charolette was my first role model and she is the one who showed me that it is possible to actually specialize in an aspect of ministry you feel most called to—such as weddings!

I have learned so much on this very colorful and diverse journey of specializing in wedding ministry. My greatest teachers have been my couples—the hundreds that I have married—and also the many others who have come to me for spiritual counsel and advice when struggling with interfaith issues. What a blessing it is to be allowed into people's lives at one of the most special and often vulnerable times and be given the chance to help them try to sort through the challenges, and honor their families, while celebrating their love.

Notes

GENERAL INFORMATION

Some names have been changed. The quotations that starts each chapter, using only first names, are from brides who filled out my Wedding Goddess survey in 2005. Every effort has been made to identify the original sources and to locate the copyright owners of the material used in this book.

PREFACE

Quotation from Daphne Rose Kingma, author of *The Future of Love* (New York: Main Street Books, 1999).

INTRODUCTION

Quotation from Ralph Waldo Emerson, *Self Reliance and Other Essays* (Scotts Valley, CA: CreateSpace, 2010), 40. Marriages per year statistic: Number of marriages is 2,162,000, according to the Centers for Disease Control and Prevention FastStats, http://www.cdc.gov/nchs/fastats/divorce.htm
Statistics on interfaith relationships and marriages from combined sources:
Rev. Susanna Stefanachi Macomb, *Celebrating Diversity in the US*, http://www.susannamacomb.com/about/celebrating_d.html and from *Joining Hands and Hearts* (New York, NY: Fireside, 2003).
Holly Lebowitz Rossi, "The Secrets to an Interfaith Relationship: How Couples Find Compromise Living with Two Gods under One Roof," *Your Tango*, http://www.yourtango.com/20071702/finding-our-religion.html

"Yet, statistics indicate this scene could play out over one in four dinner ta-
      bles across the country. More than 28 million married or cohabitating
      Americans—almost one quarter—are interfaith, according to the 2001
      American Religious Identification Survey," Steve Waldman, cofounder
      and former editor in chief of Beliefnet, updated the interfaith relation-
      ships statistic to 33,000 in a Beliefnet presentation.

Amy Sullivan, "It's Advent, Light the Menorah," *Time*, December 13, 2009.
      She cites a 2008 study by the Pew Forum on Religion and Public Life
      that reports that 37 percent of married adults in the United States have a
      spouse from another religious tradition.

The Pew Forum on Religion and Public Life provides additional statistics
      in *U.S. Religious Landscape Study, Religious Beliefs and Practices: Diverse
      and Politically Relevant,* http://religions.pewforum.org/pdf/report2-reli
      gious-landscape-study-full.pdf

Gabrielle Kaplan-Mayer, *The Creative Jewish Wedding Book: A Hands-on Guide
      to New and Old Traditions, Ceremonies and Celebrations* (Woodstock, VT:
      Jewish Lights, 2004).

David Crary, "Interracial Surge across US," *USA Today*, April 12, 2007. Accord-
      ing to the most recent U.S. Census, the percentage of couples who are
      interracial has increased sevenfold from 1970 to 2000.

http://www.usatoday.com/news/health/2007-04-12-interracial-marriage_N.
      htm

Greek Orthodox intermarriage statistics, "Interfaith Marriage," Department of
      Marriage and Family, Greek Orthodox Archdiocese of America, http://
      www.goarch.org/archdiocese/departments/marriage

CHAPTER 1

Quotation from Flower A. Newhouse, *The Meaning and Value of the Sacraments,*
      excerpted from "The Marriage Ceremony," http://www.christwardmin
      istry.com/book.asp?id=sacraments#TableofContents

CHAPTER 2

The phrase "every relationship has a dragon to slay" was spoken to me by
      Rev. Joyce Lichtenstein.

CHAPTER 3

Actors and interfaith couple Renee Taylor and Joseph Bologna wrote *Made for
      Each Other* and starred in the 1971 movie. Background information came
      from "Screen: From Therapy to a Sad and Comic Marriage," *New York
      Times,* December 13, 1971,

http://movies.nytimes.com/movie/review?res=9501E5D9163EE63ABC4B52 DFB467838A669EDE

CHAPTER 4

"Menu of Wedding Options" is my professional interpretation of how we can view the types of ceremonies. Ideas for structure and inspiration for this menu came from the New Seminary, http://www.newseminary.org, and also Daphne Rose Kingma, *Weddings from the Heart: Contemporary and Traditional Ceremonies for an Unforgettable Wedding,* 3rd ed. (Berkeley, CA: Conari Press, 2002).

Gertrud Mueller Nelson and Christopher Witt, *Sacred Threshold: Rituals and Readings for a Wedding with Spirit* (New York: Image Books/Doubleday, 1998).

CHAPTER 7

"I am my beloved's and my beloved is mine" is from Song of Solomon 6:3, English Standard Version. The Hebrew is "Ani L'Dodi, v'Dodi Li," at Hebrew Art, http://www.hebrewart.com/magen_david/ani.html

Chris and Lori adapted their vow, in part, from Roy Croft's poem "Love."

Elizabeth and Ross's vow is found in Janet Anastasio and Michelle Bevilacqua, *The Everything Wedding Vows Book: Anything and Everything You Could Possibly Say at the Altar—and Then Some* (Holbrook, MA: Adam, 2001).

Katerina and Xingmin, Brad and Karin, Tony and Summer, and Andrea and Pat vows, used with the couples' permission.

Rev. Diane Berke quotation if from an interview in 2005. She is director of One Spirit Seminary.

CHAPTER 8

Corinthians:4–7, New International Version.

"Wedding Day Prayer," *Book of Common Prayer,* Episcopal Church (1979).

"The Lord's Prayer," Roman Catholic, traditional Matthean version.

"The Lord's Prayer," Protestant orientation.

Ecclesiastes 3:1–15, New International Version.

Song of Solomon 2:10–13, English Standard Version.

"Shehecyanu," Hebrew prayer of thanks, http://judaism.about.com/od/ blessingsprayers/g/pr_shehech.htm

Zohar on soul mates, "The Zohar: The Book of Jewish Mysticism," in *Encyclopedia Britannica,* vol. 15, ed. Hugh Chisholm (Chicago, IL: Encyclopædia Britannica, Inc.), 621.

Kahlil Gibran, "On Marriage," from *The Prophet* (Ottawa, ON: Laurier Books Ltd.–AES, 2003), 7.

"Marriage Blessing from Rumi," by Jelaluddin Rumi, Kabir Helminski, and
    Andrew Harvey, from *the Rumi Collection* (Boston, MA: Shambhala,
    2005).
"The Buddha's Sermon at Rajagaha," Buddhist Scriptures, verses 19–22, from
    Paul Carus, *Buddha: The Gospel* (Charleston, SC: BiblioBazaar, 2007), 64.
"Buddhist Wedding Prayer," Lama Thubten Yeshe, 1979, http://www.fpmt.
    org/teachers/zopa/advice/pdf/weddingceremonyeditedkm.pdf
"Apache Wedding Prayer" is a popular wedding reading seen widely on the
    Internet. According to Wikipedia, it was written for the 1950 Western
    movie *Broken Arrow* by Albert Maltz, August 1950. http://en.wikipedia.
    org/wiki/Apache_Wedding_Prayer
"Classic Irish Blessing," no attribution.
"Victor Hugo Love Letter," Victor Hugo to his beloved Adele Foucher in 1821,
    from *Love Letters of Great Men,* vol. 1 (Scotts Valley, CA: CreateSpace,
    2010), 52. NA
"The Art of Marriage," by Wilfred A. Peterson, *The New Book of the Art of Liv-
    ing* (New York: Simon and Schuster, 1963). Copyright © 2004 by Lilian
    Thorpe. Used by permission.

CHAPTER 9

The Lighting of the Unity Candle: "From every human being there rises a
    light that reaches straight to heaven" is by the Baal Shem Tov, the great
    Hassidic master.
Jumping of the Broom language comes from Larry James's Web site, http://
    www.celebrateintimateweddings.com/ceremonybroom2.html
Calling in the Directions is adapted from a widely circulated Native American
    blessing.
The Sake Ceremony is adapted from an authentic Japanese wedding at the
    Ninth Annual Asian Pacific Bridal Summit, March 2, 2004, in New York
    City. Event was presented by the Association of Bridal Consultants in
    conjunction with the Asian-Pacific Bridal Federation and Japan Bridal
    Association.
The Hawaiian Sand Ceremony was inspired by several sources. Background
    information can be found online, http://www.unitysandceremony.net/
The Red String of Fate is a legend first told to me by wedding officiant Judy
    Chang. I combined it with the Red Goblet Ceremony, which I first learned
    about from Daphne Rose Kingma in *Weddings from the Heart.*
The Pagan Handfasting Blessing is from the wedding of Dena and Eugene.
Hand Wrapping is something I first learned about from Rev. Deborah Steen
    Ross when she asked me to officiate that part of her wedding ceremony
    to Rabbi Roger Ross in December 1998. The Blessing of the Hands
    used in this chapter is a mixture of pagan blessings strung together.
Tasting of Four Elements is a Yoruban custom I learned about from one of
    my brides. TheKnot.com appears to be the source. Robin Beth Schaer,
    "Ceremony: 7 Afrocentric Traditions," http://wedding.theknot.com/

real-weddings/african-american-weddings/articles/7-afrocentric-
wedding-ceremony-traditions.aspx

CHAPTER 10

Personal tributes from a friend at Jose and AnaMaria's wedding. Used by
permission.

CHAPTER 11

Minister's messages from select ceremonies tell the personal love story of the
couple.

CHAPTER 12

John Jacobs and Tina Fellows Ketubah, and Dana and Rob's Ketuba,
adapted from "Conservative Ketuba III," http://www.mpartworks.com/
conservative-ketubah-text.htm
Quaker wedding vows adapted from "Documents and Designs: Traditional
Wedding Vows, Quaker Wedding Vows I and II," http://www.docu
mentsanddesigns.com/verse/traditional_vows.htm#t2

PART FOUR

Author's note: There are certain words, phrases, and prayers I tend to use over
and over and regularly include in some form in my personalized wedding ceremonies. Having been officiating weddings for 11 years, many
of these have become a part of me, yet I am keenly aware that there
are certain expressions and prayers I learned from other authors and
sources long ago. In interfaith weddings, we must adapt the language
to suit the couple, so I apologize in advance for altering any of the original language—or removing certain specific religious references. And I
sincerely thank those who came before me and shared these inspiring
words in their books, enabling me to use them as a practicing wedding
officiant. I am listing some of the things I use fairly often and that will
appear in some of the sample wedding ceremonies in Part Four.

OFTEN USED WORDS, PHRASES, AND PRAYERS AND THEIR SOURCES

Daphne Rose Kingma, *Weddings from the Heart: Contemporary and Traditional
Ceremonies for an Unforgettable Wedding,* 2nd ed. (Berkeley, CA: Conari

Press, 1995). (Copyright 1995, 1998, and 2002, Daphne Rose Kingma and used by permission from Red Wheel/Weiser/ Conari LLC, 65 Parker Street, Suite 7, Newburyport, MA 01950. 800-423-7087. www.redwheel weiser.com).

- I use the phrase "love gathers us today" to open almost every ceremony. I first discovered it in this book as an alternative to "Dearly beloved, we are gathered here today."
- This appears in most of my Minister's Messages: "You come to this day as best friends and partners in life, united in so many ways. Yet, on this day, the journey of nourishing your love through *all* of life's cycles takes on a new dimension, as you become husband and wife. You will discover that marriage is even more than the complete joining of two lives. Not only does marriage merge two life stories and two families. It's the spiritual, physical, and emotional union of two human beings. It is the fuller opening of two hearts and the ripening of two souls. It is the opportunity for both of you to become even more of whom you are meant to be." And it is adapted from and inspired by "marriage is the joining of two lives, the mystical, physical, and emotional union of two human beings who have separate families and histories, separate tragedies and destinies. It is the merging and intermeshing not only of two bodies and two personalities, but also two life stories." From "Reflections on Marriage," *Weddings of the Heart*, 13.

Marianne Williamson, *Illuminata: A Return to Prayer* (New York: Riverhead Books, 1995).

- I open many ceremonies with "we honor the place you have made in each other's heart." This was inspired by "we welcome you to this moment in your lives and to the place you have come to in each other's hearts." From "Ceremony of Marriage," in Williamson, *Illuminata*, 261.
- I often use a variation of this phrase: "I congratulate you on the journey of your lives, on the strength and courage it has taken each of you to make your way to this place. Both of you have found a way to put away childish things and embrace a very serious love." From "Ceremony of Marriage," from Williamson, *Illuminata*, 262.
- My all time favorite prayer for ending a wedding comes also from Marianne Williamson, and I have adapted it in many different ways in my ceremonies. Usually I just use a few lines at the request of the couple:

Dear God, Please bless this couple.
May their love be nurtured, always and forever.
May this man grow even stronger in the arms of this woman.

May this woman grow even more glorious in the love of this man.
May the earth be brought closer to heaven through this love.
May they live in peace and in happiness.
And may all the world be blessed hereby. Amen.

- This is the full prayer: "Dear God, please bless this couple. May their love be nurtured by You, always and forever. May this marriage be held in Your Hands and ministered unto by Your Angels. We Dedicate this love to you. May it serve Your purposes; may it increase Your dominion. May this man grow strong in the love of this woman. May this woman grow glorious in the love of this man. May earth be brought closer to heaven through this love. May all the world be blessed hereby. Thank you very much. Amen." From "Ceremony of Marriage," from Williamson, *Illuminata,* 269.

Joan C. Hawxhurst, ed., *Interfaith Wedding Ceremonies: Samples and Sources* (Kalamazoo, MI: Dovetail, 1997).

This is a nondenominational prayer I have used many times in my ministry: "In happiness and joy, we are thankful for the gift of this marriage. May (name) and (name) have the ability to rejoice always in their love. May every wish of their hearts be fulfilled. May their eyes be open to the beauty and mystery of the love they have for each other, every day, as today. And may their life together embrace and nurture the promise of this moment. As we open our hearts in celebration, may we all be surrounded and embraced by love. May God bless and uplift this bride and groom, and all those who have come here to share in this joyous occasion. Amen."

I originally adapted it from this prayer: "Let us pray: O Lord our God, source of all blessing, in happiness and joy we thank you for the gift of marriage, which we celebrate today. May you give Tom and Helen the ability to rejoice always in their love. May you fulfill every worthy wish of their hearts. May you open their eyes to the beauty and the mystery of the love they hold for each other, every day as today. And may their life together embrace and nurture the promise of this moment, so that all who know them will call them truly blessed. Amen." From "The Wedding of Helen and Tom, June 27, 1993," from the section titled "Prayer," 30.

THE WEDDING CEREMONIES

More Christian than Jewish: Courtney and Ray

Prayer invocation adapted from *Interfaith Wedding Ceremonies: Ceremonies, Samples, and Sources.*

Wedding Reading I: Corinthians I, adapted from the New International Version.

Consecration: George Eliot quotation: George Eliot, from Adam Bede, found in *Four Novels of George Eliot* (Ware, Hertfordshire, England: Wordsworth, 2005), 361–62.

Breaking of the Glass uses one line from *Interfaith Wedding Ceremonies.*

The glass, then, is broken to "protect" the marriage with an implied prayer: "As this glass shatters, so may our marriage never break."

More Jewish than Christian: Jodi and Dennis

Opening Prayer/Invocation written by Rev. Victor Fuhrman.

"Shehecyanu," Hebrew prayer of thanks.

Traditional Hebrew prayer over the wine.

Wine ceremony: English blessing "Ceremony of the Wine Cup, Ethical Culture Society of St. Louis," Sample Wedding Vows, Blessings and Ceremonies, http://www.ethicalstl.org/eve_weddingssample.php

Minister's Message excerpts for "male officiant," written by Rev. Victor Fuhrman.

The Pronouncement and final blessing was adapted and strung together from blessings in *Interfaith Wedding Ceremonies.*

Mystical Catholic, Multicultural, Costa Rican: Annie and Arturo

"Marriage Blessing," by Jalalludin Rumi; Spanish translation by the groom.

Vows written by bride and groom; Spanish translations by the groom.

Closing Prayer, an Apache blessing, is supposed to be an authentic Native American blessing, but is also said to be from the 1950 movie, *Broken Arrow.*

Catholic, Mormon: Suzanne and Jake

Opening Prayer adapted from *Interfaith Wedding Ceremonies: Samples and Sources.*

Wedding Reading 1 is Song of Solomon 2:10–13.

The Lighting of the Unity Candle quotation is by the Baal Shem Tov.

Also in the Unity Candle ceremony is a mention of "love one another, as I have loved you." This is adapted from John 13:34–35, New International Version, "Jesus Washes His Disciples' Feet": "A new command I give you: Love one another. As I have loved you, so you must love one another. By this all men will know that you are my disciples, if you love one another."

Buddhist, Sri Lankan, Christian: Rachel and Sanith

Opening Prayer adapted from *Interfaith Wedding Ceremonies: Samples and Sources.*
Wedding Reading 1 by Kahlil Gibran from *The Prophet.*
Wedding Reading 2 is a Buddhist blessing from *The Buddhist Scriptures: The Buddha's Sermon at Raja-Gaha.*
Sri Lankan String Ceremony created with the help of the groom's family.
Closing Blessing written by Rev. Laurie Sue Brockway.

Celtic/Scottish: Elle and Eddie

Opening Blessing is adapted from *The Book of Common Prayer,* Episcopal Church, 2001.
Loving Cup Ceremony was adapted for the couple from "The Loving Cup" article on My Spiritual Wedding, http://www.myspiritualwedding.com/content/005514.shtml
The Final Prayer was adapted from "Eight Contemporary Blessings," in *Weddings: The Magic of Creating Your Own Ceremony,* ed. Henry S. Bisayne and Linda R. Janowitz (Wilsonville, OR: Book Partners, 1999).

Nondenominational Filipino: Robert and Michelle

Gold Coins, Veil, and Cord provided by bride.

Hindu, Jewish: Shari and Sanjai

Hindu and Nondenominational Prayer written by Rev. Laurie Sue Brockway.
"Shehecyanu," traditional Hebrew prayer of thanks.
The Officiant's Message starts with "an old Jewish legend tells us..." I learned about this in Susanna Stefanachi Macomb, *Joining Hands and Hearts: Interfaith, Intercultural Wedding Celebrations: A Practical Guide for Couples* (New York: Atria, 2002).
Ring Vows include "Ani L'Dodi V'Dodi Li," from Song of Solomon. The groom's family translated this in their native language as "tum hamaare priya, hum tumhare priyatama," which means "you are my love, and I am your beloved."
The Saptapadi blessing is traditional.
Blessing over the Wine is the traditional seven Hebrew blessings.
Final Blessing and Pronouncement adapts a prayer from the wedding ceremony in Williamson, *Illuminata.*

Nondenominational Chinese: Betty and David

Wedding Reading is "The Art of Marriage," by Wilferd Arlan Peterson.
Minister's Message quotes Victor Hugo's letter to his beloved.
In the Pronouncement, the phrase "may the bond that unites you be ever-
   strengthened" is borrowed from a Unitarian prayer.

Japanese, Christian: Kiko and Yoshi

The invocation is adapted from *Interfaith Wedding Ceremonies: Samples and
   Sources.*
The Japanese vows in the ring exchange were created by the bride. She offered
   this English translation:

   I marry this woman.
   I marry this man.
   I will love, console, and help this person
   Until death,
   Protecting fidelity.
   To this I swear.

Pagan, Nondenominational: Amy and Joe

Invocation/Calling the Directions is adapted from a classic Native American
   prayer.
The Wedding Reading is "Thoughts on Marriage" from *The Prophet*, by Kahlil
   Gibran.
Handfasting Prayer is a traditional pagan prayer.
The Pronouncement of "May the Highest Power bless you and keep you" is
   adapted from Numbers 6:24–26: "The Lord bless thee, and keep thee; the
   Lord make his face shine upon thee, and be gracious unto thee; the Lord
   lift up his countenance upon thee, and give thee peace," http://www.gos
   pel.com/bookmarks/LORD-bless-keep-Bible-Numbers-6–24–26/8843
   or http://www.engageworship.org/ideas/May_the_Lord_bless_you

Nondenominational Vow Renewal: Zak and Terry

Opening is from a George Eliot quotation from Adam Bede.
The Invocation/Blessing is a prayer from *Interfaith Wedding Ceremonies: Sam-
   ples and Sources.*
Wedding Reading is from *The Future of Love,* by Daphne Rose Kingma.
Theodore Parker quotation is used in the Minister's Message: widely circu-
   lated on the Internet as a wedding reading, it originated in *The Collected*

Works of Theodore Parker, vol. 14, from the section on "Marriage" (Belfast, UK: Adamant, 2001), 151.

Highly Personalized: Claudine and Michael

Opening Prayer is from *The Book of Common Prayer.*
In Honoring Family, the quotation "this family is united in a circle of love and strength" is of unknown origin.
The Lighting of the Unity Candle includes a Baal Shem Tov quotation.
The Officiant's Message starts with "an old Jewish legend tells us . . . ," from *Joining Hands and Hearts: Interfaith, Intercultural Wedding Celebrations: A Practical Guide for Couples,* by Susanna Stefanachi Macomb (New York: Atria, 2002).
In the Consecration, the prayer "Lord God, please accept our gratitude for this day" is adapted from a prayer the bride says daily.
The Seven Blessings is adapted from "Eight Contemporary Blessings," in Henry S. Bisayne and Linda R. Janowitz, eds., *Weddings: The Magic of Creating Your Own Ceremony.*
Final Blessing and Pronouncement is Corinthians I and adds John 4:7–11.
From the Holy Bible, New International Version.

PART FIVE

These were developed by Rev. Victor Fuhrman and Rev. Laurie Sue Brockway utilizing basic knowledge about the faith traditions and information from the following resources.

Jewish Sources

Helen Latner, *The Everything Jewish Wedding Book* (Holbrook, MA: Adams, 1998).

Muslim Sources

Mohammad Mazhar Hussaini, *Marriage and Family in Islam,* 1st ed. (Baltimore, MD: Al-Meezan International, 1996), http://www.soundvision.com/ info/Islam/marriage.nikah.asp

Hindu Sources

Meenal Atul Pandya, *Vivah: Design a Perfect Hindu Wedding* (Wellesley, MA: MeeRa, 2000).

Buddhist Sources

Buddhist Wedding Rituals, http://www.ayushveda.com/wedding/buddhist-wedding-rituals.htm

Catholic Sources

Explained to Rev. Laurie Sue Brockway by Father Paul Keenan, Catholic Archdiocese of New York.

Christian Sources

Mary Fairchild, Christian Wedding Traditions and Customs: Understanding the Biblical Significance of Wedding Traditions and Customs, About.com Guide, http://christianity.about.com/od/weddingceremony/a/weddingtraditions.htm

Greek Orthodox Sources

YASOU, http://www.yasou.org/church/wedding.htm
Guidelines for Marriage, http://www.saintbarbara.org/faith/sacraments/marriage/marriage_guidelines.cfm

Sikh Sources

A Sikh Wedding, http://www.sikhs.org/wedding/
Sikh Wedding Rituals at ILoveIndia.com, http://weddings.iloveindia.com/indian-weddings/sikh-wedding.html

Wiccan Sources

Inspired by a handfasting ceremony by High Priestess Phyllis Curott.
Background from Raven Kaldera and Tannin Schwarzstein, *Handfasting and Wedding Rituals* (St. Paul, MN: Llewellyn Books, 2003).

Unitarian Universalist Sources

Unitarian Universalist Web site, http://www.uua.org

Bibliography

INTERFAITH AND INTERCULTURAL WEDDING BOOKS

Hawxhurst, Joan C. *Interfaith Wedding Ceremonies: Samples and Sources.* Kalamazoo, MI: Dovetail, 1997.

Macomb, Susanna Stefanachi. *Joining Hands and Hearts: Interfaith, Intercultural Wedding Celebrations: A Practical Guide for Couples.* New York: Fireside, 2002.

Matlins, Stuart M., ed. *The Perfect Strangers Guide to Wedding Ceremonies: A Guide to Etiquette in Other People's Ceremonies.* Woodstock, VT: Skylight Paths, 2000.

Roney, Carley. *The Knot Guide to Wedding Vows and Traditions: Readings, Rituals, Music, Dances, and Toasts.* New York: Broadway Books, 2000.

ORGANIZING AND PERSONALIZING WEDDING CEREMONIES

Bisayne, Henry S., and Linda R. Janowitz. *Weddings: The Magic of Creating Your Own Ceremony.* Wilsonville, OR: Book Partners, 1999.

Fritts, Roger. *For As Long As We Both Shall Live.* New York: Avon Books, 1993.

Kingma, Daphne Rose. *Weddings from the Heart: Contemporary and Traditional Ceremonies for an Unforgettable Wedding,* 2nd ed. Berkeley, CA: Conari Press, 1995.

Leviton, Richard. *Weddings by Design: A Guide to Non-traditional Ceremonies.* San Francisco: HarperSanFrancisco, 1993.

Nelson Mueller, Gertrud, and Christopher Witt. *Sacred Threshold: Rituals and Readings for a Wedding with Spirit.* New York: Image Books/Doubleday, 1998.

Ross-MacDonald, Jane. *Alternative Weddings: An Essential Guide for Creating Your Own Ceremony.* Lanham, MD: Taylor Trade Publishing, 1997.

Warner, Diane. *Diane Warner's Contemporary Guide to Wedding Ceremonies: Hundreds of Creative Personal Touches And Tips for a Wedding to Remember.* Franklin Lakes, NJ: Career Press, 2006.

Williamson, Marianne. *Illuminata: A Return to Prayer.* New York, NY: Riverhead Books, November 1995.

WEDDING VOWS AND READINGS

Anastasio, Janet, Michelle Bevilacqua, Leah Furman, and Elina Furman. *The Everything Wedding Vows Book: Anything and Everything You Could Possibly Say at the Altar—and Then Some.* Holbrook, MA: Adams, 2001.

Ford-Grabowsky, Mary, ed. *Sacred Poems and Prayers of Love.* New York: Doubleday, 1998.

Kehret, Peg. *Wedding Vows: How to Express Your Love in Your Own Words.* Colorado Springs, CO: Meriwether, 1989.

Munro, Eleanor. *Wedding Readings: Centuries of Writing and Rituals for Love and Marriage.* New York: Viking Books, 1989.

Paris, Wendy, and Andrew Chesler. *Words for the Wedding: Perfect Things to Say for a Perfect Wedding Day.* New York: Perigee Books, 2001.

Warner, Diane. *Diane Warner's Complete Book of Wedding Vows: Hundreds of Ways to Say "I Do."* Franklin Lakes, NJ: Career Press, 1996.

Weaver, Joanna. *With This Ring: Promises to Keep.* Colorado Springs, CO: Waterbrook Press, 1984.

SPECIFIC CULTURES AND FAITHS

African American

Cole, Harriette. *Jumping the Broom: The African-American Wedding Planner.* New York: Henry Holt, 2004.

Cole, Harriette, and George Chinsee. *Vows: The African-American Couples' Guide to Designing a Sacred Ceremony.* New York: Simon and Schuster, 2004.

Christian

Wright, H. Norman. *The Complete Book of Christian Wedding Vows: The Importance of How You Say I Do.* New York: Bethany House, 2003.

Filipino

Neri, Rita M. *The Essential Wedding Workbook for the Filipina.* Self-published, 1998.

Gay and Lesbian

Toussaint, David. *Gay and Lesbian Weddings: Planning the Perfect Same-Sex Ceremony.* New York: Ballantine Books, 2004.

Hawaiian

Shepherd, Keri. *Hawaii Weddings Made Simple.* Honolulu, HI: Mutual, 2003.

Hindu

Arora, D. V. *Marriage Manual.* New Delhi: Crest, 1995.Pandya, Meenal Atul. *Vivah: Design a Perfect Hindu Wedding.* Wellesley, MA: MeeRa, 2000.
Sahai, Prem. *Hindu Marriage Samskara.* Marg, India: Wheeler, 1993.

Irish

Haggert, Bridget. *The Traditional Irish Wedding.* Dublin: Wolfhound Press, 2000.
McMahon-Lichte, Shannon. *Irish Wedding Traditions: Using Your Irish Heritage to Create the Perfect Wedding.* New York: Hyperion, 2001.

Italian

Granieri, Lori. *Abbondanza! Planning an Italian Wedding.* New York: Citadel, 2002.

Jewish

Kaplan-Mayer, Gabrielle. *The Creative Jewish Wedding Book: A Hands-on Guide to New and Old Traditions, Ceremonies and Celebrations.* Woodstock, VT: Jewish Lights, 2004.
Latner, Helen. *The Everything Jewish Wedding Book.* Holbrook, MA: Adams, 1998.
Matt, Daniel Chanan. *The Zohar: Book of Enlightenment.* Mahwah, NJ: Paulist, 1983.
Schwartzman, Ana, and Zoe Francesca. *Make Your Own Jewish Wedding: How to Create a Ritual That Expresses Your True Selves.* San Francisco: Jossey-Bass, 2004.

Pagan and Earth-Based Weddings

Franklin, Ana. *Romantic Guide to Handfasting: Rituals, Recipes, and Lore.* St. Paul, MN: Llewellyn, 2004.

Kaldera, Raven, and Tannin Schwarzstein. *Handfasting and Wedding Rituals.* St. Paul, MN: Llewellyn, 2003.

Scottish

MacGregor, Lizzie, ed. *Hanfast: Scottish Poems of Weddings and Affirmations.* Edinburgh: Scottish Poetry Library, 2004.
Merrill Budd, Eric. *Scottish Tartan Weddings: A Practical Guidebook.* New York: Hippocrene, 1999.

MIXED MARRIAGES

Crohn, Joel. *Mixed Matched: How to Create Successful Interracial, Interethnic, and Interfaith Relationships.* New York: Fawcett Columbine, 1995.
Richardson, Brenda Lane. *Guess Who's Coming to Dinner: Celebrating Interethnic, Interfaith and Interracial Relationships.* Berkeley, CA: Wildcat Canyon Press, 2000.
Rozakis, Laurie. *The Complete Idiots Guild to Interfaith Relationships.* Indianapolis, IN: Alpha Books, 2001.

Soul Mates and Marriage

Kingma, Daphne Rose. *The Future of Love.* New York: Main Street Books, 1999.
Moore, Thomas. *Soul Mates: Honoring the Mysteries of Love and Relationship.* New York: HarperPerennial, 1994.
Silbury, Lira. *The Sacred Marriage: Honoring the God and Goddess within Each Other.* St. Paul, MN: Llewellyn, 1994.
Thoele, Sue Patton. *Heart Centered Marriage: Fulfilling Our Natural Desire for Sacred Partnership.* New York: Barnes and Noble, 1996.

WEDDING TRADITIONS

Russell-Revesz, Heather. *Tying the Knot: The Book of Wedding Trivia.* New York: Barnes and Noble, 2002.
Spangleberg, Lisl. *Timeless Traditions: A Couple's Guide to Wedding Customs around the World.* New York: Universe, 2001.

Index

About the Author

REV. LAURIE SUE BROCKWAY is a widely recognized expert in interfaith, multicultural, and nondenominational weddings and bridal stress. She has an active wedding ministry in New York City and serves hundreds of couples each year. She is author of 12 books, including *Wedding Goddess: A Divine Guide to Transforming Wedding Stress into Wedding Bliss* (2005).

Rev. Laurie Sue is love, family, and inspiration editor for Beliefnet. com, the award-winning multifaith Web site that focuses on spirituality, inspiration, and faith. She also writes the "Ask the Wedding Goddess" column for Wedlok.com.

New York magazine's NY Weddings lists her as one of New York's top interfaith officiants, as does Joan Hamburg in her book *City Weddings.* The *New York Press* selected her as "Best Wedding Ceremony Provider in New York."

As a leading interfaith minister and nondenominational wedding officiant, she is known for her warm, loving, and creative approach to blessing couples of all backgrounds and faiths and for guiding them on their journey to the altar and beyond.

As a founding board member of the New York Wedding Group, she helped establish, and co-led, the New York branch of the Bridal Survival Club and cofounded the nationally acclaimed Bridal Survival School. She is also founder of the annual Wedding Goddess Blessing of the Brides and Grooms, which she officiates with her husband, Vic Fuhrman, also an interfaith minister, in Central Park.

Visit Rev. Laurie Sue online at
http://www.WeddingGoddess.com
http://www.LaurieSueBrockway.net
http://www.Beliefnet.com